D1446987

CLIMBER'S GUIDE TO THE
OLYMPIC MOUNTAINS

CLIMBER'S GUIDE
to the OLYMPIC MOUNTAINS

Third Edition

BY

OLYMPIC MOUNTAIN RESCUE

THE
MOUNTAINEERS

The Mountaineers: Organized 1906 ". . . to explore, study, preserve, and enjoy the natural beauty of the Northwest."

© 1972, 1979, 1988 by Olympic Mountain Rescue
First edition 1972
Second edition 1979
Third edition 1988

7 6 5
6 5 4 3

Published by The Mountaineers
1011 S.W. Klickitat Way, Suite 107   Seattle, WA 98134

Published simultaneously in Canada by Douglas & McIntyre, Ltd.,
1615 Venables Street, Vancouver, B.C. V5L 2H1

Manufactured in the United States of America

Edited by Barbara Chasan
Cover design by Betty Watson
Cover photograph: Mt. Cruiser. Photo by Ronald L. Sampson
Frontispiece: South Brother from North Brother. Photo by Dave Haley

Sketch on page 28 reprinted with permission from *Pages of Stone: Geology of Western National Parks and Monuments, Vol. 2: Sierra Nevada, Cascades, and Pacific Coast,* Halka Chronic (Seattle: The Mountaineers, 1986).

Library of Congress Cataloging in Publication Data

Climber's guide to the Olympic Mountains / by Olympic Mountain Rescue.
  — 3rd ed.
        p.   cm.
    Includes index.
    ISBN 0-89886-154-3 (pbk.)
    1. Rock climbing — Washington (State) — Olympic Mountains —
Guide-books. 2. Mountaineering — Washington (State) — Olympic Mountains
— Guide-books. 3. Olympic Mountains (Wash.) — Description and travel —
Guide-books. I. Olympic Mountain Rescue (Society)
GV199.42.W22048 1988
917.97'94 — dc19   88-17636
                                                                CIP

CONTENTS

Glenn A. Kelsey
1915-1988

Kelsey was a diminutive man, yet his size sparked a local legend. A founding member and past chairman of Olympic Mountain Rescue, Kelsey was forever shouldering packs that appeared far larger than himself.

He carried them with ease while bigger, younger mountaineers panted behind. Kelsey was about five feet of sinew, and he was as hard as Blue Glacier ice.

He often arrived first to comfort the lost hiker or injured climber. They might remember Kelsey the way his companions do: a giant pack with legs, churning effortlessly up a heathered mountainside.

This edition is dedicated to Kelsey — a man whose spirit was greater than the mountains he climbed.

 OLYMPIC MOUNTAIN RESCUE
Bremerton, Washington

Olympic Mountain Rescue, one of the charter members of the national Mountain Rescue Association, is composed of more than 40 skilled climbers who are dedicated to saving lives through search, rescue, and mountain safety education.

Formed in 1957, OMR works primarily on the Olympic Peninsula, but has participated in many missions in other ranges, including Alaska's Mt. McKinley on two occasions. The volunteer members pay their own expenses and provide their own personal equipment, though specialized items such as radios and stretchers are purchased with donations.

In preparing this new guide, OMR was able to draw not only on their own extensive experience throughout this beautiful range, but also on the knowledge of the National Park and Forest Services and many other organizations and climbers. OMR approached this task knowing that accurate route descriptions would decrease accidents, while increasing the enjoyment of the wilderness traveler.

We encourage anyone finding conditions other than as described here to let OMR know so corrections can be incorporated into future printings or editions of this guide. For further information on Olympic Mountain Rescue, or to submit new routes or changes in roads and trails, contact P.O. Box 4244, Bremerton, Washington 98312.

Nearing the summit (Dave Sicks)

FOREWORD

Compared to many mountain ranges, the Olympics do not occupy a large geographical area. They do, however, offer a wide variety of climbing experience ranging from alpine hiking to technical rock and ice. This variety attracts a considerable number of mountaineers, with and without experience. Occasionally a backcountry emergency arises and local climbers are asked to assist the sheriff or the National Park Service. The climbers who belong to Olympic Mountain Rescue are organized for a ready response; we get a deep sense of satisfaction from being able to help others in this unique mountain environment.

While our main function is conducting search and rescue missions, our experience with the many trails, alpine areas, and mountains on the Olympic Peninsula fits well with our other objective — mountain safety education.

Guidebooks by their very nature introduce certain elements, e.g., climbing time and difficulty, that make climbing safer by providing knowledge difficult to obtain elsewhere. There is some concern, however, in this conservation-minded era that guidebooks lead to overuse of natural resources. Yet, like bees to honey, mountaineers will be drawn to the mountains, with or without guidebooks, to escape the confinement of urbanization and to sense the experience of adventure and of perhaps being in that one spot never before trod by man.

Since its first appearance in 1972, we have continued to update and publish this guide to help mountaineers climb safely. Changes in this third edition include suggestions made by readers. We have attempted to include all new routes and to eliminate both confusion and errors. The peaks in the southern part of the Olympics were critically reviewed and many new peaks and route descriptions were added or changed to reflect the current climbing interests in that area. Since the second edition, Forest Service roads have been renumbered, extended, or closed, so new topographical maps have been introduced with changes noted in the new guide. As with past editions, we have endeavored to describe all routes with emphasis on difficulty and duration of the climb.

Olympic Mountain Rescue hopes this guidebook will help in planning your adventures and that it will help prevent accidents. Please leave the Olympics like you found them.

ROGER R. BECKETT
August 1, 1988   Chairman, Olympic Mountain Rescue

Acknowledgments

This, the third edition of the *Climber's Guide to the Olympic Mountains,* is the result of many years of continued effort that started with Fred Beckey's *Climber's Guide to the Cascades and Olympics,* published in 1949 by the American Alpine Club. The 1961 version of that publication, prepared and published by the American Alpine Club, followed. With publication of Olympic Mountain Rescue's *Climber's Guide to the Olympic Mountains,* in 1972, the first true "Olympic" guidebook became available. The second edition was published in 1979. This edition is a complete revision of the 1979 effort.

Fortunately, a nucleus of the team that worked with great dedication on the 1972 and 1979 editions returned to provide both expertise and continuity. This nucleus was joined by several new and younger members who provided both a fresh viewpoint and current knowledge on Olympic peaks and routes. Equally important was the continuing support of the Olympic Mountain Rescue membership, Board of Directors and particularly that of Chairman Roger Beckett.

Every effort has been made to acknowledge each individual who contributed to this edition. If anyone has been missed, please accept my sincere apologies. The contributors are listed in the following paragraphs.

Those responsible for research and preparation of one or more manuscript sections, the real heart of the book, were Brad "Bro" Albro, Roger Beckett, Kent Heathershaw, Jack Hughes, Paul Plevich, George Sainsbury, Dave Sicks and Keith Spencer.

Artists Kent Heathershaw and Dee Molenaar continued their fine work. Dee prepared the peak sketches. Kent prepared the sketch maps, the new section sketches and the balance of the artwork found in the book.

Photography, always a tough task, was capably handled by Dave Sicks. Fred Ewing and Ray Smutek also contributed in this regard. Fred handled the slide conversion problem and Ray opened his *Off Belay* archive to our use. Manuscript preparation typing was professionally accomplished by Frank Reh. Legal counsel was provided by Paul Williams.

Special credit must be given to Olympic National Forest (for maps and

15

other information); Olympic National Park (for pictures and other help); Tom Shindler and Little River Enterprises (for maps and other information).

A number of people contributed material or were otherwise helpful in various ways. Those who were not associated with the committee but made major contributions include: Arnold Bloomer (research on winter climbing/skiing history); Don Dooley (very valuable historical data on prewar climbing); Frank Maranville (used as a technical consultant and provided much data on the Mt. Constance area); Rich Olson, Jr. (major technical input covering the entire range); Steve Turk (technical input on the southern Olympics). Others include Diane Albro, Bryn Beorse, Bert Brown, Jack Christiansen, Allen Fries, Don Goodman, Walt Hoffman, Tom Hutchinson, Elvin "Swede" Johnson, Ed LaChapelle, Bill Larson, Harvey Manning, Kevin Page, Pete Schoening, Ira Spring, Dan Tennant, Robert Wood and Dr. Bob Yekel.

I would also like to thank Dr. Price M. Chenault, who unwittingly became a part of this revision. He skillfully patched me back together when I managed to break myself up on a guidebook field climb.

This list of credits would not be complete without acknowledging the role of The Mountaineers who, as publishers, accomplished the final critical step toward making the third edition available to the climbing public. In this regard, I wish to specifically thank Barbara Chasan, Donna DeShazo, Paul Robisch and the rest of the Editorial Review Committee of Mountaineers Books.

Last, but not least, a sincere thank you to my wife Jan who provided lodging, hospitality and patience during our countless meetings.

F. KEITH SPENCER
Chairman, Olympic Guidebook Committee
August 1, 1988

WARNING

Mountain climbing and/or wilderness travel in the Olympic Mountains Range is by its very nature hazardous because of the crumbly rock, dense vegetation, frequently inclement weather, seasonal changes, and complex drainages that render route descriptions difficult. You should recognize that these are the risks that you assume and for which we cannot be responsible when you utilize this guide. The fact that a route is described in this book is not a representation that it is necessarily safe for you, nor does the description list every possible hazard a climber may confront. Any guidebook, no matter how comprehensive, can only give you limited advice and information.

The profits from the sale of this book that flow to Olympic Mountain Rescue are used in its non-profit charitable activity as a mountain-rescue team.

Olympic Mountain Rescue
The Mountaineers

ROAD NUMBER CHANGES

Certain road numbers in the Olympic National Forest have been changed. The entries in this book do not currently reflect these changes. Refer to the latest version of the Olympic National Forest/Olympic National Park map published by the Olympic National Forest and Olympic National Park. The map can be purchased from either office.

INTRODUCTION

The Olympic Mountains occupy the center of the Olympic Peninsula, which is bounded on the south by the lowlands of the Chehalis valley, on the east by Hood Canal, on the north by the Strait of Juan de Fuca, and on the west by the Pacific Ocean. Although neither high nor extensive, they present an imposing barrier to the winds which sweep in from the sea. Captain John Meares, the English navigator who sighted the major uplift from shipboard in 1788, is supposed to have said, "If that be not the home where dwell the gods, it is certainly beautiful enough to be, and I therefore will call it Mt. Olympus." He was unaware that the Spanish navigator Juan Perez had previously named the peaks "Sierra Nevada de Santa Rosalia" in 1774. Meares' name was used by Captain George Vancouver, and as Spanish influence waned it was generally adopted by the British and extended to the whole peninsula. The mountains, however, continued to be called the "Coast Range" until 1849, when Hall J. Kelley and J. Quinn Thornton made their well-publicized attempt to change the name of the Cascades to "President's Range" and also proposed that Mt. Olympus be designated "Mt. Van Buren." The effort failed, and in 1864 the Seattle *Weekly Gazette* was successful in getting the name "Olympic Mountains" officially adopted. Thus the colorful Duwamish Indian name for the range, "Sun-a-do," and the Clallam Indian name, which translated to "Thunderbird," were forgotten among the conflicting proposals of the white man.

The Olympics stand alone, isolated from other mountains, and rise from bases just barely above sea level to heights of nearly 8000 feet. These mountains are not a "range" in the usual sense; rather, they comprise a compact cluster of steep peaks surrounded by a belt of densely timbered foothills. The drainage system is radial, with river valleys penetrating deeply into the mountain mass from all sides. The sources of most of the rivers are in the snowfields and glaciers of the higher peaks near the center of the uplift, and the mountains are deeply dissected by wild, rugged canyons carved by gushing torrents and carpeted by green jungles of slide alder, vine maple, and devil's club. Some valleys provide an extremely hostile environment for travel, notorious for box canyons and frequent cliffy waterfalls. When the downward plunge of the rushing streams eases, perhaps 1000 feet above sea level, the valleys become broader and frequently provide easier travel.

West Peak of the Anderson Massif is the hydrographic apex of the Olympic Peninsula, with its waters flowing into Hood Canal, the Strait of Juan de Fuca, and the Pacific Ocean. The major rivers draining the mountains westward to the Pacific are the Soleduck, Bogachiel, Hoh, Queets, and Quinault. The Skokomish, Hamma Hamma, Duckabush, Dosewallips, and Quilcene Rivers flow eastward into Hood Canal. The Strait of Juan de Fuca to the north receives the waters of the Elwha River, and the Dungeness River with its large tributaries, Grand Creek, Cameron Creek, and Gray Wolf River. The Humptulips, Wynoochee, and Satsop rivers drain southward into the Chehalis valley and Grays Harbor.

In the path of prevailing westerly winds, the seaward slopes of these mountains are deluged by the heaviest precipitation in the 48 conterminous states. The average rainfall at Hoh Ranger Station is 142 inches per year, and Mt. Olympus receives the equivalent of more than 220 inches annually. As a result, the western lowlands support a climax forest of spruce and hemlock. Sitka spruce, mostly below 1000 feet in elevation, averages 220 feet in height, and may reach 300 feet. Western hemlock is most common from 1500 feet to 3000 feet, and the largest known specimen is on the East Fork of the Quinault River near Enchanted Valley. Though Douglas-fir is less common in the Olympics than in the Cascades, occasional groves occur, and one includes the largest known coast Douglas-fir. Western redcedar is more infrequent, though the largest known specimen is located near Forks. The western Olympics also contain record specimens of Pacific silver fir, subalpine fir, Alaska-cedar and grand fir.

Another result of the extreme rainfall is the extensive permanent snow-fields and glaciers above 5000 feet. There are at least 70 of these, even though the highest summit in the range is less than 8000 feet in elevation. The glaciers are centered on the Mt. Olympus Massif, in the northern Bailey Range, and on Mt. Anderson, with a scattering of smaller permanent glaciers and snowfields on other peaks. Mt. Olympus ranks third in the amount of glaciation on a single peak in the 48 contiguous states, with the Hoh Glacier being the longest in the Olympics. Crevasses more than 150 feet deep and 30 feet wide are not uncommon in this area.

Most of the major peaks in the Olympic Mountains are not difficult to climb by the standard established routes. However, widely separated parts of the range provide challenging rock climbing — especially Sawtooth Ridge above Flapjack Lakes, The Needles in the Royal Basin area, and the Mt. Constance Massif. Snow and ice climbers find the greatest attraction to be the glaciers of Mt. Olympus, but many peaks provide excellent snow climbing early in the season. Mt. Constance and Inner Constance give the climber a good variety of mixed climbing, some of the routes being quite difficult. The outstanding appeal and charm of the Olympics, however, is in the abundant availability of relatively untouched wilderness, which together with the unpredictable weather and variety of terrain provides great challenges in wilderness navigation.

Though the interior is liberally crossed with access trails, these usually follow major river valleys. The better known high routes, such as the Bailey Range traverse through Cream Lake Basin, or the Glacier Meadows-Elwha Basin traverse through Blizzard Pass and Queets Basin, are now visited fairly frequently. Such relatively unknown areas as the upper Goldie or Queets drainages, the high alpine country between Mt. Christie, Mt. Anderson, and the Enchanted Valley, or the inaccessible peaks north and east of Mt. Carrie, may see only a few parties a year.

HISTORY OF EXPLORATION AND MOUNTAINEERING

The settlement of the lowlands on the Olympic Peninsula is widely recorded elsewhere. The mountains themselves, however, were almost totally unexplored until shortly before the turn of the century. Both the formal and informal penetration of the range proceeded more or less simultaneously, the former well organized, documented, and publicized, and the latter generally unknown except to the participants and their immediate friends.

The "mountain men" were mostly local settlers in the Port Angeles area, or homesteaders who staked their homesites up the verdant valleys that penetrate the north and west sides of the range. These men roamed the range partly to hunt and fish, partly because they loved the high country in the same sense as a modern climber. One of the better known "mountain men," Billy Everett, is reported to have reached Cream Lake Basin as early as 1885. A party from the Port Townsend area penetrated all the way to Queets Basin via Dodwell-Rixon Pass in 1894. The Humes brothers, Will and Grant, roamed widely throughout the Elwha drainage and the adjacent high country. No doubt these men and others like them climbed many of the less difficult peaks but left no record. Little is known of the exploits of most of the "mountain men," so their accomplishments as well as their names will probably remain unrecorded.

Lt. Joseph P. O'Neil, earliest of the leaders of organized exploration, became interested in the early 1880s, after taking part in a discussion with other Army officers concerning the lack of knowledge of the interior. He volunteered to lead an exploration and was soon dispatched from Fort Vancouver to Port Townsend with three enlisted men and two civilian engineers to undertake the task. In the summer of 1885 the first of the O'Neil parties traveled south from Port Angeles to Hurricane Ridge, followed the ridges in a southeasterly direction to the vicinity of Obstruction Point, and continued southward along the divide almost as far as Mt. Anderson. O'Neil may have climbed Mt. Claywood and Mt. Fromme — certainly he named the former for Clay Wood, the assistant adjutant general who signed his orders. He was summarily recalled in midsummer and sent east for training, but his desire to complete the exploration of the Olympics remained undimmed.

In 1888 Eugene Semple, the last territorial governor of Washington, devoted a major portion of his report to the U.S. Department of the Interior to the riddle of the Olympics. Elisha P. Ferry, first elected governor of the state of Washington, was so impressed with his predecessor's report that he called for an exploration of the Olympics, and in response an early newspaper, the *Seattle Press,* organized an expedition. Throughout the winter of 1889-1890, the Press Expedition under the leadership of James H. Christie fought against unbelievable odds up the Elwha and Goldie rivers, finally crossing Low Divide to the North Fork of the Quinault River and arriving at Lake Quinault in May. Captain Charles A. Barnes, the expedition cartographer, produced the first reasonably accurate map of the interior, and the whole epic was published in a special 24-page edition of the *Press* on July 16, 1890.

One of the reasons for haste on the part of the Press party was the fear of being "scooped." They almost were, for in October, 1889, Samuel C. Gilman and his father, Charles A. Gilman, a former lieutenant governor of Minnesota, ascended the Quinault River by canoe, then continued overland to Anderson Pass before returning the way they had come in late November. This trip was reported only in passing by the media and was not generally known until *National Geographic* published the account in April, 1896.

O'Neil had returned to the Pacific Northwest in 1887, about the time that William G. Steel organized the Oregon Alpine Club. In 1890, as agitation to explore the Olympics increased, O'Neil found his superiors cooperative, and with Steel's help he quickly assembled a party primarily composed of enlisted men and members of the Oregon Alpine Club. He was able to obtain an advance copy of the Press Expedition report and set off across the range from the Skokomish River approach. The travel was incredibly difficult, since trails had to be built for pack animals. But with the help of the Hoquiam Board of Trade, which built 30 miles of trail to meet him from the coastal approach, he eventually crossed First Divide, ascended the Duckabush River to O'Neil Pass, and descended the Enchanted Valley to Lake Quinault.

The O'Neil Expedition completed a prodigious amount of work, with side parties exploring and mapping the drainages of the Dosewallips, Duckabush, North and South Forks of the Skokomish, Humptulips, Wynoochee, Satsop, Wishkah, North and East Forks of the Quinault, and the Queets rivers. The expedition is best remembered, however, for the first attempted ascent of Mt. Olympus. The earlier reported ascent in 1854 by five white men and four Makah Indians is now generally discounted.

Lt. O'Neil dispatched N. E. Linsley and B. J. Bretherton of the Oregon Alpine Club, Sgt. F. W. Yates, and four privates, to climb Mt. Olympus. From O'Neil Pass they traveled in a northwesterly direction to Queets Basin.

At the southeast base of Mt. Olympus, Private Fisher became separated from the main party and eventually found his way out the Queets canyon to the Pacific, no mean accomplishment. The remainder of the party climbed to the head of the Jeffers Glacier and made the final climb from the south on September 22, 1890. Linsley, Bretherton, and Private Danton were in the summit party, and they left a copper box near the top containing the record of the climb, a deck of cards, two army buttons, and various other mementos as a permanent record of the first ascent. The copper box has never been located, and just which peak was ascended by the O'Neil Expedition remains a mystery to this day.

During the summer of 1890 Judge James W. Wickersham of Tacoma, who later made the first attempt on Mt. McKinley in 1903, led a party up the Skokomish with the intent of crossing the range and descending the valley of the Elwha. After great hardship, one member of the party became ill from poison ivy, and the group came out the Dosewallips valley. After the many efforts of 1890 the public considered the mountains largely explored, and they attracted little attention for the next 15 years, with few visitors other than the "mountain men" traveling beyond the foothills.

When President Grover Cleveland created the Olympic Forest Reserve of 2,168,320 acres by proclamation in 1897, the Department of the Interior ordered a survey. The U.S. Geological Survey employed Theodore Rixon and Arthur Dodwell to complete this work, and for three years, from 1898 to 1900, these men and their four assistants toiled tirelessly, working in the high country in the summer and the foothills in the winter, and climbing many of the peaks for pleasure as much as duty. In all, they surveyed 97 townships or partial townships, 3483 square miles. Only 16 of these square miles had been logged. The total was staggering — 61 billion board feet of timber in the reserve alone. The records of their ascents are lost, but their exploration was so thorough and meticulous that it can be assumed they climbed all of the peaks which were not either technically difficult or far removed from timber or alpine meadows. We believe they climbed Mt. Carrie, Mt. Queets, and Mt. Noyes, from interviews with Rixon late in his life.

In August, 1899, the Dodwell-Rixon team was encamped near Blizzard Pass high on the divide between the Hoh and Humes glaciers. After conjecture that the summit of Olympus was virgin, Jack McGlone, one of the packers, set off alone at dusk for the ascent. Reaching the top, he recorded his ascent on a clipping from a Shelton newspaper and left it in a tin box. McGlone's clipping was recovered in 1907 on the 7780-foot East Peak when the second ascent was made by a party from The Mountaineers. Dodwell and Rixon accepted McGlone's notes for their report and thus missed a chance for the highest summit, for the entire party had planned to climb it the following day.

1907 was the great year for Mt. Olympus. The Mountaineers, newly formed in Seattle, selected this still-unclimbed summit as their first major objective and carefully planned the expedition to conquer it. An advance scouting party from the club climbed Queets and Noyes in May, and trail-building crews prepared the way up the Elwha valley throughout June and July. But in mid-July, a fortnight before the scheduled arrival of The Mountaineers, a team of three representing the American Geographical Society arrived in Port Angeles from New York with the avowed intent of climbing Mt. Olympus. Little is known of Walter G. Clarke, but Professor Hershell C. Parker and Belmore H. Browne were among the foremost American climbers of the day. Browne was rapidly gaining fame as a mountain artist; Parker had been one of the founders of the fledgling American Alpine Club. Both were members of the prestigious Explorers Club and had accompanied Dr. Frederick A. Cook in his attempt on Mt. McKinley in the preceding year. With two local packers they ascended the Elwha Snow Finger, crossed Dodwell-Rixon Pass, which they named for the survey team, and placed their last camp near the foot of the Humes Glacier, which they christened for one of their packers. They gained the summit of the Middle Peak on July 17 and, thinking it to be the highest in the broken clouds, returned triumphantly to civilization and announced that Olympus had been climbed.

The newspaper publicity was extensive, and The Mountaineers were incensed, for the eastern party had hired their packers, used their approach trail, and "stolen" their peak. Parker and Browne were especially vulnerable to criticism, for they had accused Dr. Cook, a national hero, of falsifying his claim to the first ascent of Mt. McKinley, and they had not yet been able to prove their contention. Some local climbers claimed that but for the skill of Will Humes the party would not have been able to make the climb, an absurdity when one considers that in 1912 Parker and Browne came within 300 feet of the summit of Mt. McKinley. On the other hand, at least one eastern writer was still crediting them with the first ascent of Mt. Olympus as recently as 1946.

Against this emotionally charged background The Mountaineers set forth with heavy heart, for it was too late for them to change their outing to another area. After climbing a number of lesser peaks, they ascended the East Peak on August 12 and found the record of Jack McGlone's lone climb. The following day a party of 11 led by L. A. Nelson climbed the Middle Peak and located the cairn left by Parker, Browne, and Clarke, then went on to the higher West Peak, and, congratulating themselves on their unbelievable good fortune, claimed the greatest prize of all.

The hard-rock miners arrived in the Olympics in the early 1900s, and by 1906 the first claims had been staked. The range is remarkably free of valuable minerals in commercial quantities, but small deposits of manganese were discovered at various points along the valleys of the eastern front range, and most of these deposits were accompanied by copper as a secondary mineral. The American Manganese Corporation established its mine at Tubal Cain in the Dungeness valley in 1908 and worked it and the satellite mine at Tull City

The Blue Glacier — a long time ago (courtesy Olympic National Park)

at intermittent intervals through 1941. Other small deposits were located in the drainages of the Hamma Hamma, the Duckabush, and the Dosewallips, and some mining was carried out near Little Hump and well below timberline on the southeast shoulder of Mt. Constance. Several hundred men were employed during the peak of the activity in the Dungeness drainage, and they probably roamed extensively across the barren ridges near Mt. Townsend, Tyler Peak, Baldy, and the Buckhorn-Iron area, but no record of climbs has survived.

Following the ascent of Mt. Olympus many parties climbed extensively in the range, though some of the greatest summits remained unclimbed for decades. The Klahane Club was formed in Port Angeles in 1919, and The Olympians were founded in 1921 in Grays Harbor. The Bremerton branch of The Mountaineers was started in 1920, and though short-lived it contributed to the establishment of the climbing tradition in Kitsap County which eventually spawned the Bremerton Alpine Club and later the Olympic College climbing program. The Mountaineers and their branches in Tacoma and Everett continued to visit the range regularly, making the first ascent of Mt. Anderson in 1920. The Mazamas of Portland first scheduled an Olympic summer outing in 1928 and have been frequent visitors since that time.

Mt. Constance, third highest peak in the range and dominant on the eastern front overlooking Puget Sound, attracted the attention of climbers at an early time. The peak proved to be unusually complex, difficult of access even for the Olympics, and well-guarded by many nearly vertical pillow-basalt cliffs. After at least five previous attempts, it was successfully climbed in June, 1922, when A. E. "Bremerton" Smith and Robert Schellin, members of The Mountaineers, solved the approach puzzle and reached the top by a long and complex route that was not repeated for 60 years. They were immediately accused of falsifying the ascent by John "Johnny the Trapper" Clements in the Brinnon General Store before they had even returned home. Clements wrote a letter to the *Seattle Star* claiming the party had "pulled a Doc. Cook," and it was published on the front page. Two young assistant camp directors from Boy Scout Camp Parsons at Brinnon, Henry E. Thomson and Harold B. Sparks, set out to duplicate the climb and, with the aid of a sketch provided by Smith and Schellin, made the second ascent in September by a variation and returned with proof of the first ascent.

The Boy Scouts have had a long and intimate association with the range. Edmund S. Meany, commissioner of scouting in the Puget Sound region led a group of Scouts into the Olympus area in 1914, prior to the organization of local Scout councils, and is reported to have made the first ascent of Mt. Tom at that time, though some historians now consider this story apocryphal. In the following years the Seattle Council established its main camp on Hood Canal, the Tumwater Council at Lower Lena Lake, and the Twin Harbors Council on Lake Quinault. The second and third ascents of Mt. Constance were completed by Boy Scout parties in 1922 and 1923. The second ascent of Mt. Anderson and the second ascent of the South Peak of The Brothers, both in 1924, were by Boy Scouts. Over a period of several decades these groups ranged widely throughout the mountains — accounting for place names such as Lake of the Angels, Del Monte Ridge, and Scout Lake — and climbed a majority of the summits that did not require ropes and many of a more difficult nature. With the changes in national Scout policy in the late forties, provisional unit camping was eliminated, and Scout use of the remote high country decreased markedly.

Theodore Roosevelt created the Mt. Olympus National Monument by proclamation in 1909, but conservationists recognized that this did not provide adequate protection, for national monuments could be reduced in size at presidential whim. Three such reductions were made between 1912 and 1929, leaving the remaining monument barely half its original size. In 1933 national monuments were transferred from the jurisdiction of the U.S. Forest Service to the National Park Service, and during this decade pressure to create a national park mounted. The Forest Service created an adjacent primitive area in 1936, in an effort to allay the drive for park status, but this proved unsuccessful, and Congress created Olympic National Park in 1938. While the park is quite large, 914,576 acres at present, much of it is in the western lowlands and the coastal strip, and many of the most prominent peaks are on the eastern border or in Olympic National Forest.

In 1984 the Washington Wilderness Act created 23 new wilderness areas throughout the state on national forest and Bureau of Land Management property. Five of these are located in the Olympic National Forest. These areas are all roadless, and some trails that previously permitted motorized vehicles have now been closed to that use. The forest service is posting these trails, and closures are signed with a red "X". These wilderness areas effectively provide protection to all of the major peaks that are outside Olympic National Park.

In the northeast corner of the range the 45,601-acre Buckhorn Wilderness includes Mts. Fricaba and Townsend, Tyler and Maynard peaks, and Buckhorn and Iron mountains. Farther to the south The Brothers Wilderness fronts the east border of the park from the Dosewallips River to Lena Lake. This 17,239-acre area protects St. Peter's Dome and Mt. Jupiter as well as The Brothers. The 15,686-acre Mt. Skokomish Wilderness also includes Henderson, Cruiser, Pershing, Washington, Ellinor, Rose, Stone, and Copper mountains. The tiny and rarely visited 2320-acre Wonder Mountain Wilderness to the west of Lake Cushman contains not one mile of maintained trail. Almost as trailless, the 12,120-acre Colonel Bob Wilderness, farther to the west and south of the Quinault River, boasts only ten miles of trail and climbing goals of only moderate interest.

Areas providing challenging rock climbing in the range are limited, and interest developed relatively late. A group from the Bremerton Alpine Club became involved in the mid-thirties, and with a break for the Second World War, they and their successors climbed all but a few of the pinnacles on the Sawtooth Ridge. These outstanding climbers included Paul Crews, Don Dooley, Bob Henderson, Bob Layton, Ruth Carlow, Elvin "Swede" Johnson, and others. First ascents were still being made in the area as recently as 1960. The other main rock-climbing area in the Olympics, The Needles, first attracted the attention of Bremerton climbers in 1940, when George Martin and "Swede" Johnson climbed the two highest peaks. Various Seattle area climbers were also involved in rock climbing throughout the Olympics, notably the Beckey brothers, Bill and Adelaide Degenhardt, and Joe Halwax and Scott Osborne. The last major first ascent in The Needles, The Arrowhead, was not completed until 1962.

One of the most unusual aspects of the climbing history of the Olympic Mountains is that so many of the highest and most challenging summits remained virgin for so long. Despite the tremendous post-war boom in tourism and great climbing activity on scores of peaks, most climbers seem to have clung to the familiar mountains and routes. With less than 50 peaks in the range exceeding 7000 feet in elevation, half of these were still unclimbed in 1940, one quarter remained in 1950, and a few had not yet been climbed in 1960.

Today the exploration is virtually completed and all the major summits have been climbed. The wilderness remains as challenging as ever, though, and much of it is yet untrodden.

GEOLOGICAL CONSIDERATIONS

From the climber's viewpoint, there are three main geologic factors contributing to the most interesting peaks: the composition of the rock, the recency of sculpture by glaciation, and the overall height of the mountain. These three factors are not independent of each other, and on any one climb other characteristics of the rock, such as the nature of the jointing, may be important.

Some of the best climbing in the Olympic Mountains is on hard basalt lavas which form partial rings around a core of sedimentary and metamorphic rocks. The lavas erupted on the ocean bottom in horizontal layers about 60 million years ago (Lower Tertiary Era) and became interlayered with sand

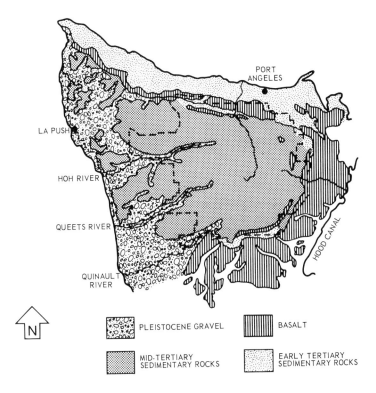

and mud. The outermost basalt layer later bulged up like the skin of a giant blister and has been broken and breached by erosion. It now forms the most extensive and continuous ring and offers some of the most challenging climbing. Peaks in this ring such as Constance, The Brothers, Pershing, and Lincoln stand high and steep above the more rounded ridges of sedimentary rock. The importance of relative hardness is shown by these mountains, for they have not been heavily glaciated recently except near their summits, and they are not in the highest part of the range.

An inner ring of basalts offers high-angle climbing of varying soundness in The Needles and Sawtooth Ridge. Even where the basalt is only present as relatively thin slivers it makes imposing pinnacles or faces, such as Piro's Spire, some fangs on Cameron Creek, and Steeple Rock. Very thin slivers of basaltic rock deeper in the core of the range hold up bold faces or ridges on Mt. Fromme and Mt. Claywood and on the north ridge of Mt. Ferry.

All three factors have operated to make challenging climbs of the hard sandstone peaks of Mt. Olympus and its flanking retinue of smaller summits. Summits of phyllite or slate, on the other hand, offer very little exciting work even in the Mt. Olympus area, though they may present some imposing faces smoothed by glaciers, such as the east side of Mt. Dana or Dodger Point.

Although these factors govern the major pattern of the mountains, the details of the climb are commonly determined by the nature of the jointing. Joints are cracks formed as internal pressures release when the rocks become exposed to the earth's surface by erosion. Closely spaced joints cause the peaks to crumble into relatively easy heaps of rubble. Widely spaced joints leave flawless monoliths and pinnacles on the ridge tops. The basalts of Sawtooth Ridge and The Needles have widely spaced joints. Meany, Queets, and Anderson are sandstone peaks with imposing summit blocks.

WEATHER

The Olympics lie in the storm belt of the Pacific and are notorious for their highly changeable weather. Even on the leeward side of the range, precipitation is heavy and weather patterns shift with alarming rapidity. Since most of the more rewarding climbs in the range require a minimum of two to three days, it is always advisable to prepare for summer storms. Temperature variations can be as much as 70 degrees in a 24-hour period in the high interior, and it is not uncommon to experience clear skies and debilitating heat followed by clouds, rain, and driving sleet, in the course of a single summer afternoon. The so-called "rain shadow" of the Olympics is an exception to this pattern, and weather in this sheltered area, which is protected by the high mountains to the west and south, is much more stable and salubrious. This belt comprises the lower drainages of the Gray Wolf, Cameron, Grand, Dungeness, and Quilcene rivers, as well as all of the rock-climbing areas in The Needles.

Changes in weather patterns in the interior of the range are frequently of relatively long duration. It is not uncommon to have several days or weeks of splendid weather followed by an extended period of more than a week of heavy summer rain and chilling temperatures. Storms usually blow in from the southwest or west, though there are occasional exceptions. Typical signs of weather change consist of an advancing and thickening line of cirrus or cirro-stratus clouds, often followed within 24 hours by a frontal system. Thunderstorms seldom occur in these mountains, though lightning, if it occurs, is as great a hazard here as elsewhere.

ACCESS

The Olympic Peninsula is easily reached from Puget Sound cities by car, using cross-Sound ferries and the Olympic Highway (U.S. 101) which surrounds the mountains. The Aberdeen-Hoquiam area and Port Angeles are served by scheduled flights, and bus service is available on the Olympic Highway. Spur roads from the Olympic Highway follow various river valleys into the interior. The Hurricane Ridge road, the Sol Duc Hot Springs road, and the Hoh River road are paved. Other roads are gravel and are generally in fair condition. All roads end at low elevations except the Deer Park and Hurricane Ridge roads. Detailed information on access to specific climbing areas is included in the introduction to each climbing section.

Exact distances on both roads and trails are given in decimals. Approximate distances are given in fractions.

MAPS

One of the advantages enjoyed by climbers in this range is complete coverage by relatively high-quality maps. The USGS is currently engaged in remapping all of the portion of the range covered with 15' quads and will be issuing the new maps in 7½' format. Some of these new maps are now available. The USGS also publishes a topographic map of Olympic National Park in both regular and shaded-relief editions. The date of issue of currently available USGS maps in the mountainous areas of the peninsula is as follows:

7½' Quadrangles		15' Quadrangles	
Mt. Muller	1978	Mt. Tom	1956
Lake Crescent	1978	Mt. Olympus	1956
Lake Sutherland	1978	Mt. Angeles	1944
Elwha	1978	Tyler Peak	1946
Port Angeles	1979	Kloochman Rock	1956
Slide Peak	1978	Mt. Christie	1947
Bogachiel Peak	1950	Mt. Steel	1947
Mt. Carrie	1950	The Brothers	1947
Hurricane Hill	1950	Quinault Lake	1955
Mt. Washington	1985	Grisdale	1955
Mt. Jupiter	1985	Mt. Tebo	1953
The Brothers	1985		

A free index to topographic quadrangles in Washington can be obtained on request from the Distribution Section, Geological Survey, Federal Center, Denver, Colorado 80225. The quads can also be purchased from this center as well as from most map and outdoor stores in northwestern Washington.

Little River Enterprises of Port Angeles started producing *Custom Correct Maps* in 1984 and has brought out 11 maps of the mountainous portions of the peninsula to date. These are based on USGS quads with updated material on roads and trails. They differ from other similar efforts in that each map covers a specific area of interest to the user, such as a sub-range or watershed, without regard to the borders of USGS quadrangles. These high-quality maps are available at most western Washington outdoor stores. Additional maps will probably be available by the time this book is published.

Green Trails Maps of Bellevue, Washington, produce 15′ quadrangles with contour lines at a slightly smaller scale than the corresponding USGS quads, but with more recent trail and road conditions superimposed. These cover the mountainous areas of the peninsula and are widely available at map and outdoor stores. Their Olympic Peninsula maps are currently undergoing revision and will probably be available by the time this book is published.

Pargeter's Picture Map-Guide to the Olympic Mountains, updated to 1983 by Richard Pargeter, and *The Olympic Peninsula Pictorial Relief Map,* updated to 1983 by Dee Molenaar, are both excellent shaded relief maps of the overall range which are available at most outdoor and map stores.

The planimetric Olympic National Forest/Olympic National Park map can be purchased through Olympic National Forest headquarters in Olympia, Olympic National Park headquarters in Port Angeles, or at ranger stations for a nominal fee. This map is normally updated at two-year intervals.

Olympic National Forest now produces maps of each district which are topographic and include the latest road numbering. They also produce planimetric fireman's maps at regular intervals with updated road changes, helispots, and other information for internal use. The fireman's maps are not normally available to the general public. All updated road information in this book is taken from the 1983 fireman's maps.

BACKCOUNTRY REGULATIONS

Olympic National Park has no climbing regulations, but both the park and forest recommend registering for climbs. The park and forest do enforce some rules pertaining to backcountry usage, primarily regarding fire management, domestic animals, sanitation, and protection of wildlife and wilderness. Open fires are widely prohibited in the high country and discouraged throughout the park and forest, for small stoves leave no scar. If a fire is necessary it should be kept small and built in a place where fires have been built before. Backcountry use permits are issued at no cost but are required

Olympic Rock (Rich Olson)

throughout the park and wilderness areas for overnight stays. Group size is limited to 12, to reduce human impact on the fragile high country.

Quotas have been established for 20 persons per day at Lake Constance and 30 persons per day at Flapjack Lakes from June 15 through Labor Day. Telephone reservations may be made for half the quotas for each area by calling Staircase, (206) 877-5569, between 8:00 A.M. and 5:00 P.M. The remaining reservations are available on a first-come first-served basis. Reserved permits must be picked up by 11:00 A.M. on the day of entry at the ranger station nearest your destination.

Regulations throughout the park and forest service wilderness areas are virtually identical. All litter must be packed out. Human waste should be disposed of at least 200 feet from the nearest water in a hole no deeper than 8 inches and covered with dirt. Tents must not be ditched. No motorized equipment is allowed other than battery-powered devices such as shavers and cameras.

The general philosophical underpinning of these regulations can best be explained by citing the definition of wilderness in the Wilderness Act of 1964, which states: "A wilderness . . . is hereby recognized as an area where the earth and its community of life are untrammeled by man, where man himself is a visitor who does not remain."

RATING SYSTEM

The Modified NCCS, a marriage of the National Climbing Classification System and the Sierra Decimal System, was selected for use in this guidebook because it was felt that it most nearly satisfied the rating problems found in the Olympics, such as an abundance of snow, long arduous approaches, the relative difficulty in route finding, and the heavy forest growth often extending into the technical portions of the route. It is the system in use in volumes I, II, and III of the *Cascade Alpine Guide,* and it is the system best understood by most currently active climbers in the Pacific Northwest.

Overall Difficulty. The overall difficulty of the route is represented by a Roman numeral from I through VI, with the difficulty increasing in ascending order. This rating, known as the "Grade," takes many factors into account — the length of the route in terms of both time and distance; the average difficulty of all the individual pitches; the ease of escape or retreat, if required; the extent of the weather problem, either in estimating it or in the effect of rain or snow on the route; the various objective dangers, such as avalanche or rockfall; the route-finding difficulty; and, somewhat more vaguely, the challenge or degree of commitment required by the route.

Since many factors are used to establish the overall difficulty rating, one should not expect, for example, to be able to climb all Grade III climbs just because he has been successful on one Grade III route. An experienced climber might apply the same Grade to two climbs, even though one involved a 5.8 pitch, while the second had no pitches exceeding 5.4 in classification.

Individual Pitch Free-Climbing Difficulty. Never applied to an entire climb, this rating, known as the "Class," indicates the severity of the most difficult free pitch of the route, and is signified by Arabic numbers applied in ascending order of difficulty. These numbers are loosely defined as follows.

> 1 — Walking
> 2 — Scrambling, some use of the hands required
> 3 — Advisable to rope up, occasional belaying
> 4 — Continuous belaying required for safety
> 5 — Placement of protection required for safety

Class 5 is further subdivided into tenths to more accurately identify the difficulty of technical climbing. A comparison of the Grade of overall difficulty with the Class of the most difficult pitch will give an experienced climber a fairly accurate indication of what can be expected.

Individual Pitch Aid-Climbing Difficulty. The classification of the most difficult direct aid pitch is represented by the letter "A" (for aid) followed by an Arabic number from 1 to 5. A1 and A2 climbs can usually be done using standard hardware, while specialized equipment or techniques will normally be required for A3, A4, or A5 climbs. Since few routes in the Olympics require direct aid, this part of the rating is usually absent.

Applying the System to the Olympic Range. Many Olympic climbs are started only after miles of approach by trail; this distance is not included as part of the rating. The classification of a route starts where the party leaves the trail, or, in a few instances, the road, if that is where the climb begins.

The Olympics are not especially well suited to the technical specialist, and most routes included in the guide provide an overall mountaineering experience. Therefore the overall difficulty Grade as applied in this guide places increased emphasis on route finding, wilderness travel, brush beating (some of it vertical), length of the route, friability of the rock, and objective danger, and slightly less emphasis on pure technical difficulty. This can be contrasted with the Teton Range, more suited to the technician, where the guidebook has given primary emphasis to technical climbing and less emphasis to the relatively simple and straightforward approaches.

These ratings apply to good summertime conditions. Any climb obviously increases in difficulty as conditions deteriorate. Assignment of a rating to each route was made only after considerable discussion and was done as objectively as possible. Since ratings are, by their nature, subjective, it is expected that all climbers will not agree with the rating assigned to every route. Novices will be inclined to feel that some routes are underrated, while experts may take the opposite position.

STANDARD CLIMBS

OVERALL ROUTE DIFFICULTY, OR "GRADE"

I Mt. Buckhorn (low in grade)
   Mt. Angeles, easiest route
   Mt. Carrie, from Heart Lake
   Mt. Washington, south side
      routes
   Mt. Anderson, Flypaper Pass
      route
   The Brothers, South Couloir
      (high in grade)

II Mt. Olympus, from Glacier
      Meadows (low in grade)
   Mt. Johnson, all routes
   Mt. Constance; Mountaineer,
   College, and Mazama routes
   Mt. Cruiser, West Face
   The Brothers; North Peak and
      Great Basin routes
   Chimney Peak
   West Peak, Anderson Massif
      (high in grade)

III Mt. Constance; West Arête and
      Northeast Ridge
   Mt. Constance, Red Dike
      (high in grade)

IV Mt. Constance, North Face

INDIVIDUAL FREE-PITCH DIFFICULTY, OR "CLASS"

1. Mt. Townsend
    Sentinel Peak
    Mt. Lena
    Mt. Appleton

2. Mt. Ellinor, easiest route (low
       in class)
    Mt. Angeles, easiest route
    Mt. Carrie (from Heart Lake)
    Mt. Lincoln, easiest route

3. Mt. Washington, south side
       routes (low in class)
    The Brothers, South Couloir
       (low in class)
    Mt. Olympus, from Glacier
       Meadows
    Mt. Constance; Mountaineer,
       College, and Mazama
       routes
    The Fin, South Ridge

West Peak (Anderson Massif)
   (high in class)

4. Inner Constance, Route 1 (low
       in class)
    Mt. Johnson, Route 1A
    Chimney Peak, Route 2
    Mt. Mathias

*This is where the average party
   begins to use protection.*

5.0 The Bandersnatch
     Castle Spires, West Face

5.1 Mt. Johnson, Route 1B

5.2 Sweat Spire
     The Fin, Northeast Face

5.3 The Royal Shaft
     The Arrowhead

STANDARD CLIMBS —
INDIVIDUAL FREE-PITCH DIFFICULTY, OR "CLASS"

5.4 Mt. Constance, West Arête
     Mt. Cruiser, Route 1A

5.5 Mt. Cruiser, West Face
     The Horn, West Face

5.6 Mt. Cruiser, Northeast Face

5.7 Mt. Cruiser, East Face
     Mt. Cruiser, WSW Corner

RECOMMENDED CLIMBS

The following climbs are representative of the best that the Olympic Mountains have to offer. While not necessarily the longest, the highest, or the most difficult, they provide a typical cross section of the types of climbing available and are generally enjoyable and worthwhile.

ONE-DAY CLIMBS

Mt. Angeles. A short, pleasant climb with a variety of routes. Provides an excellent view of both the interior and the Strait of Juan de Fuca.

Mt. Ellinor. Popular in any season, this short climb, mostly on good trail, is readily accessible and offers an excellent view of the interior.

Mt. Stone. This scenic climb provides enough elevation gain to give a feeling of accomplishment and an excellent view of the interior.

Mt. Washington. One of the most popular summits in the range. Washington has a variety of routes, some quite challenging, and good mixed climbing in season.

TWO-DAY CLIMBS

The Brothers. A popular scenic climb in the eastern front range. Not difficult. The traverse is an excellent route in early season.

Mt. Constance. Even the "dog routes" are challenging, the summit is high, the scenery is superb, and the tough routes are the most difficult in the range.

Cruiser. The Olympic's best-known and most frequently done rock climb, on excellent Sawtooth pillow lava. The summit is airy, the tough routes are hairy.

Warrior. Infrequently done, this peak deserves more attention for both beauty and climbing enjoyment.

The Horn. A short but excellent rock climb on pillow lava in the scenic Sawtooth Ridge above Flapjack Lakes. A choice of routes is available.

CLIMBS OF THREE OR MORE DAYS

Mt. Anderson. Located in the geographic and hydrographic center of the Olympics, this scenic glaciated peak reminds one of a miniature "major."

Mt. Mathias. Perhaps the least known of the more difficult peaks in the Olympics. Mathias is challenging by either route and provides good mixed climbing.

The Needles. A visit to Royal Basin, in the protection of the rain shadow, is a must for those who would know the Olympics. Mt. Clark is the best climb, but Johnson, The Incisor, and Arrowhead are all worthwhile.

Mt. Olympus. The monarch of the range, Olympus can be a pleasant glaciated climb in good weather or a nightmare of route-finding problems and crevasses in fog or sleet. The scenery is superb.

REFERENCES

Across the Olympic Mountains — The Press Expedition 1889-90, by Robert L. Wood, The Mountaineers, Seattle, second edition, 1976. 220 pages.

Gods & Goblins — A Field Guide to Place Names of Olympic National Park, by Smitty Parratt, C P Publications, Inc., Port Angeles, 1984. 223 pages.

Guide to the Geology of Olympic National Park, by Rowland W. Tabor, University of Washington Press, Seattle, 1975. 144 pages.

Lakes of Washington — Volume 1, Western Washington, by E. E. Walcott, Department of Ecology, Olympia, third edition, 1973. 619 pages.

Men, Mules and Mountains — Lieutenant O'Neil's Olympic Expeditions, by Robert L. Wood, The Mountaineers, Seattle, 1976. 483 pages.

Off Belay, Volume 1, Number 4, special edition on the Olympics, Renton, August, 1972. 60 pages.

Olympic Mountains Trail Guide — National Park and National Forest, by Robert L. Wood, The Mountaineers, Seattle, 1984. 317 pages.

100 Hikes in the South Cascades and Olympics, by Ira Spring and Harvey Manning, The Mountaineers, Seattle, 1985. 240 pages.

Trips and Trails 2, by E. M. Sterling, The Mountaineers, Seattle, third edition, 1983. 224 pages.

A number of publications, such as the *American Alpine Journal, Mountaineer,* and *Mazama,* contain helpful articles on specific peaks and routes. Where applicable, specific references to these publications are provided in the climbing routes at the end of each peak's route description coverage.

CLIMBING ROUTES

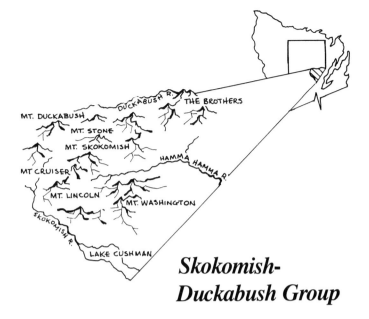

Skokomish-Duckabush Group

The southern mountains of the eastern Olympics are deeply dissected by three rivers flowing into Hood Canal: the Hamma Hamma, the Duckabush, and the North and South Forks of the Skokomish. Above Lake Cushman the North Fork of the Skokomish River flows south from its sources which, along with the Duckabush River, form a natural boundary virtually enclosing this group. West of the North Fork Skokomish River drainage, water flows into the Quinault River on its way to the Pacific Ocean.

While the general peak elevation is less than that of other parts of the Olympics, the contours are no less rugged. Near timberline, many lakes are nestled in parklike meadows and heather. Active glaciers have vanished long ago, but large snowfields persist on northern slopes all summer. The jagged Sawtooth Ridge just east of Flapjack Lakes has a number of prominent pillow-lava pinnacles, offering some top challenges for rock climbers.

Its proximity to metropolitan areas, with generally good climbing terrain and relatively accessible peaks, makes this group by far the most frequently climbed in the Olympic Range.

APPROACHES

1. *Skokomish River (North Fork).* This approach provides entrance to Lake Cushman and the beautiful Staircase area of the Olympic National Park. The Sawtooth Ridge, Mt. Steel, Mt. Lincoln, and Copper Mountain are the

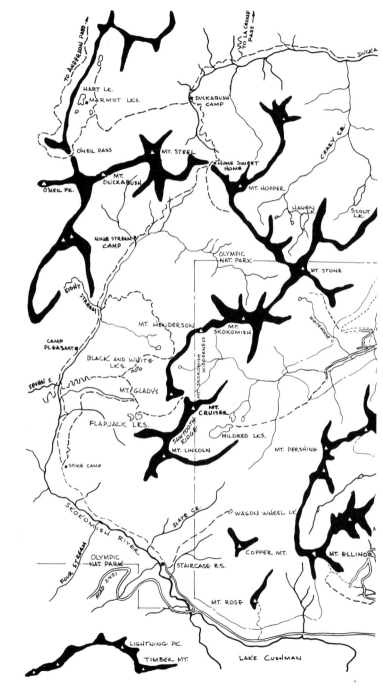

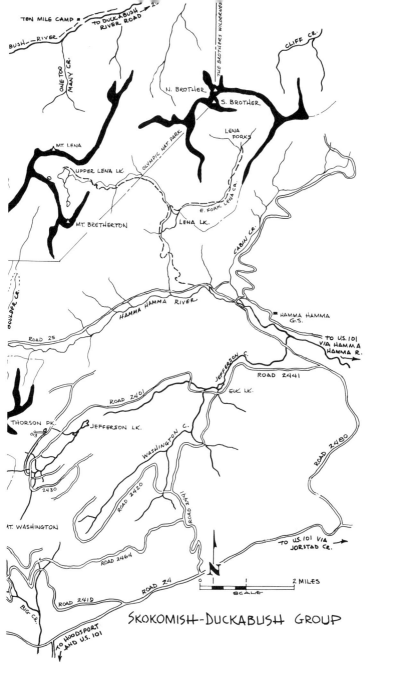

SKOKOMISH-DUCKABUSH GROUP

main peaks accessible from the Staircase area. This approach also leads to Lightning Peak and the eastern climbing routes of Mt. Ellinor and Mt. Washington.

Two roads lead into this area from U.S. 101 on Hood Canal: the Lake Cushman road (a paved road from Hoodsport), and the Jorstad Creek road.

1a. The Lake Cushman road leaves U.S. 101 at Hoodsport (16 miles N of Shelton). Drive W on paved road for 9 miles to the "T" intersection with Forest Service road # 24. Turn left and continue 6½ miles past the lake to the end of the road at the Staircase Ranger Station (770 ft.) in Olympic National Park.

Several enjoyable trails branch into the Olympics from the Staircase Ranger Station. (Note: Mileages in this paragraph are from the Ranger Station.) The most popular is the Skokomish River trail which follows the river and then climbs to First Divide (12.9 miles, 4688 ft.) where it connects with the Duckabush River trail. Campsites are at Spike Camp (3.4 miles, 1500 ft.), Camp Pleasant (6.7 miles, 1530 ft.), Nine Stream (9.6 miles, 2090 ft.), and Home Sweet Home (13.2 miles, 4200 ft.).

Three trails branch off the Skokomish River trail. The one to Black and White Lakes (4500 ft.) and Smith Lakes (3900 ft.) leaves the main trail at 5.3 miles. The Six Ridge trail, which may be followed to the Quinault River, leaves the Skokomish River trail after it crosses the river at 5.6 miles. The Flapjack Lakes trail starts at 3.4 miles (Spike Camp) and extends 4.1 miles to Flapjack Lakes (3900 ft., campsites) and then continues 1.4 miles to Gladys Divide, the starting point for many climbs in the Sawtooth Ridge, including Mt. Cruiser.

1b. The Jorstad Creek road leaves U.S. 101 2 miles S of Eldon (at the Jorstad Creek bridge). The road becomes Forest Service road # 24 after 1.2 miles, and it connects with the Lake Cushman road in another 7.3 miles.

The Big Creek logging road, # 2419 (used for the eastern approaches to Mt. Ellinor and Mt. Washington), branches from the Jorstad Creek road (# 24) 7 miles from U.S. 101. This road can also be easily reached by turning right at the "T" intersection of the Lake Cushman road with road # 24. Drive 1.5 miles more and turn hard left at the "Y".

2. *Hamma Hamma River.* Though one of the shorter rivers of the Olympics, the Hamma Hamma flows through a scenic subalpine region. Its waters, flowing from many peaks including The Brothers, Mt. Stone, Mt. Skokomish, and Mt. Bretherton, are augmented by Jefferson Creek, the principal drainage of Mt. Washington and Mt. Pershing. All of those peaks except Mt. Washington are best reached via this approach. Like the Skokomish, this area may be reached by two roads.

2a. The Hamma Hamma River road (Forest Service road # 25) branches W from U.S. 101 13½ miles N of Hoodsport. The Hamma Hamma campground is reached after 6 miles. The road continues ½ mile to a junction with road # 2480, turns right, and then gradually climbs for 7 miles to where it crosses the Hamma Hamma River and immediately ends in a parking area. An ungraded 5-mile trail leads from here to Mildred Lakes, the western approach to Mt. Pershing and the eastern approach to the Sawtooth Ridge. The popular Lena Lakes trail begins on this road 7.7 miles from U.S. 101. Lena Lake (1800 ft., campsites) is reached after 3 miles of well-graded trail; the trail then continues 4.3 miles to Upper Lena Lake (4600 ft.). For the standard climbs of The Brothers, cross Lena Creek at the head of Lena Lake and proceed up the East Fork Lena Creek through the Valley of Silent Men to Lena Forks campsite (3000 ft.) at 6.2 miles from the road.

2b. The Jorstad Creek road leaves U.S. 101 2 miles S of Eldon (at the Jorstad Creek bridge). After 1.2 miles, the road forks. The right fork (# 2480) continues for 8.9 miles where it connects with the Hamma Hamma River road (# 25) after crossing the river.

The Jefferson Creek road, used for the N and W approaches to Mt. Washington and the E and S approaches to the Pershing-Thorson Massif, is reached by turning left off road # 2480 about 6.5 miles from U.S. 101. Follow the Washington Creek road (# 2441) for 3 miles and hold to the right on the Jefferson Creek road (# 2401). Jefferson Lake is 3 miles farther.

3. ***Duckabush River.*** The 6.1-mile Duckabush River road begins just N of the Duckabush River bridge on U.S. 101 (22 miles N of Hoodsport and 3.6 miles S of Brinnon). In about 4 miles it becomes Forest Service road # 2515, and at about 6 miles it turns left and becomes the Murhut Creek road (# 2530). At this point, spur road # 011 continues upriver about 0.1 mile to a parking area below Little Hump. From here, the Duckabush River trail climbs steeply over Big Hump and then follows the river, eventually connecting with the Skokomish River trail (17.7 miles, 2695 ft.). Campsites are located at Tenmile (10.6 miles, 1500 ft.), Upper Duckabush (17.7 miles, 2695 ft.), Marmot Lakes (21.1 miles, 4300 ft.), and Hart Lake (21.7 miles, 4800 ft.).

RANGER STATIONS

Hoodsport — both USFS and NPS (just off U.S. 101), Staircase (end of Lake Cushman-Staircase road). Guard Stations: Hamma Hamma (Hamma Hamma River road), Interrorem (Duckabush River road). Note: Check with ranger regarding limits on size of party and use of campfires.

CAMPGROUNDS

U.S. 101: Potlatch State Park, el. 20 ft. (3 miles S of Hoodsport).

Lake Cushman-Staircase Road: Lake Cushman State Park, el. 750 ft. (7 miles W of Hoodsport); Staircase, el. 770 ft. (16 miles W of Hoodsport).

Hamma Hamma River Road: Hamma Hamma, el. 600 ft. (6 miles W of

U.S. 101); Lena Creek, el. 600 ft. (7.8 miles W of U.S. 101).

Duckabush River Road: Camp Collins, el. 200 ft. (4.1 miles W of U.S. 101).

Lake Cushman-Jorstead Creek Road: Lilliwap Creek, el. 950 ft. (5 miles N of Lake Cushman State Park on road #24).

VANTAGE POINTS

Mt. Ellinor, Jefferson Ridge, and Mt. Jupiter are accessible by trail. An impressive closeup view of Mt. Washington, Mt. Pershing, Thorson Peak, and Mt. Stone may be seen by continuing up logging roads past Jefferson Lake to points on both sides of the Jefferson Creek valley.

MAPS

Olympic National Forest/Olympic National Park; USGS 30-minute Olympic National Park and Vicinity; the following 15-minute USGS and Green Trail quadrangles: The Brothers, Mt. Steel, Mt. Christie, Mt. Tebo, and Grisdale; the following Custom Correct Maps: The Brothers-Mount Anderson, Enchanted Valley-Skokomish, and Mount Skokomish-Lake Cushman.

THE BROTHERS   6866 (2093 m)

This double-summit peak, the most imposing feature of the eastern skyline of the Olympics, is located 2 miles north of Lena Lake on the Duckabush-Hamma Hamma River divide. It was named after the Fauntleroy brothers in 1856 by Professor George Davidson. First ascent of the South Peak 1912 by I. Collier, O. Corkenill, W. Dehn, W. Fish, E. Goldsmith, and H. Trumbull. First ascent of the slightly lower North Peak 1908 by C. Hill and W. Hill. First ascent of both peaks was made from the Duckabush via Cliff Creek (very brushy).

South Peak   6866 (2093 m)

Route 1 (South Couloir). I, 3. Follow the Lena Lake trail (leaves Hamma Hamma River road 7.7 miles from U.S. 101, 685 ft.) 3 miles to Lena Lake (1800 ft., campsites). Continue on trail around the head of the lake and up the East Fork of Lena Creek through the Valley of Silent Men to the Lena Forks campsite (3.2 miles, 3000 ft.). From here, follow a faint trail in the general NW direction of the left (W) fork of the creek. In about 30 minutes, a small avalanche meadow just below the first cliff is reached. Cross the meadow and ascend W across a minor tree-covered ridge to a rocky or snow-filled gully. Climb this gully which opens into a snowfield or broad open slope. Bear slightly right ascending easy slope to a headwall (ca. 5000 ft.) where it is best to climb right (E) on minor ledges to an open rocky slope below a group of small trees (Lunch Rock). This passes under a steep narrow gully called the

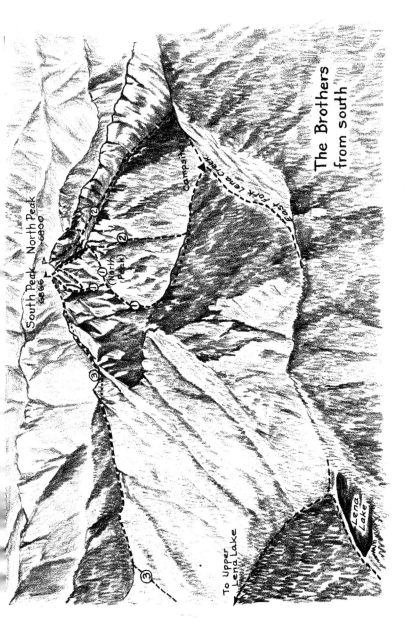

The Brothers
from south

South Peak North Peak
6866   6800

① (North Peak)

②

③

Campsite

EAST FORK LENA CREEK

To Upper
Lena Lake

Lena Lake

"Hourglass" which collects falling rocks and avalanche debris from the entire south couloir. Climb N about 200 yards and then bear slightly left into the narrow upper couloir which is followed to about 6000 ft. where the slope broadens. From here, either bear right under the summit block to the ridge or go straight up through a narrow chute. Climb to the summit by either route on broken and loose rock. Time: 8 hours up from road.

Route 2. I, 4. From the meadow of Route 1, climb the steep cliffs directly to a SE spur ridge. Follow the spur to the summit. The upper part of the route is steep and exposed. Time: 8 hours up from road.

Route 3 (SW Ridge). II, 3. Climb after an approach via the lower half of the Upper Lena Lake trail and a difficult brush crash to the Mt. Lena-Brothers saddle. This, the early popular route, is very long. Time: 9 hours up from saddle.

North Peak   ca. 6800 (2073 m)

Route 1. II, 3. After reaching Lunch Rock on Route 1, South Peak, traverse upward toward SE spur and contour into the eastern Great Basin. An alternate route is to descend from the South Peak summit into the same basin, dropping below the prominent buttress. From the basin, ascend a couloir and moderate rock to the small summit. Time: 9 hours up from camp at Lena Creek forks.

Route 2. II, 3. This route should be done in early season because of later heavy brush. From camp on the East Fork of Lena Creek (see Route 1, South Peak), proceed up the far right branch of the East Fork about ¾ mile. Near the upper end of the valley, climb westerly up into the eastern Great Basin. From the basin, climb the snow couloir of Route 1 or make an ascending traverse around to the N slope of the peak, and proceed up the N ridge to the summit. Time: 9 hours up from camp.

Route 3. II, 4. First ascent 1970 by R. Beckett, H. Pinsch, L. Triboulet, and R. Yekel.
Take the Murhut Creek logging road, #2530 (see Duckabush River approach) to where it reaches the saddle between Cabin Creek and the E fork of Cliff Creek (ca. 4100 ft.). Ascend wooded ridge W and S until reaching a narrow rocky ridge (ca. 30 minutes) which extends all the way W to the summit. At about 4900 ft., the ridge's gendarmes may be bypassed by crossing to the N side and traversing to the meadow on the N slopes of the peak. Continue as in Route 2. Time: 10 hours up from road; 10 hours down.

Brothers Traverse

First traverse S to N in 1939 by R. Carlow, D. Dooley, B. Henderson, W. Ingalls, E. Johnson, and S. Nelson. A sporting III, 4 traverse can be made from either summit to the other in 3-4 hours.

MT. LENA (MT. BALDY)   5995 (1827 m)

Located ½ mile north of Upper Lena Lake.

Route. I, 1. From Lena Lake, proceed on the trail 4.3 miles to Upper Lena Lake (ca. 4500 ft.). Walk N and W up easy slopes to the top. Time: 6 hours up from road.

MT. BRETHERTON   5960 (1817 m)

An elongated double-summited peak located 1 mile south of Upper Lena Lake.

Route 1. I, 2. From Upper Lena Lake proceed S past Milk Lake and ascend the higher (S) summit via a saddle and upper basin traverse. As an alternate route from Upper Lena Lake, ascend the N ridge and cross the N summit to the higher S summit. Time: 2 hours up from Upper Lena Lake.

Route 2. I, 2. From the Hamma Hamma River road near the Boulder Creek bridge (12.1 miles from U.S. 101) follow the Putvin trail to where it crosses an old logging road (1.3 miles). Follow the old road (ca. 2½ miles) N until it crosses Boulder Creek. Leave the road, climbing E along edge of logging area until ridge crest is reached. At ridge, cross N of large gendarme to E side of ridge. Work N along the ridge just below crest to the saddle between peak 5464 and the main ridge to the W. Proceed N through the saddle and descend a snow slope to bypass a buttress on its E side. Work back to ridge crest crossing to W side. Continue N to the higher S summit. Time: 7 hours up from road.

MT. STONE   6612 (2015 m)

A sharp, multiple-peaked mountain located at the head of the Skokomish River, Crazy Creek, and Whitehorse Creek; it has several permanent snowfields on the north and west faces.

South Peak   6612 (2015 m)

Route 1. I, 3. From the Hamma Hamma River road near Boulder Creek bridge (12.1 miles from U.S. 101), follow the Putvin trail, crossing an old road. Pick up trail again just down hill. Trail soon steepens emerging in open meadow. Continue on right side of meadow to headwall (3 miles from Hamma Hamma). A steep rocky way trail to the right leads to a bench. Continue northwesterly up past a small pothole to a second bench. Ascend to right through brush and scree toward the obvious pass known as St. Peter's Gate. Bear left below the pass following the natural line along the base of the cliffs to the west ridge which can be climbed to the E. The final pitch involves a short rock scramble. Time: 6 hours up from road.

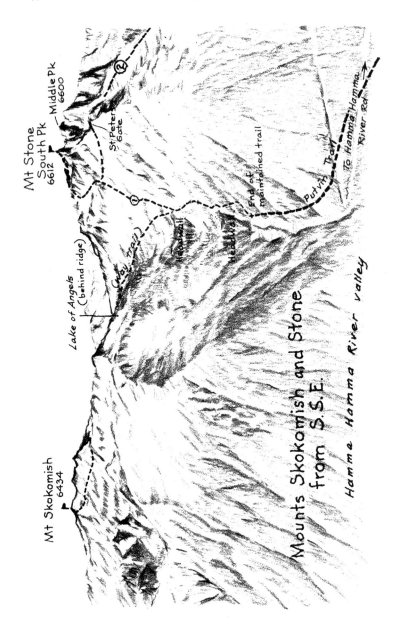

Mounts Skokomish and Stone
from S.S.E.

Route 2. I, 3. Follow Route 2 Mt. Bretherton until the old road crosses a wood bridge (3.5 miles). Just beyond bridge, pick up a way trail leading to the left, this trail follows a steep ridge to the alpine area E of Mt. Stone (ca. 4300 ft.). Avoid the creek bed to the left of the way trail because of brush. This creek drains several small lakes known as Ullin's Bathtubs. Continue upward to the 5900-ft. pass in the SE ridge of Mt. Stone (St. Peter's Gate). Proceed through the pass and join Route 1. Time: 6-7 hours up from road.

Route 3. I, 3. From First Divide take the Mt. Hopper way trail to the saddle S of Mt. Hopper and then follow the ridge SE about 2 miles to the saddle S of Hagen Lakes. From here, climb E up snowfields to the base of the summit tower.

Middle Peak   ca. 6600 (2012 m)

This double-summited peak is located just north of the main South Peak of Mt. Stone. First ascent 1932 by C. Ullin and party by Route 1.

Route 1 (Y-Couloir). I, 3. From Route 1, South Peak, turn off to the pass known as St. Peter's Gate (ca. 5900 ft.) on the SE ridge of Mt. Stone. Proceed NE through this pass, descend about 300 ft., and contour N ¼ mile on snow or rock to steep snow (crampons may be needed) below a Y-shaped couloir. Ascend the right branch past a large chockstone to the notch SSW of the summit gendarmes. Make the final ascent of the S Middle Peak by the SSW ridge, using ledges on the E side to bypass a short vertical section. Although the register is on the N Middle Peak, the summit gendarmes are very close to the same height. Time: 7 hours up from road.

Route 1A (Double-Y). I, 3. Proceed to the Y-shaped couloir in Route 1 (above). Take the left branch of the Y, then the right branch of an upper Y to an upper chockstone which is passed on the left face. Climb down to the notch S of the S Middle Peak and join the Y-Couloir route.

Route 2 (North-Northeast Ridge). I, 3. First ascent 1952 by J. H. Eliason and L. F. Maranville.

Follow Route 1 (above) to the base of the Y-couloir. Turn NNE up a steep rock and heather ramp to gain the NNE ridge. Turn SSW up the ridge, and near the top follow a wide crack which forms a convenient ledge on the WNW side for 200 ft., just below the crest. Climb 50 ft. to the crest just NNE of the N Middle Peak, and continue to its summit via a short pitch on the NW face. To attain the S Middle Peak, drop back to the NNE side of the N Middle Peak, traverse a ledge on its E side to the saddle between the two gendarmes, descend a crack system in the W face, traverse the wide crack SSW under the S Middle Peak, and scramble back up easy rock to the summit. Time: 8 hours up from the road.

Route 3 (West Side). I, 3. From the 6000-ft. notch in the ridge to the W of Mt. Stone (South Peak) via Route 1, descend a snow finger N and traverse ¼

mile to the basin on the WNW side of the Middle Peak summits. The basin is about 200 ft. higher than that on the ESE side. Climb the short snow or rock couloir to the notch of the Y-Couloir route. This notch appears as the lowest point between South Peak and the S Middle Peak. From here proceed as in the previous routes. The North-Northeast Ridge (Route 2 above) may also be gained from the W side by continuing NNE in the basin and ascending easy snow or scree up a narrow defile between vertical cliffs. Time: 8 hours up from the road.

North Peak   ca. 6400 (1951 m)
First ascent 1935 by T. Martin, C. Ullin and party.

Route 1. I, 2. Traverse from the Middle Peak via the rocky connecting ridge.

Route 2. I, 2. From the Scout Lake way trail, ascend SW over talus or snow to a prominent pass in the long ridge N of North Peak. A long traverse over and around the gendarmes of the N ridge leads to the summit.

The Bandersnatch   ca. 5300 (1615 m)
This 150-ft. spire is east of the north ridge of Mt. Stone (Jabberwocky Ridge) and is prominently visible to the north from the small lakes east of Mt. Stone. First ascent 1958 by D. N. Anderson, J. Richardson, and E. Rodgers.

Route 1. I, 5.0. Approach the spire from the small lakes (4600 ft.) at the E base of Mt. Stone. A rising traverse on the N ascends to the spire's SW base. A chimney leads to a platform below the notch between the two summits. Traverse past a tree to a belay point behind a big rock. The last pitch is an 80-ft. high-angle lead where protection was used. The rappel rope should be tied to the tree before ascending and stretched across the top.

Route 2. I, 5. 6. First ascent 1983 by K. Page and J. White.
From the notch between the two summits, climb an obvious open book and face. If the rappel procedure of Route 1 isn't used, a long sling is required.

MT. SKOKOMISH   6434 (1961 m)
A rather massive peak on the Skokomish-Hamma Hamma River divide. There are three summits; the south peak is the highest, but the north peak (I, 3) is a better climb. The rock is very rotten in places.

Route 1. I, 2. Follow description of Route 1, Mt. Stone (South Peak) until above second bench. Continue westerly on way trail to Lake of the Angels (4800 ft.). Climb southwesterly on ridges and benches to the shoulder of N Skokomish. Continue to a snowfield or scree on the SE side. Traverse to the SW, turn right, and ascend over rock to the summit. Time: 6 hours up from road.

North Peak of Mt. Stone from Shoulder of Mt. Stone (Dave Sicks)

Route 2. I, 2. From Flapjack Lakes and Gladys Divide (5000 ft.), traverse 2½ miles northerly past Mt. Henderson to the summit. Perhaps faster than this ridge traverse would be descent to the N of Gladys Divide followed by a direct ascent up the peak.

This route has also been followed from above Smith Lake after an approach via the Black and White Lakes trail.

MT. HENDERSON   ca. 6000 (1829 m)

Located nearly a mile southwest of Mt. Skokomish and 1½ miles north-northeast of Mt. Gladys.

Route. I, 1. An ascent may be made either from Mt. Gladys or from above Smith Lake after an approach via the Black and White Lakes trail.

PERSHING MASSIF   6154 (1876 m)

A group of rock summits located between the Hamma Hamma River and Jefferson Creek, 1¼ miles north-northwest of Mt. Washington. Approach can be made via the Jefferson Creek road (#2401) or the Hamma Hamma River road (#25). See Hamma Hamma River approach for details.
Reference: 1972 *Mountaineer*.

Mt. Pershing (South Peak)   6154 (1876 m)

First ascent 1939 by D. Dooley, R. Henderson, W. Ingalls, and R. Mandelhorn via Middle Peak and Route 4 saddle. The three peaks were done in one day.

Route 1. II, 3. First ascent 1966 by A. Bloomer, R. Etten, and K. Spencer.

Leave the Jefferson Creek road (#2401) 2.5 miles past Jefferson Lake (just beyond intersection with road #2430) and contour W through timber just above the S side of an extensive marshy area to a large (300 yards wide) avalanche basin beneath Mt. Washington's NE cliffs (40 minutes). Next, climb westerly under the cliffs on the N side of Mt. Washington, staying high along the SE side of the valley to avoid heavy brush. After passing two wooded sections and an avalanche slope, cross the valley just above the large scree slide which lies under the cliffs of Mt. Pershing's S ridge. Continue up the valley to the Lake Ellinor cirque, with its gigantic overhanging rock (ca. 2 hours from road, 3900 ft.). Turn hard right and climb N ¼ mile to a low spot in Pershing's S ridge (5450 ft.). Descend slightly on the W side of the ridge and contour N far enough to bypass "Mt. Ben" (a minor summit on the S ridge, 5650 ft.). Next, climb ledges, snow, and easy rock to the ridge crest and then follow the narrow exposed arête to the summit. Time: 8 hours up from road.

Route 2. II, 4. First ascent 1967 by H. Pinsch, B. West, and M. West (see Route 7 for alternate approach to small lake).

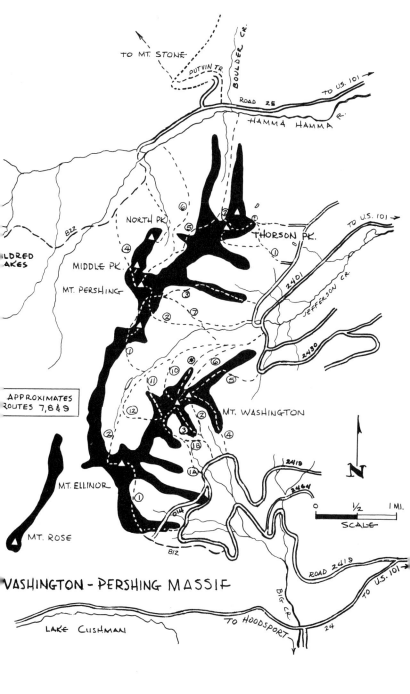

TO MT. STONE

PUTVIN TR.

BOULDER CR.

ROAD 25

TO U.S. 101

HAMMA HAMMA R.

812

MILDRED LAKES

NORTH PK.

⑥

⑧

②

⑧

THORSON PK.

TO U.S. 101

①

④

MIDDLE PK.

2401

JEFFERSON CR.

MT. PERSHING

③

⑦

②

2430

⑨

★

⑥

⑩

⑤

⑪

APPROXIMATES ROUTES 7,8 & 9

⑫

②

MT. WASHINGTON

②

③

④

⑬

N

①

1A

2419

2461

MT. ELLINOR

①

0   ½   1 MI.

SCALE

914

MT. ROSE

812

ROAD 2419

TO U.S. 101

WASHINGTON - PERSHING MASSIF

BIG CR.

TO HOODSPORT

24

LAKE CUSHMAN

Leave the Jefferson Creek road (# 2401) as in Route 1. Travel W through the jungle past the right side of a small lake formed by Jefferson Creek. Continue westerly up a broad couloir to a narrow bench (ca. 5200 ft.) keeping the S ridge of Mt. Pershing directly on the left. Contour N and into another couloir, cross the head of this couloir to the N side, and ascend left (W) to the narrow, exposed ridge of Route 1. Continue on to the summit. Time: 8 hours up from road.

"Mt. Ben" (ca. 5650) may be ascended by continuing past the bench in the first couloir to the ridge crest. Climb the open book of a small pinnacle, or contour to the left of the base. Continue N on easy rock to a short chimney which ends at the summit. One may descend N and continue on to the summit of Mt. Pershing from here.

Route 3 (East Ridge). II, 3. First ascent 1959 by D. Bechlem, J. Christiansen, R. Etten, and R. Wood.

Follow road # 2401 about 3 miles past Jefferson Lake to where the road contours the E end of Mt. Pershing's E ridge. Climb westerly to the ridge crest and then travel W along the S side of the timbered crest to about 5000 ft. The summit can be seen to the W from this point. Descend about 300 ft. into a basin and proceed W toward the summit. Ascend the E side of the S ridge of Pershing via an obvious snow gully and follow the narrow exposed ridge of Route 1 to the top. Time: 8 hours up from road.

Route 4. II, 3. From the end of the Hamma Hamma River road (# 25) where it has crossed the river, take the Mildred Lakes trail for about 2 miles or to where the trail recrosses the creek. Leave the trail and climb SE over scree to a point just S of cliffs of the Middle Peak. Next, climb E to the saddle between the Middle and South peaks. From here, the main summit can be reached either by moderate rock scrambling on the right-hand ridge or by way of a more difficult rock gully directly left of the ridge. Time: 8 hours up from road.

Route 5. II, 3. First ascent 1952 by A. Filion and J. Murray.

Leave the Hamma Hamma River road (# 25) at the Boulder Creek bridge (ca. 5 miles above its junction with road # 2480). Cross the river and proceed S up the gully on the hillside through brush, scree and over snow (early in the season) to a basin at about 4000 ft. Continue climbing to the head of the basin and then cross the 5000-ft. pass in the N ridge of Thorson Peak. Drop slightly and contour westerly along the NW side of the Pershing-Thorson ridge. Climb to the saddle (5600 ft.) between the South and Middle peaks, and continue S to the summit as in Route 4. Time: 8 hours up from road.

Route 6. II, 3. Drive 6.6 miles up the Hamma Hamma River road (# 25) from its intersection with road # 2480 or about a mile past Boulder Creek. Walk toward the river, to an old logging road. Follow the logging road until it meets the river. Cross on any available logs. Follow S through brush, then SE along the right side of the creek bed, reaching a basin at 4000 ft. Continue southerly and somewhat to the right, reaching a second basin at about 5000 ft. Proceed SW up this basin to the Middle-South Peak saddle (5600 ft.). Traverse S to the rocky ridge. Proceed E to the summit. This route is quite brushy. Time: 7 hours up from road.

A variation in this route can be accomplished by climbing S from the 4000-ft. basin through a notch in the E ridge and ascending directly up the E face of the summit.

Route 7. II, 3. Leave road #2401 (see Route 1) on the N side of the valley between Mt. Washington and Mt. Pershing, traveling W along the N side of Jefferson Creek in fairly open timber. Just before reaching the small lake, which shows on The Brothers quadrangle as part of Jefferson Creek, turn NW up the steep hillside through open timber and about 50 yards of brush, and proceed left into the bottom of the 4000-ft. basin. Continue NW across the basin toward the lowest notch in the ridge. Turn W about 100 yards short of this notch, climb through a higher notch, and proceed to the summit as in Route 3. Time: 7 hours up from road.

Middle Peak   ca. 5800 (1768 m)
First ascent 1939 by D. Dooley, B. Henderson, W. Ingalls, and R. Mandelhorn via Route 2.

Route 1. I, 2. Climb from the South-Middle Peak saddle after an approach via Route 4, South Peak. Time: 6 hours up from road.

Route 2. I, 3. Use the approach of Route 4, South Peak, until under the obvious cliffs of the Middle Peak (ca. 1½ hours from road). Climb these cliffs directly, generally following the line of easiest passage to the summit. Time: 5 hours up from road.

North Peak   ca. 5600 (1707 m)
First ascent 1939 by D. Dooley, B. Henderson, W. Ingalls, and R. Mandelhorn by traverse from Middle Peak.

Route 1. I, 3. From the end of the Hamma Hamma River road, take the Mildred Lakes trail about ½ mile to where it switches back. From this point, climb SSE over brush and scree to the base of the cliffs of the North Peak. Climb E under these cliffs around to the SE side of the peak. From here, the final 200 ft. is over steep but pleasant rock. Time: 5 hours up from road.

Route 2 (North Couloir). I, 3. First ascent 1982 by C. Miller and R. Bozelle.

This couloir is obvious from the end of the Hamma Hamma road. Approach as in Route 1 to the base of the cliffs. Enter the couloir through a narrow gap (ca. 4100 ft.) and ascend snow and ice directly to the summit. This route is best done early in season but avalanche conditions could be extreme. Descend by Route 1. Time: 5 hours up from road.

Thorson Peak (Jefferson Peak)   ca. 5700 (1737 m)

Located between Jefferson Creek and the Hamma Hamma River, 1½ miles
northeast of Mt. Pershing. Named for R. Thorson, who lost his life on The
Brothers in 1948. The summit rocks will affect compass bearings. First ascent
1958 by D. N. Anderson, R. Oram, R. Peterson, and K. Spencer via Route 2.

Route 1. I, 3. First ascent 1962 by A. Bloomer, D. Butler, A. Filion, J.
Horn, R. Harniss, R. Oram, J. Pinsch, and K. Spencer by alternate route.

Follow road #2401 10.5 miles past its intersection with road #2480. Turn
left at house-sized rock. This leads to near the top of a logged area. The E
peak is in full view from this spot. Ascend steep timber, contouring left
through slide alder and climb W to prominent saddle on the left side of
Thorson. Ascend N and E up easy rock to the W peak (highest). This route
has considerable avalanche activity in winter and early spring. Time: 3 hours
up from vicinity of Goober Pond. For an alternate route, ascend directly
toward E peak through timber to an open meadow of gigantic boulders. Bear
slightly to the right, up scree or snow, and onto the ridge E of E peak. See
Route 3.

Route 2 (North Couloir). I, 3. Thorson Peak is the high point ahead and
slightly to the left when entering the basin in Route 5, Mt. Pershing. From this
basin, ascend the steep snow couloir on the left of the peak to the col on the
ridge. From this col, turn right and climb easy rock to the summit. Time: 6
hours up from road.
Reference: 1963 *Mountaineer.*

Route 3. I, 3. Follow road #2401 for 11.7 miles from its intersection with
road #2480. Turn left on side road at ridge crest and go 1 mile W toward
Thorson. From end of road, ascend N through logged area to ridge crest (15
minutes). Follow ridge left through steep timber to open ridge of easy snow or
rock slab to base of E peak of Thorson (1½ hours from road). Near middle of
wall take ramp up and left under large overhanging rock to a stand of large
dead trees. Bear right and follow gulley and easy rock to E peak. Follow
sharp broken ridge to W peak (¼ mile). Time: 4 hours up from road end.

Tran Spire   ca. 4900 (1494 m)

Located directly north of Thorson Peak. First ascent 1958 by D. N. Anderson
and R. Peterson.

Route. I, 5.3. From the basin (4000 ft.) in Route 5, Mt. Pershing, walk E a
short distance to the base of this prominent 250-ft. spire. Two long leads on
the rotten rock of the SE wall gain a large ledge on the S corner. Here a stunted
tree provides an anchor for the 130-ft. rappel necessary for the descent. From
this point, the summit is easily reached. Several smaller towers in the area
offer ascents. Time: 6 hours up from road.

MT. WASHINGTON   6255 (1907 m)

This peak is the highest point overlooking Lake Cushman and is named for its resemblance to George Washington's profile. The "chin" is the summit. Due to easy access and a variety of routes (snow and good rock) it is a popular peak. In years of heavy snowfall, the steep slopes are prone to avalanches; early climbs should be undertaken with caution. East-side routes are approached from the Big Creek logging road (#2419). North- and west-side routes are approached from the Jefferson Creek road (#2401) and are long.

Route 1A. I, 3. Take the Big Creek logging road (#2419) for 6.3 miles to just short of its second crossing of Big Creek (prominent waterfall). Park car 100 yards S of Big Creek, and take the way trail leading westerly up through timber, scree, or snow slopes to a large basin (4500 ft.). Continue W up a steep rock or snow chute to a headwall; bear right until the broad ridge stretching N is reached. Continue N to the summit block. The summit block may be climbed either directly up the rock or by contouring to the right on a rocky ledge and up the steep slope on the N side. Time: 4 hours up from road.

Washington's "nose" NE of the summit is a short exposed rock scramble. A group of rock pinnacles on the left side of upper Big Creek basin (S of Route 1) offers moderate to difficult rock climbs.

Route 1B. I, 3. Continue past the second crossing of Big Creek for 0.3 mile to where timber starts. Ascend through trees to a rocky ridge. Climb this tree-covered ridge for about 200 ft. elevation gain, then contour left into Big Creek basin. Continue as in Route 1A. Time: 4 hours up from road.

Route 2. I, 3. Continue past the second crossing of Big Creek, and ascend through trees as in Route 1B. Where Route 1B bears left, continue up the rocky ridge (staying somewhat to the right) to a large buttress (ca. 4500 ft.). Traverse N through a notch in a minor ridge, keeping the buttress on the left. Ascend directly W up steep snow slopes to the summit. Time: 4 hours up from road.

Route 3 (Southeast Ridge). I, 4. When reaching the buttress of Route 2, climb on ledges to the crest of the ridge. Stay quite close to the crest, following the ridge westerly. Route finding may be a problem, and two rappels are necessary to continue. Continue to the summit block where the ridge joins Route 1. Time: 6 hours up from road.

Route 4 (East Ridge). II, 4. Continue on logging road 0.3 mile past the second crossing of Big Creek. Take the Mt. Washington trail, which leads N to Jefferson Pass, the saddle between the Big Creek and Jefferson Creek drainages (3850 ft.). Turn left (W) and continue to the base of the E ridge. Climb the steep wooded ridge which becomes rock and turns northward. Follow the narrow ridge crest, bypassing some of the gendarmes on the right

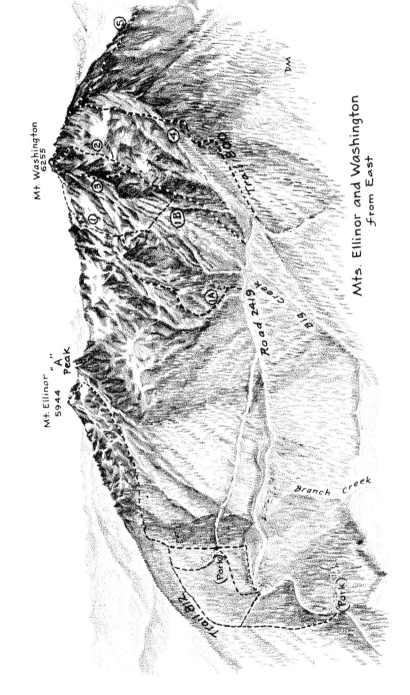

Mt. Ellinor "A" Peak 5944

Mt. Washington 6255

Mts. Ellinor and Washington
from East

Trail 812

(Park)

(Park)

Branch Creek

Road 2419

Big Creek

Trail 809

to a huge buttress. This difficulty is overcome by traversing left into a large cirque. Follow the head of the cirque to a narrow gully with a 30-ft. chockstone. After climbing a wall to the left of the chockstone, take one of two choices: either proceed straight up the wall, or up another chockstone chimney. An interesting variation can be made by bearing right near the 30-ft. chockstone into a poorly defined open book. Ascend this until it fades, and continue exposed scramble to the ridge top. Descend to N or E slightly only to avoid impasses. Follow the ridge until meeting with Route 4. The regained ridge crest is broad and rounded all the way to the "nose." From here, a rappel or a short exposed descent leads to the summit. Time: 5 hours up from road.

Reference: 1960 *Mazama*.

Route 5 (Northeast Ridge). I, 3. First ascent 1964 by D. N. Anderson and L. Scott.

From where the Jefferson Creek road (#2401) branches with road #2430 (2¼ miles past Jefferson Lake), leave the car and scramble SW up the hillside to the ridge crest overlooking the N face. Ascend the NE ridge, bypassing

(Foreground ridge hides start of routes)

Mt. Washington from north

most of the buttresses on the left. The final scramble skirts the wall on the E face and ends atop the "nose." Continue to the summit as in Route 4. Time: 5 hours up from road.

Route 6 (Northeast Face). II, 3. First ascent 1959 by D. N. Anderson, A. Bloomer, R. Harniss, R. Hebble, N. Jacques, J. Koch, and K. Spencer.

Take the Jefferson Creek road (# 2401) 2.5 miles past Jefferson Lake to just beyond the intersection with road # 2430. Contour W through timber just above the S side of an extensive marshy area to a large (300 yards wide) avalanche basin beneath the NE cliffs (40 minutes). Ascend through the lower cliffs on their left side about 500 ft. to an upper basin; thence traverse right to the chute emptying over the lower cliffs. Ascend to the head of the chute and then climb directly to the obvious notch near the confluence of the NE and N ridges over steep snow or slab. From here, bear left to the summit of the "nose" and join Route 4. Time: 5 hours up from road.

Route 7 (Great Groove). II, 4. First ascent 1961 by A. Bloomer, T. Coon, and R. Harniss.

Approach as in Route 6. Start on the right (W) side of the large avalanche basin. Follow the rib up steep timber to a cliff band, traverse left on a ledge above the waterfall and follow the shelf to the base of the upper cliffs on the right side of the NE face. Here enter a great groove worn by a former water course parallel to the present stream. Climb and stem about 700 ft. up this groove on sound clean rock. Continue over onto easy rock (plane wreckage scattered about), and join Route 6 at the top of the basin. An alternative to joining Route 6 would be to climb right to the crest of the N ridge joining the culmination of Routes 8 and 9. Time: 6 hours up from road.

Route 8 (North Ridge, Diagonal Snowfield). II, 4. First ascent 1974 by J. P. Gray and L. F. Maranville.

This route utilizes a prominent diagonal snowfield across the northern cliffs. Visible from the road, this snowfield normally persists into July. Follow the Route 7 approach to the ledge above the waterfall, turn right up rock into a tree-choked gully which leads to the crest of the rib. Cross the next chute to an obvious ledge on the next rib about 100 ft. below the waterfall coming from the diagonal snowfield. From the far end of the ledge ascend through trees and cliffs to the crest of the second rib and emerge on a platform below a 50-ft. rocky section of the rib. Climb this difficult section to the diagonal snowfield, and on up to its head. From here, four horizontal leads to the right from tree to tree, along a narrow downsloping ledge between a 50-ft. cliff band above and the main northern cliffs below brings one to a break in the upper cliff band. Climbing steep snow through trees for several hundred ft. leads to the foot of the rocky central spine of the N ridge. This central section of the ridge is delightful Class 3 or 4 climbing with superb views. It ends at a saddle a short distance from the summit, joining Routes 6 and 7. Time: 8 hours up from road.

Route 9 (North Ridge, Yellow Cedar). II, 4. First ascent 1972 by J. H. Eliason and L. F. Maranville.

Approach as in Route 6. From large avalanche basin traverse SW through about 100 yards of open timber to a snow-and-slide-alder slope (1 hour from road) and climb to its head. Gaining the wooded ridge to the right at the highest convenient point, scramble up to the shelf at the bottom of the next cliff band near a waterfall. Wet rocks on the right side of the lower section of the waterfall provide access to a second shelf. Above this shelf, ascend a long series of cliff bands slightly to the right of the waterfall. Between the cliff bands are narrow downsloping ledges supporting a great number of trees, usually Alaska Yellow Cedar, which provide both holds and belays, but at times protection of the leader is minimal. After topping the waterfall, continue up the steep timbered slope just below the crest of the rounded lower ridge to the base of the rocky central spine of the N ridge joining Route 8. Time: 8 hours up from road.

Route 10 (North-Northwest Face). II, 3. First ascent 1960 by D. N. Anderson, A. Bloomer, K. Heathershaw, J. Newman, and D. Blitz.

Approach as in Route 6. From the large avalanche basin, contour SW just below the cliffs, crossing two wooded sections and one snow-and-slide-alder slope to a second snow slope. Ascend this about 500 ft. until a ledge allows a traverse left to avoid the cliffs above and below. Contour right, above the upper cliffs (5000 ft.) and continue until able to turn left. Thence climb directly up to either the "nose" or the summit. Time: 6 hours up from road.

Route 11 (Shangri-La Valley). II, 3. First ascent 1973 by L. Gosser and L. F. Maranville.

This valley, which bottoms in a cliff, lies at about 5500 ft. between the NW ridge and the W buttress (the buttress tees into the Washington-Ellinor ridge just S of the saddle from which Route 1A starts up Mt. Washington's summit block). From the foot of the NNW face (Route 10) traverse along the base of the western cliffs into the Lake Ellinor cirque to a snow chute just S of the W buttress. Ascend this chute E about 1000 ft. to a platform (ca. 5000 ft.) at the base of the W buttress. From this platform follow an airy ascending ledge N, then E across the face of the W buttress to the bottom of the valley, and thence up snow to join Route 1A at the saddle. The upper valley may be exited on the right. Later in the year, a traverse over Mt. Ellinor and a snow descent to the base of the W buttress is better to avoid brush. Time: 7 hours up from road.

Route 12 (Southwest Snowfields). II, 3. First ascent 1967 by D. Baker, R. Etten, G. Sinrud, and K. Spencer.

From a huge overhanging rock in the meadow just below Lake Ellinor (see Mt. Pershing, Route 1, for approach), proceed S past Lake Ellinor toward the head of the cirque. About ¼ mile S of the lake is a break in the eastern cliffs. Climb E through this break, then climb NE over snow or talus to the base of a broad couloir. Climb this couloir to the ridge saddle and a junction with Route

1 just below the summit. Time: 8 hours up from road.
References: 1972 *Mountaineer;* August 1972 *Off Belay.*

MT. ELLINOR   5944 (1812 m)

The southernmost high peak of the ridge overlooking Lake Cushman from the north was named in 1856 after Ellinor Fauntleroy of Seattle. First ascent 1879 by D. Utler, H. Esteps, and Mr. and Mrs. J. Waughop from Lake Cushman.

Route 1. I, 2. Take the Big Creek logging road (#2419) for 6.2 miles to spur road (#014). Turn left, taking the road for 1 mile to a hogback ridge at 3500 ft. Proceed up the ridge to connect with the Mt. Ellinor trail at about 4000 ft. Follow way trail through open woods to a point some 300 ft. above a large prominent rock. Angle right, leaving the ridge and entering a small meadow. Across the meadow, an easy 1000-ft. chute leads to a basin about 250 ft. below and N of the summit. From the basin, bear slightly left to the summit. An interesting variation is to proceed up the hogback beyond the big rock to the S ridge of the mountain and then follow this large ridge to the summit. Time: 3 hours up from road.

Alternate approaches include the 1.7-mile Mt. Ellinor trail (4.8 miles on #2419) or, when conditions prevent use of the upper spur road, a hike up the hogback ridge from the road at 0.6 mile past the Mt. Ellinor trailhead. Also, from the end of road #014, a way trail leads to an intersection with the Mt. Ellinor trail.

Route 2 (West Arête). II, 3. First ascent 1967 by K. Jensen, R. Oram, G. Sinrud, and K. Spencer.

From the huge overhanging rock at the lower end of Lake Ellinor (see Mt. Pershing, Route 1, for approach), proceed S past the lake toward the head of the cirque. Ascend southerly over snow or talus slopes to a saddle, the lowest point in the sharp ridge running between Mt. Ellinor and Mt. Pershing (4½ hours from road). From the saddle, climb the ridge E over rock and snow. The only difficulty, a 200-ft. buttress, can be passed on the S via gullies and some interesting rock pitches. Time: 7 hours up from road.

Ellinor-Washington Traverse

To accomplish this interesting traverse, descend the chute of Route 1 (ca. 200 ft.) and cross the ridge that forms the N side of the gully. Next, traverse a minor basin to Big Creek basin. Continue on to Washington's summit via Route 1, Mt. Washington. Time: 3 hours from Mt. Ellinor. In the summer, this traverse offers a full day's climb by ascending the ridge at the *Horse's Mouth* (I, 3) formed by the intersection of Ellinor and Washington ridges. Either follow the ridge, crossing between the rock pinnacles, or (more interesting) stay on the ridge top (I, 4).

The prominent rock pinnacle NE of the head of the Mt. Ellinor chute,

Mt. Ellinor from Mt. Washington (Harold Pinsch)

known as *"A" Peak* (I, 4) offers a short rock scramble.
References: 1972 *Mountaineer;* August 1972 *Off Belay.*

COPPER MOUNTAIN   5425 (1654 m)

Located 2 miles west of Mt. Ellinor, this peak has some spectacular cornices
in the spring.

Route. I, 2. From the Staircase Ranger Station (770 ft.), take the 2.9-mile
trail to Wagonwheel Lake (4100 ft.). From the lake, proceed S (right) up a
wooded ridge to 4600 ft. Traverse SE for ½ mile to the basin N of the summit.
Climb directly to the E (highest) summit, or ascend to the right through a
notch in the ridge with a S approach to the rocky top. Time: 6 hours up from
road.

SAWTOOTH RIDGE   6104 (1860 m)

This ridge of sharp summits, for the most part solid rock, is known to local
climbers as some of the best climbing in the Olympics. Its pillow-lava
formations provide good handholds but few cracks. The vertical pitches of
this peculiar rock offer an interesting challenge for the experienced climber.

This popular climbing area is best approached from the west via the
7.5-mile trail to 3900-ft. Flapjack Lakes and its 1.4-mile continuation to
Gladys Divide. An alternate approach is from the east via the ungraded
5-mile Mildred Lakes way trail. Considerable brush is encountered in climbing from Mildred Lakes to the ridge crest. This approach is better when snow
covered.

Most of the following route descriptions start on the west side, at or above
Flapjack Lakes. The major summits and pinnacles are listed in groups, with
common approaches starting at Mt. Lincoln on the south and continuing
northeast along the ridge to Noodle Needle.
References: 1963 *Mountaineer;* August 1972 *Off Belay.*

Mt. Lincoln   5868 (1789 m)

Located on the Madeline Creek-Slate Creek Divide. First ascent 1932 by K.
Soult and F. Harmon.

Route 1. I, 2. The timbered lower parts of this route were burned over
during the 1985 Beaver Fire, which burned from the river to the ridge south of
Mt. Lincoln. While this is a direct route, the trail was partly obliterated and is
not maintained. Leave the North Fork Skokomish River trail 2.4 miles
beyond Staircase Ranger Station and climb NE to about 3300 ft. where the
trail ends. Climb ENE directly up and to the right of the ridge crest. Pass to
the E of the false summit, and continue on the moderate slope for ¼ mile to
the summit block. The summit is reached via an interesting rock scramble on
the S side. Time: 8 hours up from ranger station.

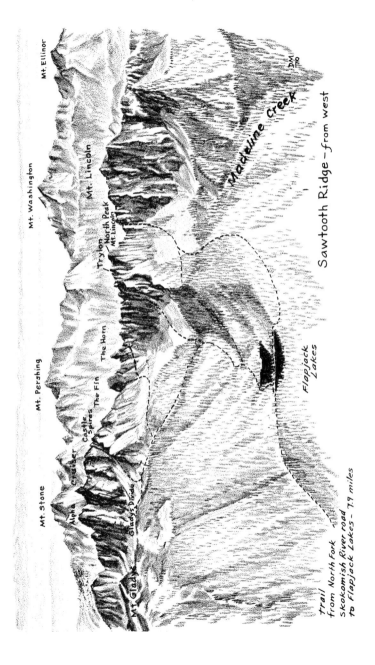

Mt. Ellinor

Mt. Washington

Mt. Pershing

Mt. Stone

Mt. Lincoln

Tryton
North Peak
Mt. Lincoln

The Horn

The Fin

Castle Spires

Cruiser

Alpha

Gladys Divide

Mt. Gladys

Madeline Creek

Flapjack Lakes

Sawtooth Ridge — from west

trail
from North Fork
Skokomish River road
to Flapjack Lakes — 7.9 miles

DM
70

SMITH LK.

MURDOCK LKS.

BLACK & WHITE LKS.

OLYMPIC NAT PARK

MT. SKOKOMISH WILDERNESS

MT. GLADYS △

GLADYS DIVIDE

NOODLE NEEDLE

DONAHUE CR.

← TO SKOKOMISH RIVER RD.

NEEDLE PASS

ALPHA

MT. CRUISER

NEEDLE

CASTLE SPIRES

SAWTOOTH PASS

FLAPJACK LKS.

HARNISS CHUTE

FIN

HORN

TO HAMMA HAMMA R.

RECTAGON

CLEAVER

SLAB TOWER

MILDRED LAKES

TRYLON

PICTURE PINNACLE

N. PK. MT. LINCOLN

MADELINE CR.

MT. LINCOLN

0   ½ MI.

SCALE

SAWTOOTH RIDGE

SLATE CR.

Route 2. I, 3. From Flapjack Lakes, either contour to the right around, or climb E and then S over, a forested ridge to the head of Madeline Creek basin. From here, some exposed rock scrambling leads to the N ridge. Follow this ridge to the summit. The prominent 5700-ft. N summit of Mt. Lincoln seen from the lakes should be kept to the left. Time: 3 hours up from Flapjack Lakes.

Route 3. I, 2. Cross to the E side of Sawtooth Ridge through the notch at the head of Harniss Chute. To reach Harniss Chute, leave the Gladys Divide trail about ¼ mile above Flapjack Lakes. Proceed through timber, soon reaching a small meadow. From here, a prominent rock slide marks the entrance of Harniss Chute. After reaching the ridge crest, descend the E side several hundred feet and contour S. Ascend the prominent couloir on Mt. Lincoln's ENE face. The left-hand peak is the summit. Time: 5 hours up from Flapjack Lakes.

Mt. Lincoln (North Peak) 5700 (1738 m)

Route 1. I, 3. Approach via Harniss Chute (see Route 3, Mt. Lincoln). Descend the E side several hundred ft. and contour SW bypassing the gendarmes on the right. After The Trylon, scramble up easy rock to the summit. Time: 4 hours up from Flapjack Lakes.

Mt. Lincoln from Flapjack Lakes (Frank Chapin)

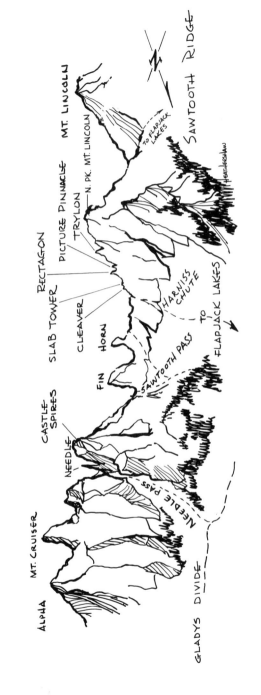

Route 2. II, 5.5. First ascent 1983 by J. Siler, K. Cornia, and M. Borgers.

Approach as for Route 2, Mt. Lincoln to head of Madeline Creek Basin. Ascend the left-hand gully system and some exposed rock to the notch below the S arête. Descend slightly E until a ledge system can be followed upward (large blocks are not as loose as they appear) to a large ledge at the base of a right-facing corner. Ascend wide crack in corner, crux 5.5, until corner ends, then scramble up and left to tree. Continue W across the gully and two large horns to gain the crest of the arête. Follow the crest (little or no protection) until a small ledge with good cracks is reached just left of the crest. Continue along crest to its end. Drop 15 ft. to the base of summit rocks; scramble to the top. Descend to the E and contour S, over exposed scree and easy rock until an exposed ledge system is reached, which leads back to notch at base of arête. Make a tight exposed squeeze between a small tree and rock, to gain easy access to notch; descend to Madeline Creek basin.

APPROACH NOTE

The following 5 gendarmes are best approached via Harniss Chute (see Route 3, Mt. Lincoln). They are described in order from the ridge notch southwest toward the north peak of Mt. Lincoln.

The Cleaver and Slab Tower

Each rock tower has a simple one-pitch ascent.

Rectagon   ca. 5600 (1707 m)

Route. I, 4. Ascend a ledge leading around the NW face. At the end of the ledge, turn and climb the single pitch on downsloping slab to the summit. Time: 4 hours up from Flapjack Lakes.

The Trylon   ca. 5700 (1737 m)

A short three-sided gendarme seen prominently from Flapjack Lakes, located just north of the north summit of Mt. Lincoln. First ascent 1951 by F. Beckey and H. Beckey.

Route. I, 4. Climb the SE side with a tricky start from a high handhold. Time: 4 hours up from Flapjack Lakes.

Picture Pinnacle   ca. 5650 (1722 m)

First ascent 1941 by F. Beckey and H. Beckey.

Route. I, 4. Ascend a narrow chimney on the SE side.

APPROACH NOTE

The next two summits on this interesting ridge, The Fin and The Horn, are seen quite prominently from Flapjack Lakes. Although this is the lowest part of the ridge, some of the best Sawtooth climbs are on these two peaks. The easiest approach is to follow the Gladys Divide trail above Flapjack Lakes for about 1 mile to an open meadow on the right. Leave the trail and travel east, crossing a small rocky hump. The first narrow chute to the left of The Fin leads to a notch in the ridge called Sawtooth Pass. For routes on The Horn, contour directly below the west face of The Fin to a ledge on the west side of The Horn.

The Fin   ca. 5500 (1676 m)
First ascent 1939 by R. Carlow and D. Dooley via Route 2.

Route 1. I, 3. Climb the gully to Sawtooth Pass (notch in ridge N of The Fin). Cross Sawtooth Pass and contour around to the E side. Climb easy rock to the summit. Time: 3 hours up from Flapjack Lakes.

Route 2. I, 3. Contour beneath the W face of The Fin to the notch in the ridge S of the peak. Climb directly up the exposed S ridge. Time: 3 hours up from Flapjack Lakes.

Route 3 (West Face). I, 5.5. First ascent 1959 by D. N. Anderson and R. Harniss.
Leave the gully that leads to the S ridge just below the notch and traverse left (N) about 40 ft. to the first break in the shallow overhang above. Climb up a superficial chimney, and traverse a few ft. to the left. Climb the very strenuous crack (slightly overhanging) to an excellent belay behind a flake. Scramble along the flake to a point where an easier section gives access to the notch a few ft. S of the summit. The first pitch is quite difficult. Time: 3 hours up from Flapjack Lakes.

Route 4 (Northeast Face). I, 5.2. First ascent 1966 by H. Pinsch and G. Tate.
From about 50 ft. E of Sawtooth Pass, climb directly up the face for 30 ft. Make an ascending traverse to the left, to the base of a deep chimney. Two pitons and two runners were used in the first ascent for this long lead. Stem the chimney to its top, which is within 50 ft. of the summit. Time: 3 hours up from Flapjack Lakes.

The Horn   ca. 5500 (1676 m)
First ascent 1939 by R. Carlow, D. Dooley, R. Henderson, and E. Johnson.

Route 1. I, 4. Contour beneath the W faces of The Fin and The Horn to the ridge notch S of the objective. Cross the ridge to the SE and climb an open book with cannon hole, or a vertical chimney, to a platform 40 ft. below the top. From here, traverse to the right to a good belay spot, and then climb the nearly vertical E face. Time: 3 hours up from Flapjack Lakes.
As an alternate route from the platform, climb the direct overhang or traverse to the left and up (5.3).

Route 2 (West Face). I, 5.5. Just before reaching the ridge notch of Route 1, turn left and climb up behind a small gendarme. From the ledge just N of the

The Fin and The Horn — Sawtooth Ridge (Dave Sicks)

gendarme, climb directly up the W face to a secure point behind a flake. From here, either climb left to the summit or scramble to the right up to a platform of Route 1. Time: 3 hours up from Flapjack Lakes.

APPROACH NOTE

The summits north of The Fin are commonly approached from Needle Pass. Needle Pass is at the head of the long snow finger visible from Gladys Divide.

Castle Spires   ca. 5800 (1768 m)

This peak is the irregular mass between Sawtooth Pass and Needle Pass. First ascent 1952 by N. Jacques, L. Nothwang, and D. Smith via Route 2.

Route 1. I, 3. Scramble to the summit from Needle Pass.

Route 2. I, 3. Ascend the couloir on the SE corner (from the E side of Sawtooth Pass) and scramble on exposed terrain to the highest of the gendarmes. As an alternate route, climb directly up the ridge from Sawtooth Pass.

Route 3 (West Face). I, 5.0. First ascent 1962 by A. Filion and K. Spencer.

From ¼ mile below Gladys Divide, climb to the lone green tree at the base of the W face. Traverse a few feet S past the tree to the base of a shallow gully. Ascend the gully and its left face until it narrows into a chimney. Climb the chimney and traverse left to a heather patch. Ascend cracks and ribs to the summit. Time: 3 hours up from Flapjack Lakes.

Route 4 (North Face). I, 5.0. First ascent 1964 by N. Howe, E. Kishida, and R. Rossiter.

From halfway up the chute to Needle Pass, bear right and enter a large and deep chimney. Difficulty in crossing moat may be experienced in late summer. Two vertical steps are encountered in this chimney, the first terminating at a cannon hole. Above, a large open-book formation culminates near the summit which is then reached directly over broken rock.

The Needle   ca. 5800 (1768 m)

A sharp spire located at Needle Pass.

Route. I, 4. Climb with a single 130-ft. lead to the summit.

Mt. Cruiser   6104 (1860 m)

A towerlike summit near the north end of Sawtooth Ridge; it is the highest point on the ridge. First ascent 1937 by P. Crews and R. Layton (Route 1 via 1A). The peak is named for the Bremerton Ski Cruisers.

Route 1 (South Corner). I, 5.0. From Flapjack Lakes, take the 1.4-mile trail toward Gladys Divide. Just before reaching the divide, turn right and ascend the 700-ft. chute to a notch in the ridge crest (Needle Pass). Take crampons, as this chute is steep and usually icy. Traverse E on the left side of the pass for 50 ft., then turn to the N and ascend to the ridge crest. Follow on the W side of the ridge northeasterly for ⅛ mile, then cross to the E side and descend a gully just before reaching Mt. Cruiser. Traverse NE on rocky ledges to a small chimney with a cannon hole at its top. Climb through the cannon hole, or over the top, to a platform. Traverse E across the platform and, from a ledge, ascend directly up the face to the ridge crest with a good belay spot. There is a ¼-inch bolt about halfway up and slightly to the left of

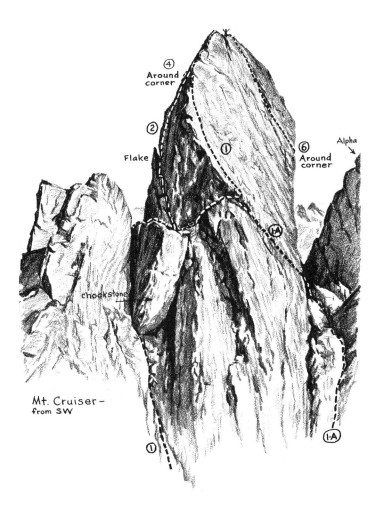

Mt. Cruiser –
from SW

this 70-ft. lead. Follow the ridge to the summit. Two ropes are needed for the rappel. Time: 3½ hours up from Flapjack Lakes.

Route 1A. I, 5.4. Instead of traversing on the rocky ledges of Route 1, continue down the gully to the scree slope. Contour N along the base of the peak and then ascend a short, broad chimney. Next, stem the vertical crack on the E face and traverse left on a narrow ledge. A crack in the overhang provides for hardware placement. One move gains a ledge leading to the platform of Route 1.

Route 2 (West-Southwest Corner). I, 5.7. First ascent 1957 by D. N. Anderson, J. Koch, and J. Richardson.

From the SW platform of Route 1, climb the flake on Mt. Cruiser's W face. From the lower (S) end of the flake, climb directly upward to the ridge crest. Two bolts are in place for protection on this difficult pitch.

Route 3 (Northeast Face). II, 5.6. First ascent 1958 by D. N. Anderson, R. Hebble, and J. Richardson.

From Gladys Divide, go up and slightly left to a steep crack and gully system in the wall below Mt. Cruiser. Cross the moat and ascend moderate rock for several leads. Higher up, the angle eases off for an exposed scramble to the ridge top. Traverse SW along the crest and then through a tunnel to a platform at the base of a gendarme on the NE face. From the platform, lead up and slightly left to the ENE corner, following that to a belay spot just below the summit. A 150-ft. rope is necessary for this difficult lead. Time: 6 hours up from Flapjack Lakes.

Route 4 (West Face). II, 5.5. First ascent 1959 by D. N. Anderson and R. Harniss.

Climb up immediately to the N (left) of the Needle Pass snow chute of Route 1, until it is possible to scramble up and left (N) to tree-studded ledges. Next, climb a short, mossy gully to the first flake. Move up behind the flake, and drop about 20 ft. on the N side to a shallow, open chimney. Ascend the chimney to a good belay stance behind a second flake (from here, a short scramble up and to the right leads to the platform of Route 1). Climb left (N) behind the flake until a large crack pierces the overhang above. Ascend this crack to the top of a third flake. From near this flake's N end, a long lead gains the ridge very close to the summit. Pitons were placed on three pitches. Time: 6 hours up from Flapjack Lakes.

Route 5 (West Face, Wandering Minstrel). IV, 5.7. First ascent 1975 by S. R. Moss and A. Pettit.

From Gladys Divide, climb about 300 ft. to the top of a snowfield in the center of the W face. From the first big ledge about 100 ft. up, go right to a break in the wall above the ledge. Go up and right to a left-leading steep ramp which intersects a right-leading ramp split by a wide crack which is not visible from below. Climb the two ramps about 150 ft. to the end of the second ramp. Next, go left up an easy inside corner past one chimney to a second chimney. Ascend the second chimney about 200 ft. to the top, passing a large, overhanging chockstone. Climb a short 30-ft. wall above, then descend left about 50 ft. until an open book is encountered. Climb the open book about 75 ft. to the base of the summit pyramid, about 200 ft. below the summit. Climb an overhanging 4-5 inch crack or go left and traverse back right into the crack above the overhang. At the top of the crack, go right and down a flake about 15 ft. to the right (S) side of the summit block and ascend about 30 ft. to the summit ridge where Route 1 is joined. Time: 10 hours up from Gladys Pass for first ascent.

Note. — Hardware on first ascent included small nuts through # 8 hex, but larger sizes would be helpful. Rock helmets recommended as stonefall was experienced.

Route 6 (East Face). II, 5.7. First ascent 1959 by D. N. Anderson and J. Koch.

Climb onto this triangular wall in its center, and make a left-ascending traverse for 20 ft. Next, climb directly over very difficult rock to a small stance. Continue directly up, crossing a side of the triangle on the SE face which leads to the top. Time: 6 hours up from Flapjack Lakes.

Route 7 (Southeast Face). II, 5.5. First ascent 1967 by D. Benedict and P. Karkiainen.

Climb from the lowest point of the SE face directly to a point about 20 ft. left of the summit. This route is to the right of Route 1 and includes a 140-ft. lead to a 6-inch standing-belay ledge.

Alpha   ca. 6100 (1859 m)

Located directly northeast of Mt. Cruiser. First ascent 1956 by R. Harniss, C. Mecklenburg, and J. Newman.

The approach is made by continuing north past the east face of Mt. Cruiser (see Route 1A, Mt. Cruiser) or continuing north from Gladys Divide to the Alpha-Cruiser col.

Route 1. I, 2. Ascend a gully on the SE face to the summit.

Route 2. I, 2. Ascend the ridge from the Alpha-Cruiser col.

Route 3 (West Face). I, 5.5. First ascent 1957 by J. Duenwald and J. Koch.

Start from a ledge 200 yards N of the route to the Alpha-Cruiser col, and continue up a series of ledges and open chimneys to a prominent tree-covered ledge in mid-face. A short chimney, followed by an exceedingly long, high-angle pitch, and then several easier pitches, gains the summit. Good cracks are scarce. Time: 4½ hours up from Gladys Divide.

Noodle Needle   ca. 5600 (1707 m)

Located below and on the west side of the ridge top opposite the basin north of Alpha. First ascent 1957 by D. N. Anderson, J. Koch, and J. Richardson.

Route. I, 5.4, A1. From Gladys Divide, drop slightly and contour into a short gully leading to the basin N of Alpha. The route is on the E side where Noodle Needle connects with the adjoining *Fag Crag*. Ascend an angling crack.

MT. GLADYS   5600 (1707 m)
Located immediately northwest of Gladys Divide.

Route. I, 1. Ascend heather slopes from either Gladys Divide or Black and White Lakes.

MT. HOPPER   6114 (1864 m)
Located between the Skokomish and Duckabush rivers 1 mile southeast of First Divide (4688 ft.).

Route. I, 2. From First Divide, a faint trail contours the S slope to the pass (5010 ft.) ½ mile S of Mt. Hopper. Follow this trail about 1 mile, and then ascend directly to the top over easy heather and talus slopes. An alternate route is a pleasant climb directly up the valley from Home Sweet Home.

MT. STEEL   6233 (1900 m)
A rocky peak located about 1¼ miles west-northwest of First Divide.

Route 1. I, 1. From First Divide, follow meadows to the E face and ascend this face to the summit. Time: 3 hours up from First Divide.

Route 2. I, 1. Leave the Marmot Lake trail where it leaves the river about 3 miles above Duckabush Camp. The route follows a creek into a little amphitheater on the W side of the summit, where easy slopes lead to the top.

OVERLOOK PEAK   ca. 5700 (1738 m)
This double-summited peak is located immediately northwest of O'Neil Pass.

Route. I, 2. From O'Neil Pass, scramble up steep heather near ridge to the false summit. The true summit is a short and easy scamper to the N.

O'NEIL PEAK   5758 (1756 m)
Located 1½ miles southwest of O'Neil Pass on a spur west of Mt. Duckabush.

Route. I, 3. From O'Neil Pass, traverse southward across upper O'Neil Creek on a bench to gain the E-W ridge between Mt. Duckabush and O'Neil Peak. Follow this lengthy tree-covered ridge W. Climb onto the rocky portion of this ridge to a prominent notch. Two long rope pitches lead to the broad summit that is crowned with three bench markers. Time: 4 hours up from O'Neil Pass.

Mt. Steel (Dave Sicks)

MT. DUCKABUSH   ca. 6250 (1905 m)

Located at the head of Nine Stream, Upper O'Neil Creek, O'Neil Creek, and the Duckabush River; the rocky southwest peak is the summit. The 6233-ft. northeast peak is identified as Mt. Steel on the 1947 Mt. Steel quadrangle. First ascent 1899 by L. F. Murdock.

East Peak   6233 (1900 m)

Route. I, 3. From O'Neil Pass, travel SE about ½ mile to ascend the eastern (left) of the twin snowfields. Climb up a prominent, steep and long, N-facing snow finger to the saddle between the E and middle peaks. Scramble NE up heather slope to the summit. Time: 3 hours up from O'Neil Pass.

Middle Peak   ca. 6225 (1898 m)

Route. I, 3. From the saddle (see East Peak), climb W up rotten rock to the summit. Time: 3 hours up from O'Neil Pass.

West Peak   ca. 6250 (1905 m)

Route 1. I, 4. From the summit of Middle Peak, climb W along the exposed ridge to the summit. Time: 4½ hours up from O'Neil Pass.

Route 2. I, 4. First ascent 1956 by G. Sainsbury, D. Bechlem, and N. Blamey.

Behind ridge

Behind ridge

② ③

①

Trail

Hart Lake

Mt. Duckabush from NW

D.Molenaar '76

From O'Neil Pass, travel SE about ½ mile to ascend the westernmost of the twin snowfields. Ascend to the ridge top and contour through brush on the SW face; cross numerous minor gullies, and continue to gain altitude on moderately difficult rotten rock. After reaching the S ridge, climb directly to the summit.

Route 3. I, 3. First ascent 1937 by N. Bright.

Ascend the steep rock arête between the two glaciers directly to the summit.

BUMBERSHOOT PEAK   5786 (1764 m)

This double-summited peak is located 2 miles south of O'Neil Pass.

Route. I, 2. From O'Neil Pass, traverse southward across upper O'Neil Creek on a bench to gain the E-W tree-covered ridge between Mt. Duckabush and O'Neil Peak. Follow numerous elk trails past Lake Ben and over ridge to lake at source of west fork of Nine Stream. Ascend snowfield to Bumbershoot Pass, about 5450 ft. Scramble up easternmost of two adjacent summits. Time: 6 hours up from O'Neil Pass.

SCRAMBLER PEAK   ca. 5700 (1738 m)

This pyramid-shaped peak is located southwest and adjacent to Bumbershoot Peak. First ascent 1986 by B. Larson, F. Ratliff, and J. White.

Route. I, 3. Climb rotten rock on a 120-ft. rope lead on NE ridge to the summit. Time: 1 hour up from Bumbershoot Peak.

ROVER PEAK   ca. 5700 (1738 m)

Located southwest and adjacent to Scrambler Peak. First ascent 1986 by B. Larson, F. Ratliff, and J. White.

Route. I, 2. Scramble up easy rock on NE ridge to the summit. Time: 1 hour up from Scrambler Peak.

YONDER PEAK   ca. 5200 (1585 m)

Located 1½ miles south of Bumbershoot Peak and ¼ mile northeast of Peak 5289. It is the source of Eight Stream. First ascent 1986 by B. Larson, F. Ratliff, and J. White.

Route. I, 3. From the pass N of Peak 5289, contour eastward. Scramble up steep heather to gain notch on W ridge. Climb near the ridge to reach the summit.

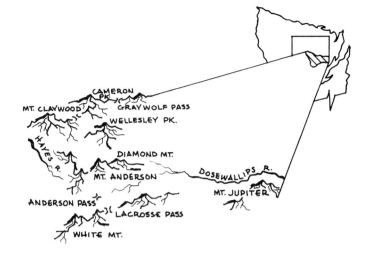

Dosewallips Group

The Dosewallips River, with its two main branches, drains a large section of rugged terrain approximately in the middle of the eastern Olympics. Seventeen miles above its mouth in Hood Canal the river branches, the West Fork flowing from Anderson Pass and the main fork from Hayden Pass. Between the two streams is the Anderson Massif with its large glaciers and rugged cliffs. Peaks on the Duckabush-Dosewallips divide, and those adjacent to Hayden Pass, are of gentler contour and lack glaciers. With the exception of the Anderson Massif (7365 ft.), the general peak elevation averages about 6600 ft.

1. ***Dosewallips River.*** This is the primary approach for all peaks of this group. It is also used for the S side routes of Mt. Constance, Inner Constance, Mt. Deception, and Mt. Mystery (see Constance-Buckhorn and Gray Wolf-Hurricane Ridge groups, pages 97 and 131 respectively).

The Dosewallips River road leaves U.S. 101 ½ mile N of the river near Brinnon on Hood Canal and extends 15½ miles to Muscott Flat (1540 ft.). Large trailers are not permitted beyond Elkhorn campground (11.2 miles). The Dosewallips River trail continues 15.4 miles to Hayden Pass (5847 ft.), with campsites at Dose Forks (1.5 miles, 1736 ft.), Camp Marion (8 miles, 3350 ft.), Bear Camp (11 miles, 3900 ft.), and Dose Meadows (12.8 miles, 4450 ft.). The West Fork trail branches from the Dosewallips River trail near

Anderson Massif and Eel Glacier (courtesy Olympic National Park)

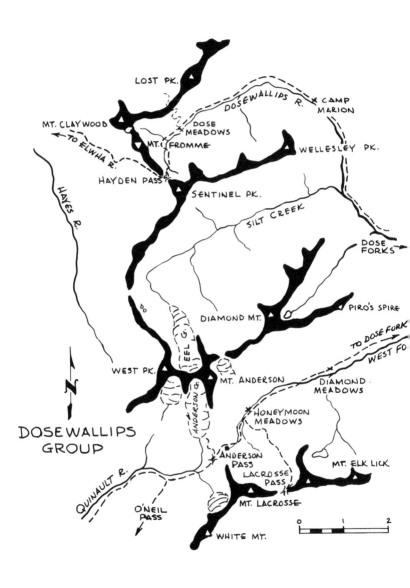

Dose Forks and reaches Anderson Pass (4464 ft.) 10.5 miles from road end. Campsites are located at Big Timber (4.2 miles from the road end, ca. 2300 ft.), Diamond Meadow (6.7 miles, 2692 ft.), Honeymoon Meadows (8.9 miles, 3527 ft.), Anderson Pass (10.5 miles, 4464 ft.), and on the heather slopes above Anderson Pass.

2. **Quinault River.** While this approach is used primarily for access to the southern peaks of the Quinault Group, it can also be used to reach the Anderson Massif and adjacent peaks, including Mt. La Crosse (see Quinault Group, page 187, for approach details).

RANGER STATIONS

Dosewallips (Dosewallips River road), Graves Creek (Quinault River road). Guard Station: Corrigenda (Dosewallips River road). Note: Check with ranger regarding limits on size of party and use of campfires.

CAMPGROUNDS

U.S. 101: Dosewallips State Park, el. 20 ft. (at Brinnon).
Duckabush River Road: Camp Collins, el. 200 ft. (4 miles W of U.S. 101).
Dosewallips River Road: Elkhorn, el. 600 ft. (11 miles W of U.S. 101); Dosewallips, el. 1540 ft. (15.5 miles).
Quinault River Road: Willaby, el. 200 ft. (2 miles E of U.S. 101); Falls Creek, el. 200 ft. (2½ miles); Graves Creek, el. 540 ft. (18.5 miles).

VANTAGE POINTS

Mt. Jupiter can be reached by a 7-mile trail (no water); Sentinel Peak (near Hayden Pass).

MAPS

Olympic National Forest/Olympic National Park; USGS 30-minute Olympic National Park and Vicinity; the following 15-minute USGS and Green Trail quadrangles: Mt. Angeles, The Brothers, Mt. Steel, and Tyler Peak; the following Custom Correct Maps: The Brothers-Mt. Anderson and Gray Wolf-Dosewallips.

PIRO'S SPIRE   6301 (1921 m)

The easternmost peak in the string of summits located between the West Fork Dosewallips River and Silt Creek. Named for R. Piro, who was killed in the Italian Campaign in 1945. First ascent 1947 by D. Dooley, E. Johnson, and N. Johnson from Diamond Meadow.

Route. I, 3. First ascent 1956 by F. Armstead, G. Campbell, W. Jacobsen, and K. Spencer.

Take the West Fork trail to just short of the top of a grade about 2 miles beyond Dose Forks. Turn N up the wooded hillside to the E ridge (ca. 2 hours from the trail). A faint wash may be followed to avoid brush on the lower slopes. Follow the ridge W, and traverse into a prominent basin on the N side when it becomes jagged. From the basin, regain the ridge by climbing a shallow gully on the E end of the main massif (two westerly gullies blank out). Traverse the S side of the summit to a platform just below the short summit tower. The ascent of the tower on its W (easier) or S side is somewhat exposed. Time: 8 hours up from road.

The peak has been climbed using an approach from the SW (Diamond Meadow). This route is long, circuitous, and nasty. To avoid the worst of the extensive cliffs on the SW side, traverse easterly, gaining the ridge crest well E of the summit. While the ridge can be climbed, it appears easier to descend to the N slope as described in the previous paragraph.

DIAMOND MOUNTAIN   ca. 6800 (2073 m)
A high point located on the northeast side of the Anderson Massif.

Route. I, 2. Climb the long mountainside above Diamond Meadow (6.7 miles from road end) on the West Fork trail. The ascent involves gully, broken rock, and heather scrambling.

MT. ELK LICK   6517 (1987 m)
Located on the Duckabush River-West Fork Dosewallips River divide, 1½ miles east of La Crosse Pass.

Route 1. I, 3. First ascent 1971 by B. Burns, H. Favero, F. King, P. Robisch, and J. Stout.

Leave the Duckabush River trail at an elevation of 2100 ft. approximately 3 miles above Tenmile Camp. This is 0.1 mile above the point where large and noisy Crazy Creek joins the opposite side of the river and somewhat before another stream crossing. Camp can be made in the vicinity. Obtain water before leaving the trail. Climb due N up steep timbered hillside keeping to the right of the stream on the left. Continue climbing N past timberline (ca. 5000 ft.) to about 5500 ft. From this point, ascend a ridge NNW to about 6000 ft. where a very steep snow chute is climbed. Continue up the E shoulder to the summit. Time: 7 hours up from Tenmile campsite.

As an alternate approach route, the aforementioned ridge may be gained following a 2-mile traverse E on the S side of the ridge from La Crosse Pass.

Route 2. I, 2. Reach the W side of the peak by leaving the West Fork trail at Diamond Meadow (6.7 miles) and follow Elk Lick Creek through forest and heavy brush. The climb is long.
Reference: 1972 *Mountaineer*.

Route 3. I, 2. From about the 5625-ft. pass ⅓ mile ENE of La Crosse Pass, descend to SE and then traverse E at the 5000-ft. level to S side of Mt. Elk

Lick. Gain W ridge just E of prominent gendarme and scramble up the ridge to the broad summit area.

MT. LA CROSSE   6417 (1956 m)

Located at the head of the West Fork and just west of La Crosse Pass. First recorded ascent 1928 by R. Paulson, W. Ryer, P. Wiseman, and F. Woodworth.

Route 1. I, 2. From Camp Siberia ½ mile NE of Anderson Pass, climb S up a basin on talus and snow to the ridge top just SE of the summit at 6000 ft. Climb moderate rock and heather to the summit. Time: 3 hours up from Siberia.

Route 2. I, 3. Leave the talus and snow in the basin (see Route 1), and ascend a prominent snow gully between the N face and the lower NW summit to a loose rock face on the W side of the summit. Time: 3 hours up from Siberia.

Route 3. I, 2. From La Cross Pass (5566 ft.), climb W up the ridge (1 mile) to the SE base of the summit, and proceed as for Route 1. Time: 2 hours up from trail.

The ridge can be traversed from Mt. La Crosse to White Mountain.

WHITE MOUNTAIN   ca. 6400 (1951 m)

Located on the Duckabush-Quinault River divide.

Route 1. I, 2. From Anderson Pass (4464 ft.), make a traversing ascent S 1½ miles to the edge of the White Glacier. From here, climb easy rocks to the summit. Time: 4 hours up from Anderson Pass.

Route 2. I, 3. From Mt. La Crosse, cross the saddle to the lower NW summit of La Crosse and traverse the serrated ridge 1 mile to White Mountain.

Route 3. I, 2. From Lake La Crosse, travel cross-country NE to Buck Lake and then to the little lake at about 5800 ft. on the Mt. Steel quadrangle (Pocket Lake). N of Pocket Lake, descend the small glacier to its N side, then ascend steep snow or grass slopes NE toward the summit of White Mountain, gaining its N ridge just below the summit. Follow this ridge to the summit pinnacle. Time: 3 hours up from Lake La Crosse.

ANDERSON MASSIF   7365 (2245 m)

This prominent massif bears several large glaciers, which are the sources of the West Fork of the Dosewallips River, Silt Creek, the Quinault River, and the Hayes River. West Peak is the hydrographic apex of the Olympic Peninsula, with its waters flowing into Hood Canal, the Strait of Juan de Fuca, and

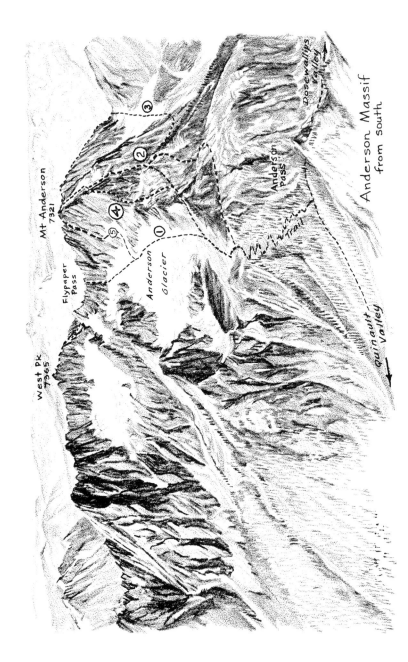

West Pk
7365

Mt Anderson
7321

Flypaper
Pass

③

②

④

⑤

①

Anderson
Glacier

Dosewallips
Valley

Anderson
Pass

Trail

Quinault
Valley

Anderson Massif
from south

the Pacific Ocean. Mt. Anderson was named for General T. M. Anderson, the conqueror of Manila in 1898.

West Peak   7365 (2245 m)
First ascent 1930 by E. B. Hamilton.

Route. II, 3. From Anderson Pass (4464 ft.), 10½ miles from the Dosewallips River road, ascend the heather ridge on the N via a way trail to the Anderson Glacier moraine (1 hour). There is a campsite near the moraine, in addition to Camp Siberia, ½ mile NE of Anderson Pass. Cross the moraine and follow the right side of the glacier about 1 mile to the base of a steep snow finger (ca. 35°). Ascend this finger to Flypaper Pass (6500 ft.) at the head of the glacier. The prominent summit immediately SW of Flypaper Pass, sometimes confused with West Peak, is 7100-ft. *Echo Rock*.

From Flypaper Pass descend onto the Eel Glacier. The bergschrund may be a problem in late summer. Traverse NW over the glacier until directly under the steep rotten flank of the N ridge. Do not climb to the ridge at this point!

Hanging Glacier and West Peak (courtesy Olympic National Park)

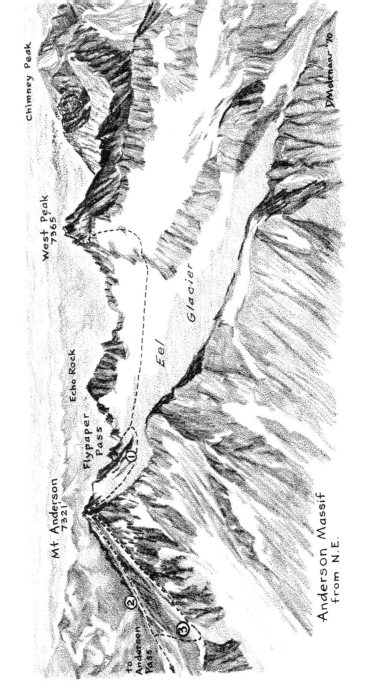

Chimney Peak

West Peak
7365'

Echo Rock

Mt. Anderson
7321'

Flypaper Pass

Eel Glacier

① ② ③

to Anderson Pass

DWolenaar '70

Anderson Massif
from N.E.

This common mistake leads to an impasse. Instead, traverse N about 300 yards, descending slightly to an obvious scree ledge leading to the NE shoulder. Climb the shoulder westerly until a notch in the horseshoe-shaped ridge is reached. Cross the ridge and climb on the W side about 700 ft. Here the ridge narrows, and the only practical route is along the rotten, exposed knife-edge over several false summits. The westernmost summit is the highest. Time: 7 hours up from Anderson Pass. The approach can also be made from Hayden Pass (see High Alpine Traverses Section, page 241).

Mt. Anderson   7321 (2231 m)
First ascent 1920 by F. B. Lee and party of 20 from Hayden Pass.

Route 1. I, 3. From Flypaper Pass (see Route 1, West Peak), drop 200 ft. onto the Eel Glacier and traverse to the right for a few hundred ft. Climb E up glaciated slopes to a saddle just left of the summit and go S to the summit. Time: 5 hours up from Anderson Pass.

The approach can also be made from Hayden Pass (see High Alpine Traverses Section, page 241).

Route 2. I, 2. From Anderson Pass, take the way trail to its end at the Anderson Glacier moraine. Cross the wooded ridge to the right and contour around on heather and snow about ⅓ mile to a view down a basin with lakes. Descend to the lakes (excellent campsite), then contour past the lakes and climb heather and snow to a col about ½ to ¾ mile beyond the lakes. Above and left of the col, take a steep gully system about 800 ft. to scree and snow on the SE side of the peak. From here, climb snow to the summit rocks. The upper part of this route can also be reached using the approach of Route 3. Time: 5 hours up from Anderson Pass.

Route 3. I, 2. First ascent 1932 by N. Bright and C. Ullin.
From Anderson Pass, take the way trail to Anderson Glacier moraine, and cross the ridge to the NE at the lowest point (ca. ½ mile). Contour N on alpine meadows and easy snow-covered benches to the ridge NNE of the summit. Ascend WSW to the summit on moderate snow slopes. Time: 5 hours up from Anderson Pass.

Route 4. I, 3. First ascent 1930 by E. B. Hamilton and party.
Follow Route 3 to the low point in the ridge (ca. ½ mile) and on 200 to 300 yards to bypass a buttress just N of the notch. Double back W (left) as soon as practical to regain the ridge. Follow this a short distance to the base of a second buttress. Gain the buttress via a steep gully just E (right) of the ridge crest. Follow the crest N to the summit (2 hours from here). Time: 5 hours up from Anderson Pass.

Route 5. I, 3. First ascent by L. F. Maranville and N. A. Townsend.
Ascend the Anderson Glacier about ⅔ mile to a point where a snow finger can be ascended up the SW face for about 200 ft. A short traverse NW above

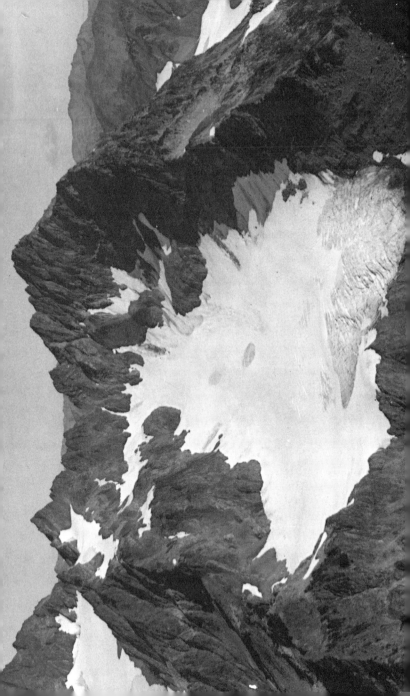

cliffs leads to a steep couloir (rockfall may be a problem) and a scramble over easy rock to the summit. Descent by Route 1 is desirable. Time: 4 hours up from Anderson Pass.

References: 1920 and 1975 *Mountaineer,* 1932 *Trail and Timberline,* 1943 *American Alpine Journal,* August 1972 *Off Belay.*

SENTINEL PEAK   6592 (2009 m)
Located on the south side of Hayden Pass.

Route. I, 1. From Hayden Pass climb SE up an easy talus ridge. Time: 2 hours up from Dose Meadows.

MT. FROMME   6655 (2028 m)
Located 1 mile northwest of Hayden Pass. Named for R. L. Fromme, an early supervisor of Olympic National Forest.

Route 1. I, 1. Climb a gentle talus ridge to the top from 5847-ft. Hayden Pass. Time: 2 hours up from Dose Meadows.

Route 2. I, 1. Climb the W ridge from 1 mile NW of Hayden Pass on the Hayes River trail. Time: 2½ hours up from Dose Meadows.

MT. CLAYWOOD   6836 (2084 m)
Named for Clay Wood, the adjutant general who ordered Lt. O'Neil on his first Olympic expedition. The USGS names Mt. Claywood as the northerly of two summits northwest of Hayden Pass, though this is in conflict with some references.

Route 1. I, 1. From Mt. Fromme, drop to a lake between the 2 summits. A talus shoulder falling to the NE provides an easy final ascent. The lake can be reached directly by climbing steep gully slopes from Dose Meadows. Time: 2 hours up from Mt. Fromme.

Route 2. I, 1. From Hayden Pass, follow the Hayes River trail about 1 mile to the point where it turns away from the peak down a ridge. Climb northerly up meadow, talus, and easy rock to the summit. Time: 3 hours up from Dose Meadows.

Reference: 1920 *Mountaineer.*

LOST PEAK   6515 (1986 m)
A prominent though subsidiary peak located north of Dose Meadows.

Route. I, 1. Take the trail N from Dose Meadows to Lost Pass (the 5500-ft. pass just SW of the summit). Ascend easy talus slopes E, swinging around to the E side of the summit near the top. Time: 2 hours up from Dose Meadows.

Mt. Anderson, Echo Rock, and Anderson Glacier (courtesy Olympic National Park)

CAMERON PEAK   7192 (2192 m)

Named for Cameron Creek which was in turn named for A. B. Cameron, an early settler, hunter, and guide. It is the highest point on the ridge north of Lost Peak.

Route. I, 2. Follow the ridge NE from Lost Peak to the main ridge and contour W to the first summit. Time: 2 hours up from Lost Peak.

WELLESLEY PEAK   6758 (2060 m)

Named for Wellesley College, this pointed peak stands 2 miles northwest of the Silt Creek-Dosewallips junction.

Route. I, 2. From Dose Meadows, follow the trail toward Hayden Pass ½ to ¾ mile to the end of the long switchback going E. Climb up and left to the Thousand Acre Meadows. Traverse diagonally across the meadow as streams permit to the ridge overlooking Silt Creek. Follow this ridge easterly past an intervening NW-SE ridge to the SW ridge of Wellesley. Scramble along ridge about ½ mile to the top. Time: 4 hours up from Dose Meadows.

MT. JUPITER   5701 (1738 m)

The closest high peak to Hood Canal, located between the lower Dosewallips and Duckabush rivers.

Route 1. I, 1. Take 7.2-mile trail (no water) to the summit from the end of the Mt. Jupiter road. This 6.3-mile road leaves U.S. 101 about ⅓ mile N of the Duckabush River. Time: 7 hours up.

Route 2 (Jupiter Cliffs). II, 5.5. First ascent 1967 by H. Pinsch and G. Tate.
Walk up the Duckabush River trail 1 mile (an abandoned logging road) to near the summit of little hump. Where the abandoned road stops and the real trail starts, turn right (N) where there is faint evidence of an old logging road. Follow this tree-covered road for about 30 minutes and the start of the climb. Start climbing at about 1000 ft. just left of a springtime waterfall bed. From this point, the route is via chimneys and ledges and is somewhat restrictive. The climbing eases at 4300 ft. An easier descent can be made by traversing E to avoid the worst of the cliffs. Time: 9 hours to pass the last difficulty.
An easier route is to follow the overgrown road as it climbs easterly another ½ mile. Leave the road and climb N to the E ridge and an intersection with the trail of Route 1.

Olympic elk (Jan Burger)

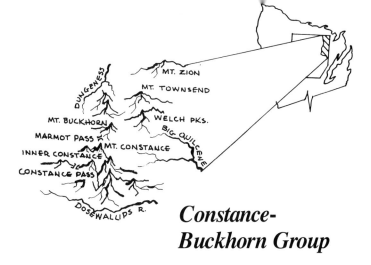

Constance-Buckhorn Group

This impressive uplift is located in the northeast corner of the Olympic Peninsula. It is bordered on the east by Hood Canal, and on the south and west by the Dosewallips and Dungeness rivers respectively. The Quilcene and Little Quilcene rivers on the east side are the remaining significant drainage systems. The general peak elevation exceeds that of the mountains to the south and rivals both the Gray Wolf-Hurricane Ridge and Mt. Olympus-Bailey Range groups to the west.

The southern half of this group is characterized by steep and lofty Mt. Constance and its jagged satellite peaks. Northward, the vertical walls gradually give way to high barren ridges with rocky summits.

This group offers some of the best alpine climbing in the range. The rock is fairly sound, particularly in the southern portion. A variety of climbing is available, including steep snow and high-angle rock. Most of the Grade III and IV climbs in the range are on Mt. Constance. Numerous climbs for the novice are also available.

In recent years, as logging roads have been extended up the thickly timbered valleys, this group has for the most part become fairly accessible. Since this area lies in the Olympic rain shadow, snowfall is the lightest in the range and glaciation is minimal.

APPROACHES

1. ***Dosewallips River.*** This approach is used for the S side routes of Mt. Constance, Inner Constance, and Desperation Peak. See Dosewallips Group, page 83, for approach details.

2. *Big Quilcene River-Townsend Creek.* This approach comprises a complex system of logging roads covering all major tributaries of the Big Quilcene River including both Tunnel Creek and Townsend Creek. It is used primarily for access to the N and E routes on Mt. Constance, the upper Quilcene River peaks, Warrior Arm, and Mt. Townsend. The upper Dungeness River can also be reached via this approach. Since this is a complicated approach, the main access road, including junctions, is described first. Succeeding paragraphs cover the major branch roads.

Leave U.S. 101 1.4 miles S of the town of Quilcene (0.4 mile N of the U.S. fish hatchery) on the Penney Creek road. At 1.4 miles, take the left branch which becomes Road #2812 (Big Quilcene River-Townsend Creek road). Road #2812 contours 3.2 miles to a junction with the Tunnel Creek road (#2743) and then climbs 6.1 miles to a junction with the upper Big Quilcene road (#2720). From this point, #2812 climbs 5 miles to Skaar Pass (3650 ft.) and then descends into the Little Quilcene River drainage.

The North Fork Tunnel Creek is used to reach the N and E sides of Mt. Constance and as the eastern approach to Warrior Arm. To reach North Fork Tunnel Creek, take Road #2743 (off road #2812) 6.5 miles and turn right on road #2762, which follows the N side of North Fork Tunnel Creek 2 miles to its end.

The Tunnel Creek trail starts where road #2743 crosses the S Fork (7 miles from #2812) and climbs about 4 miles to the ridge crest separating Tunnel Creek and the Dosewallips River (5000 ft.). The trail then descends approximately 3½ miles to the Dosewallips River road. The Tunnel Creek Shelter is at 3800 ft. about 2.5 miles in from the road.

The upper Big Quilcene River road (#2720) provides access to a number of peaks, including Mt. Buckhorn, Iron Mountain, Boulder Ridge, and Ridge of Gargoyles. This road climbs 4.7 miles to the start of the Quilcene River trail, then crosses the river, and eventually ends in logged-off areas. The Quilcene River trail climbs 5 miles to Marmot Pass (6000 ft.), and then descends 1.5 miles to the upper Dungeness River trail. Established campsites are Shelter Rock Camp (2.5 miles, 3600 ft.), Camp Mystery (4.5 miles, 5400 ft.), and Boulder Shelter Camp (SW from Marmot Pass on the Dungeness River trail, 4500 ft.).

Spur road #2764 leaves the main road (#2812) 4.2 miles above the 2812/2720 junction (0.8 mile below Skaar Pass). This spur road descends 0.8 mile, ending at the start of the S side Mt. Townsend trail (#839).

The trail ascends 3 miles, passing Camp Windy, to a fork. One branch continues 1.2 miles to the summit of Mt. Townsend, the other descends westerly to Silver Lake.

3. *Little Quilcene River.* This approach is of interest only for access to Mt. Townsend and the Dirty Face Ridge area.

The Lords Lake road (Forest Service road #2909) leaves U.S. 101 1.9 miles N of the town of Quilcene. It then climbs 7.7 miles to a junction with road #2812. Road #2812, the left fork, follows the Little Quilcene River, climbing 5.1 miles to Skaar Pass.

Note that road #2909 continues past the junction over Bon Jon Pass (2960 ft.) to the Dungeness River, 10.1 miles from the junction. When travel between the Quilcene and Dungeness drainages is necessary, it is much quicker to use the cutoff than to drive back out to U.S. 101 and around.

4. *Dungeness River.* This approach can be used to reach most of the peaks of the group, including Inner Constance, Warrior Peak, Alphabet Ridge, and Mt. Buckhorn. Mt. Constance is the major exception. See Gray Wolf-Hurricane Ridge Group, page 133, for approach details.

RANGER STATIONS

Dosewallips (end of Dosewallips River road), Quilcene (on U.S. 101 just S of Quilcene). Note: Check with ranger regarding limits on size of party and use of campfires.

CAMPGROUNDS

U.S. 101: Seal Rock, el. 50 ft. (2 miles N of Brinnon); Rainbow, el. 800 ft. (5 miles SW of Quilcene); Falls View, el. 450 ft. (4 miles SW of Quilcene); Sequim Bay State Park, el. 100 ft. (4 miles SE of Sequim).

Dosewallips River Road: See Dosewallips Group, page 83.

Big Quilcene River-Townsend Creek Road (Forest Service road #2812); Big Quilcene, el. 1700 ft. (4.9 miles from U.S. 101).

Dungeness River Road: See Gray Wolf-Hurricane Ridge Group, page 133.

VANTAGE POINTS

Mt. Walker can be reached by road. Mt. Jupiter and Mt. Townsend can be reached by trails.

MAPS

Olympic National Forest/Olympic National Park; USGS 30-minute Olympic National Park and Vicinity; the following 15-minute USGS and Green Trail quadrangle: Tyler Peak; the following Custom Correct map: Buckhorn Wilderness.

CONSTANCE AREA

The Constance area includes all peaks surrounding Lake Constance and Avalanche Canyon extending north from Lake Constance to Crystal Pass. Mt. Constance and its satellites on the east side of the canyon will be described first. Inner Constance and subsidiary peaks on the west side will be covered next. Within each grouping, the peaks will be reported from north to south.

The best approach is via the very steep but well-marked way trail that leaves the Dosewallips River road 14.2 miles in from U.S. 101. The 2-mile trail climbs 3350 ft. Camp is best located near Lake Constance at 4650 ft.

Mt. Constance

Desperation
Peak

Crystal
Pass

Point
Harroh

Peak 7022

②

④

The
Thumb

② ③

①A

To Inner Constance

Avalanche Canyon

①

④

Route
Toward
summit of Constance from S.E.

①

Mount Constance (7743')
above Lake Constance (4700'),
Eastern Olympics, from south,
showing route to
main massif.

"Trail" from
Dosewallips Rd | 2 miles, 3400' elevation gain

Alternate approaches are via the upper Dungeness River and North Tunnel Creek. Two traverses between Lake Constance and Boulder Shelter Camp on the Dungeness River can be made. The first, a col between Inner Constance and Desperation Peak, provides access to the west side of Warrior Peak and the Dungeness River. The second, Crystal Pass and a traverse north to the Warrior Peak-Brave col, provides access to Warrior Arm, Alphabet Ridge, and the Charlia Lakes way trail which leads to the Dungeness River.

CAMPING RESTRICTION

Because of excessive use, the National Park Service has imposed an overnight camping limit at Lake Constance. A summer ranger station is established near the lake. Lake Constance use quota is 20 persons per night between June 15 and Labor Day. Check with ranger concerning quotas and fire restrictions.

Mt. Constance   7743 (2360 m)

Mt. Constance is the highest and most massive peak in the eastern front range. Located northeast of Dose Forks, on the Dosewallips River, it is drained mainly by Tunnel Creek to the east and Constance Creek to the south. The first ascent was made from the east in 1922 by R. Schellin and A. E. "Bremerton" Smith via Route 7.

APPROACH NOTE

Three chutes climb easterly from Avalanche Canyon at points between ⅔ and 1 mile north of Lake Constance. Selecting the proper chute to gain the main ridge crest is a major key to the climb.

About ⅔ mile above the lake, the broad south chute (Route 1) climbs easterly to the low point in the main ridge. Several hundred yards farther north, the middle chute leads to an impasse and should be avoided. The narrow, steep north chute (Route 1A) climbs southeast out of the bowl located just below Crystal Pass and about 1 mile north of Lake Constance. The north chute provides the most direct route. The south chute is slightly easier and is less likely to be icy. Take crampons, as either chute may be icy into early summer. Route 1 should be considered as a primary descent route.

Route 1 (South Chute). II, 3. Follow Avalanche Canyon N from Lake Constance about ⅔ mile. The base of the broad S chute is characterized by a very broad scree fan and a large rock outcropping near the bottom. It is located opposite the S end of the The Thumb. Past this point, the walls of the canyon become nearly vertical. Climb E up this chute to a notch (Chute's Notch) in the ridge crest, gaining about 1200 ft. The top few feet of this chute are hidden, but above on the N side is a distinctive rock called Cat's Ears. Cross to the E side of the ridge and traverse N about 200 yards, passing close under a pillow-lava cliff to the base of a broad scree gully. Ascend this gully system to an obvious notch in a minor E-W ridge. Cross through this notch

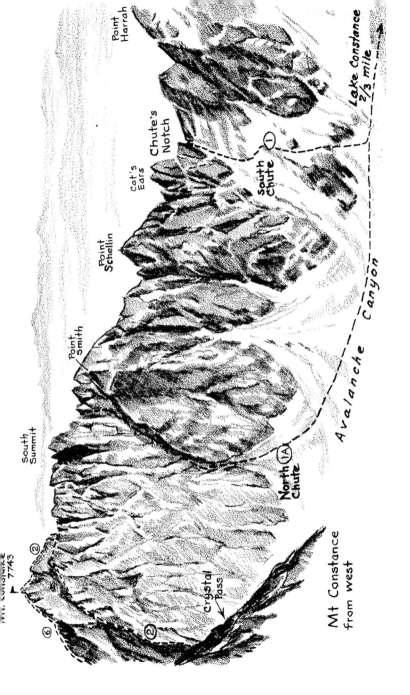

Mt Constance
from west

Point Harrah

Chute's Notch

Cat's Ears

Point Schellin

Point Smith

South Chute
①

North Chute ⑴ᴬ

Avalanche Canyon

Lake Constance 2/3 mile

South Summit

Crystal Pass

Mt Constance 7743

②

⑥

②

and descend a short distance to a scree or snow ledge. Next, contour N ¼ mile, crossing heather or snow slopes, gullies, and finally a steep cirque (the Terrible Traverse). From here, climb an ascending ledge, then past rock outcropping to open slopes just SE of the summit. Continue to the 60-ft. summit block which is climbed on the N side. Time: 7 hours up from Lake Constance, 4 hours down.

Route 1A (North Chute). II, 3. From Lake Constance, follow Avalanche Canyon N past the broad S chute (Route 1) and the middle chute. Continue past the point where the valley walls become nearly vertical, to a basin about 200 yards S of Crystal Pass (ca. 1 mile above the lake). At this point, N of the N end of The Thumb on Inner Constance, the steep, narrow N chute leads southeasterly to the main ridge crest. It is the last chute before reaching Crystal Pass. Note that this chute, unlike the S chute, cannot be seen until one is at its base. Climb past a large house-sized boulder and continue up this long, steep chute to the notch at the ridge crest. Go through this notch, turn left, and then traverse a short distance over ledges on the E side of the massif to the notch in the minor E-W ridge where this route joins Route 1.

Route 1B (Finger Traverse). II, 3. First ascent 1923 by L. Chute and W. Thomson.

Through the notch in the minor E-W ridge, descend several ft. and then scramble up westerly, bypassing a minor buttress on the left. Contour slightly upward and N around a depression in the E face below the main ridge to the S side of a second buttress. Continue to the right of this buttress, dropping slightly to the E side where a narrow sloping ledge (the Finger Traverse) permits passage. Traverse northerly over another minor buttress to the main ridge, or descend a narrow gully onto a permanent snowfield which should be crossed. From here, climb any one of several rock gullies or chimneys to the ridge crest and follow it to the summit block. Time: 7 hours up from Lake Constance; descent via Route 1 is 4 hours.

Route 2 (West Arête). III, 5.4. First ascent 1957 by D. N. Anderson, R. Knight, and J. Richardson.

From camp at the head of Avalanche Canyon, climb N to the pass with the small pinnacle in it (Crystal Pass). From behind the small pinnacle, climb the right-hand buttress to the arête and continue at or near its crest. At the large wall that cuts the arête ⅔ of the way up, traverse up and right on a narrow rotten ledge for 20 ft. and then climb straight up to a wide tilted ledge. Next, climb up a chimney to another exposed ledge leading to a final steep pitch. The arête joins the main ridge ¼ mile S of the summit, which may be reached by traversing the ridge crest on the E side. Note: This route is difficult and very exposed. Retreat would be problematical in bad weather. Time: 4-7 hours up from Crystal Pass; descent via Route 1 is advisable.

Route 3 (Red Dike Route). III, 5.5. First ascent 1959 by D. N. Anderson, R. Hebble, and J. Richardson.

Summit of Mt. Constance (Frank Chapin)

From camp in the upper valley (see Route 2), cross Crystal Pass and descend the glacier past the larger bergschrund. Just above the level part of the glacier a red dike leads up the wall. Slightly broken rock on the right of this dike permits upward advance. A long initial lead, with one difficult pitch about 80 ft. up, leads to a spot where an anchor protects the next advance over slightly easier rock. From this point, scramble up and right to the highest point on the slabby ledge. Next, climb to the left and up a short pitch of red loose-appearing rock to another ledge. Above, on the left, climb another band of very difficult, unstable-looking red rock with a traverse into a narrow chimney. Above the chimney, scramble up along the red dike to a point just 200 ft. short of the W ridge. Climb back left and up, making several zigzags to avoid major difficulties. Go around the corner on a grassy ledge to the final part of the W arête which can be ascended to its junction with the summit ridge and Route 1. Time: 6-10 hours up; descent via Route 1 is recommended.

Route 4 (North Face). IV, 5.7. First ascent 1976 by J. Olson and K. Pearce.

Start the climb 200 yards N of the red dike (see Route 3) at the base of three prominent cracks. These cracks are below and to the right of a west-facing

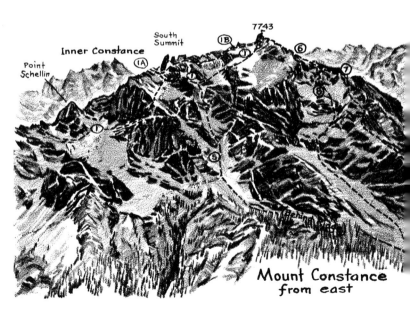

Mount Constance
from east

open book. Work up two pitches (mostly Class 5) to the book. Thirty ft. to the right of the book is a small bush. Belaying from this bush, work up and right until an 18-inch ledge is reached. Traverse the ledge right to its end and then move directly up over a bulge on loose rock (5.7). Moving from the bulge, work up and right to a left-running crack; a belay bolt was placed in this system. Follow the obvious crack up through a chimney to easier ground and another belay bolt. Work left, then up, then left again to a ridge. This ridge (Class 4 and easier) joins the main NE ridge several hundred yards N of the summit.

Long runouts and poor protection make this route precarious. The difficulty is compounded by extreme rockfall encountered throughout the face. Water running through the major crack would make the ascent very difficult at any time other than dry periods. Time: 9-10 hours up from camp; descent via Route 1 is recommended. Time on this route is highly subjective and will vary greatly depending on the party and conditions.

Route 5 (Southeast). II, 3. First ascent 1932 by J. Kiley, R. Pollock, and B. Winiecki via Dosewallips River-Tunnel Creek Divide.

Leave the end of the North Fork Tunnel Creek road # 2762 and contour W for about 1 mile following game trail. Bear S 100 yards, crossing the Charlia Lakes drainage. Continue S, following game trail along creek to large tarn at about 4100 ft. (ca. 3 miles from end of road). Good campsites can be found here. Continue SSW into upper drainage 1 mile and then climb W to snow or scree gullies and up the E face. Near the 6000-ft. level, ascend SW to a broad snow/scree ramp E of Cat's Ears where the route joins Route 1. As an alternate, continue directly up toward the Terrible Traverse route (beware of rockfall in gullies). This route can also be approached through the two passes NE of Lake Constance and then through the pass on Tunnel Creek Divide (Cunningham Pass). Time: 6 hours up from tarn campsite. The easiest and safest descent route off the E side of Constance is the broad snow or scree ramp E of Cat's Ears.

Route 6 (Northeast Ridge). III, 4. First ascent 1958 by K. Heathershaw, R. McKee, R. Oram, and K. Spencer.

From the 3800-ft. level of Route 5, proceed westerly about ¼ mile to a fairly large level meadow (ca. 4000 ft.). From the meadow, ascend SW up a brush or snow slope. Next, climb the right-hand narrow gully to a large basin (ca. 5000 ft.). Ascend to the head of the basin and traverse to the right until the ridge is reached. Climb along the ridge a short distance until it becomes difficult, then contour SW over very steep slab on the NW face to a shallow gully. Ascend the gully to just below a prominent spire on the ridge crest. The summit can be attained in 1 hour by climbing along the ridge crest, bypassing the gendarmes on either side. The ascent is long, and involves careful route finding. Time: 9 hours up from road, 4 hours down (a descent via Route 5 or Route 1 is recommended).

Mount Constance
from E.N.E.

Route 7 (S. Spur NE Ridge). III, 4. First ascent 1922 by A. E. Smith and R. Schellin. Approach was via the Dosewallips River-Tunnel Creek Divide. The descent was similar to Route 6.

From the tarn (see Route 5 approach) ascend NW to talus or snow fan 300 yards N of waterfall below the E face (Great Amphitheater). From the rock fan, climb a chute 900 ft. to a cul-de-sac (ca. 5400 ft.). Continue right over a ridge to the next chute and ascend to its head. Traverse right to a third chute which drains N. Climb to the NE ridge (staying on S side of ridge crest) where the route joins Route 6. Time: 6 hours up from tarn area (descent via Route 5 or Route 1).

Route 8 (Great Amphitheater). III, 4. First ascent 1981 by L. F. Maranville and R.B. Nelson. The amphitheaterlike formation is the most prominent feature of Mt. Constance viewed from the east.

This classic climb starts directly above the tarn mentioned in previous routes. Ascend large avalanche basin at the base of the headwall, following stream or couloir (depending on condition and season) to headwall (ca. 6000 ft.). From here, the route climbs the face divided by three rock bands to the right of the headwall. The rock bands are climbed via their right side, which involves mixed climbing with short rock pitches (some Class 4 or 5). Above the rock bands, continue up and left to gain the NE ridge. Continue along ridge to summit via Route 6. Time: 6 hours up from tarn; descend via Route 5 or Route 1.

References: 1922, 1926, 1959, 1972, 1974, 1981, and 1983 *Mountaineer;* 1943 *American Alpine Journal;* August 1972 *Off Belay.*

South Summit   ca. 7600 (2316 m)

Located immediately north of the notch at the head of the Constance north chute. First ascent 1958 by T. Hovey and D. Keller.

Route. II, 4. Follow Mt. Constance Route 1B to the depression in the E face below the main ridge. Climb upward and westerly until the S side of the peak is reached. Climb the obvious chimney to a wide ledge and then traverse left into a second gully to a large rock slab forming a tunnel. Go through the tunnel. A short rock pitch then leads to the flat summit. Time: 4 hours up from Lake Constance.

Point Smith   ca. 7100 (2164 m)

This prominent rampart is located immediately south of the Constance north chute and 200 yards west of the main ridge. Named after A.E. Smith, who made the first ascent of Mt. Constance in 1922. First ascent 1983 by S. Baker, K. Page, and A. Sande.

Route. I, 3. From the top of Constance N chute, climb S a short distance and then descend W on the N side of the ridge. Cross to S side of the ridge and continue to the summit. Time: 30 minutes up from top of N chute.

South summit of Mt. Constance from the east (Rich Olson)

Point Schellin   ca. 6850 (2088 m)

A prominent rampart located 100 yards north of the Constance south chute on the main ridge. Named after R. Schellin, who made the first ascent of Mt. Constance in 1922. First ascent 1923 by L. Chute via south wall. The second ascent was in 1983, 60 years later. Chute's register was found by the party.

Route. I, 3. First ascent 1983 by K. Page and J. White.

From the top of S chute (Chute's Notch), contour N under E side of Cat's Ears and E side of Pt. Schellin. Climb to notch on N side, then scramble directly to summit. Time: 45 minutes up from Chute's Notch.

Cat's Ears   ca. 6650 (2027 m)

A distinctive rock tower located immediately north of Chute's Notch on the main ridge.

Point Harrah   ca. 7000 (2134 m)

Located ⅔ mile northeast of Lake Constance and 200 yards south of Chute's Notch. Named after D. Harrah, leader of the Inner Constance first ascent party. First ascent 1983 by K. Page and J. White.

Route. I, 4. From Chute's Notch traverse S to top of next knob and then downclimb directly into notch N of summit. Traverse E under summit to gully system, then climb up gullies and slabs to the summit. Time: 1½ hours up from Chute's Notch.

Peak 7022 ca. 7022 (2140 m)

Located approximately ½ mile northeast of Lake Constance.

Route. I, 2. Follow Avalanche Canyon N from Lake Constance about ½ mile and then climb SE over snow or scree, keeping left of the rocky buttress forming the W face of Peak 7022. Continue to the base of the short gully with a rock finger on its left side. Climb the gully and then contour right beneath a rock wall to the ridge which is followed SW a short distance to the summit. Time: 3 hours up from Lake Constance.

Destroyer ca. 6550 (1996 m)

This rock spire is located northeast of Peak 7022, ½ mile from 6300-ft. Tunnel Creek Pass (Cunningham Pass) on the northeast-southwest Tunnel Creek divide. First ascent 1980 by D. Bogucki, L. F. Maranville, and P. Reagan.

Route. II, 5.4. Take the Tunnel Creek Trail (# 841) to the stream crossing a short distance above Tunnel Creek Shelter Camp. Leave the trail and continue up valley on the right side of creek to a level area (ca. 4900 ft.), then turn right through trees into a boulder field at the foot of cliffs. Ascend steep chute in cliffs at the right. Climb rocky slope above cliffs and then traverse left SW to the foot of Destroyer. Climb left on a 50-ft. sloping ledge (Class 5) to the notch on the SW side of the summit tower. Cross broad downsloping ledge to the NW corner. Climb easy rotten chimney to platform. A knifeblade piton was used to protect the final lead to the summit. Rappel from summit. Time: 5 hours up from Tunnel Creek Shelter Camp. A variation can be done by climbing left from the NW corner to a crack. Ascend open book to chockstone. Continue up closing book to the platform (5.6).

Enigma ca. 6550 (1996 m)

Located immediately southwest of Destroyer on the Tunnel Creek divide. First ascent 1979 by L. R. Maranville, W. McCleary, and R. Nelson.

Route 1. II, 4. From the notch between Destroyer and Enigma (see Destroyer route), climb to ledge on NE face and then climb slab to ridge which is scrambled to the summit.

Route 2. II, 5.3. First ascent 1979 by L. F. Maranville and P. Reagan. Climb the SE face diagonally over broken rock directly to the summit.

The Nun ca. 5450 (1661 m)

Located on the north edge of the Dosewallips River-Tunnel Creek Divide, east southeast of Destroyer and at an elevation just 700 ft. above the South Fork of Tunnel Creek. Although low in elevation, this inconspicuous but noble little peak is a challenging climb. First ascent 1978 by L. F. Maranville and J. Wilson.

Route 1. II, 4. Use the same approach as for Destroyer and turn S, crossing the creek at about 4800 ft. (¾ mile above trail). Continue until The Nun's E ridge is gained and then climb to the tree at base of the summit block. Turn right on a descending traverse, then proceed W for 200 ft. on exposed slab. Next, climb rock to the summit ridge and traverse W to summit. Time: 3 hours up from Tunnel Creek Shelter Camp. Rappel E side 120 ft.

Route 2. II, 5.0. First ascent 1983 by D. Colwell, K. Page, J. Renfro, A. Sande, and J. White.

From the tree (Route 1), proceed directly up a near vertical pitch on pillow basalt. Then scramble to the summit on W end.

April Peak   ca. 6350 (1935 m)

This peak is the highest point on the Dosewallips River-Tunnel Creek Divide. It is located ¾ mile southeast of Peak 7022. Several other peaks east of April offer some good Class 3 climbs. They are March (ca. 6100), Lenten (ca. 6100) and February (ca. 5301).

Route. II, 3. Follow the S Tunnel Creek approach (see Destroyer), passing The Nun on the left to the 5000-ft. level. Turn left (300 yards past The Nun) and ascend the basin to the col between March and April peaks. From the col, climb the E side of April and angle left on a ledge which leads to the upper ridge and summit. Time: 3 hours up from Tunnel Creek Shelter Camp. April Peak and the other summits along the ridge can also be reached by traversing the Dosewallips River-Tunnel Creek Divide from Tunnel Creek trail above Harrison Lake.

Desperation Peak   ca. 7150 (2179 m)

A subsidiary peak located at the north end of Avalanche Canyon and immediately northwest of Crystal Pass. First ascent 1940 by W. Ingalls, B. Henderson, R. Carlow, and D. Dooley.

Route. I, 3. From Lake Constance, ascend N up Avalanche Canyon to Crystal Pass. Climb NW over broken rock to the jagged SE ridge, and follow the ridge to the false summit. Descend 30 ft. on the W side and cross the col between the false and true summits. Traverse to the N side of the summit face and ascend 40 ft. to the top. The S face offers short Class 4 climbing in chimney systems. Time: 4 hours up from Lake Constance.

Rottenrockel Spitz   ca. 6500 (1981 m)

The easternmost of three pinnacles on a spur ridge extending northwest from the north ridge of Inner Constance (see Route 5, Inner Constance, for approach). The pinnacle is identified by a huge cleft completely bisecting it. First ascent 1962 by B. Gordon, J. Lindsay, and P. Schoening.

Route. I, 4. From the N ridge of Inner Constance, traverse the spur ridge NW for several hundred yards to the base of the pinnacle. A chimney stem then leads to the E ridge which is climbed to the top.

Inner Constance   ca. 7670 (2338 m)

A high massive peak located directly west of Mt. Constance. First ascent 1939 by D. Harrah and party.

Route 1. II, 4. From Lake Constance, proceed N up Avalanche Canyon for about ¾ mile, until just S of The Thumb. From this point, climb W ascending one of several shallow gullies for about 750 ft. until reaching a large snow basin. Continue W crossing the basin and then climb a broad, steep snow chute to the ridge crest just S of The Pyramid. The chute is sometimes icy, and crampons may be needed. Cross to the W side of the ridge, turn right, and follow the ragged ridge N, skirting The Pyramid on its W side. The summit block is located on the N end of the massif. The top is attained by climbing 100 ft. of steep rotten rock from the S side. If desired, this final pitch may be avoided by following a ledge system around to the right (E) where the final pitch of Route 2 is joined. Time: 4 hours up from Lake Constance.

Route 2. II, 3. First recorded ascent 1974 by J. Gray, J. Hinck, F. Maranville, W. McCleary, H. Munson, T. Sloan, and T. Weston.

Leave Avalanche Canyon just N of The Thumb and climb SW to the bowl between The Thumb and Inner Constance. Next, climb obliquely right up a

Inner Constance
from S.E.

snow finger and rock to the west end of a horizontal snowfield. Angle left up steep snow to an upper bowl at about 7000 ft. From here, climb right, up a steep snow couloir to the notch on the E side of the summit block which is climbed by the E face. Time: 4 hours up from Lake Constance.

Route 2A. II, 3. From the bowl between The Thumb and Inner Constance (see Route 2), climb NW up the steep snow gully leading to the notch immediately N of The Pyramid. About halfway up this gully turn right, up a narrow snow-filled defile hidden by the cliffs below. From here, a gentle snow ridge leads to the upper bowl of Route 2. This is an excellent descent route. Time: 4 hours up from Lake Constance.

Route 3. II, 3. Leave Avalanche Canyon just N of The Thumb. Climb NW directly to what appears to be a ledge rising to the N. This is actually a steep, rock-filled chute. Climb the ridge immediately right of the chute to a headwall, then switchback to the S on a broad ledge around a buttress. From this point, climb N up a short chute reaching a small meadow. Turn SW and climb a ridge to the easy summit block. Time: 4 hours up from Lake Constance.

Route 4 (Northeast Face). II, 3. First recorded ascent 1972 by D. Bently, B. Brown, M. Dodd, E. Hutt, L. Kinsey, R. Jamison, and G. Olson.

Follow Avalanche Canyon N from Lake Constance for about 1 mile to the bowl just below Crystal Pass. From the middle of the bowl, climb westerly up a snow finger, past a moat and then over rock. Next, angle left then right to a snowfield at the base of the cliffs below the NE ridge. Ascend the snowfield to the saddle in the ridge which is followed to the summit. Time: 4-5 hours up from Lake Constance.

Route 5 (North Buttress). II, 4. First ascent 1957 by R. Harniss and J. Newman.

From the cirque between Inner Constance and Warrior Peak (see Warrior Peak for approach) ascend the right-hand buttress SSW up steep rock and snow to the ridge, which leads to the summit. Time: 7 hours up from Home Lake or Boulder Shelter Camp.

Route 6 (Southwest Ridge). II, 4. From Constance Pass, follow the broad shoulder NE, bypassing several rock towers on the E side. When stopped by a prominent wall at about 6700 ft., traverse left on steep snow or rock and then climb a twisting gully to regain the flat ridge crest ½ mile S of the main summit (between C-141 and Stasis). Descend slightly and contour N, bypassing Stasis on the E side, to join Route 1 near the top of the chute. Time: 4 hours up from Constance Pass.

Route 7 (Southwest Face). II, 4. First ascent 1975 by R. Olson, Jr., K. Pearce, and B. Albro. This climb was accomplished under extreme winter conditions during the rescue operation after the 1975 C-141 crash.

Inner Constance Ridge from Mt. Constance; from left: Stasis, The Pyramid, Inner Constance
(Richard LaBelle)

From Home Lake, climb E up snow or scree slopes to a large bench. Continue up a steep couloir (schrunds late in the summer) and then traverse left to a gully and ledge system which is climbed to a point level with the shoulder mentioned in Route 6. Here, the route joins Route 6 just below the ridge crest. Time: 4 hours up from Home Lake. Descent via Route 6 is recommended.

The Thumb   ca. 6600 (2012 m)

A prominent rock thumb located approximately 1 mile north of Lake Constance on the east shoulder of Inner Constance immediately above Avalanche Canyon.

Route 1 (Northwest Couloir). I, 2. Leave the valley just N of The Thumb and climb to the snow basin between Inner Constance and The Thumb. When reaching the NW corner, climb a 400-ft. 30° snow or rock couloir to the rounded summit. Time: 2 hours up from Lake Constance.

Route 2 (West Ridge). I, 3. Continue past the couloir of Route 1 several hundred ft. to the W ridge. Bypass the initial vertical step via gullies on the left side, and then follow the exposed ridge to the summit. Time: 2 hours up from Lake Constance.

Route 3 (South Face). I, 4. First ascent 1973 by R. LaBelle, G. Sterr, and H. Sterr.

From the valley floor, follow Route 1 of Inner Constance approximately 30 minutes to the base of the S face. Climb the obvious fault line found at the center of the face. Six pitches, mostly Class 4, lead to the summit. Time: 4 hours up from Lake Constance.

The Pyramid   ca. 7650 (2332 m)

A pointed summit on the Inner Constance ridge crest about ⅓ mile southwest of the main summit block and immediately north of the notch at the top of the Inner Constance Route 1 chute.

Route. I, 3. Follow Route 1 of Inner Constance to the top of the chute at the ridge crest. Proceed W through the notch and traverse several hundred ft. N on the W side to the saddle at the N side of the peak. Climb over snow and broken rock to the summit. Time: 3 hours up from Lake Constance.

Stasis   ca. 7500 (2286 m)

Located on the main Inner Constance ridge crest between C-141 Peak and the notch at the top of the Inner Constance Route 1 chute.

Route. I, 3. From the notch, climb S over snow or rock several hundred yards to the summit. Time: 3 hours up from Lake Constance.

C-141 Peak   7339 (2237 m)

Located approximately 1 mile northwest of Lake Constance. It is the high point at the south end of the main Inner Constance ridge. This peak is dedicated to the 17 servicemen who perished in the U.S. Air Force C-141 crash, March 1975.

Route 1. I, 3. After reaching Lake Constance, proceed up Avalanche Canyon until it narrows (ca. ½ mile). Continue 400 ft. inside the canyon's mouth and climb westerly up an obvious chute. Near the top of the right branch, climb out to the right over rock and then angle NW into a prominent basin. From the basin, climb westerly to the flat saddle between Aeterna Tower on the left and C-141 Peak on the right. Climb the ridge N to the top, bypassing several rock buttresses on the E or W side. Time: 3 hours up from Lake Constance.

Route 2. I, 3. From about halfway up the chute of Inner Constance Route 1, make a climbing traverse southwesterly several hundred yards over snow or scree to the broad saddle on the N side of the peak. Climb the ridge S over snow or broken rock. Time: 3 hours up from Lake Constance. C-141 Peak can also be climbed via Inner Constance Routes 6 and 7.

Aeterna Tower   ca. 6700 (2042 m)

A rock tower located ⅔ mile northwest of Lake Constance and ⅓ mile southeast of C-141 Peak. First ascent 1974 by P. Carney, R. LaBelle, and M. Martin.

Route 1. I, 3. From the flat saddle between Aeterna Tower and C-141 Peak (see C-141 Peak, Route 1), proceed SE to the short but steep summit block. Time: 3 hours up from Lake Constance.

Route 2. I, 3. First ascent 1986 by J. Diianni and T. Rae.

Follow Avalanche Canyon to the point where it narrows. Proceed up the first steep couloir on left (snow in early season). At the top of the couloir, angle NW over open slopes to a bowl. Climb N to the SW ridge of Aeterna Tower. Follow the ridge crest NE to the summit block. Time: 3 hours up from Lake Constance.

WARRIOR PEAK   7300 (2225 m)

A rocky double-summit peak located 1 mile north-northeast of Inner Constance on the Tunnel Creek-Dungeness River divide. First ascent of both summits 1945 by F. Beckey.

Southeast Summit   7300 (2225 m)

Route 1. I, 3. Leave the Dungeness River trail about 2 miles S of Boulder Shelter Camp (ca. 1½ miles N of Home Lake) near where the creek flows out of the Warrior Peak-Inner Constance cirque.

Climb E alongside the creek to reach the mouth of the cirque. From here, Warrior Peak is due N; it is the peak bisected by a prominent couloir. Climb this couloir via snow or steep talus to the saddle between the two summits.

Warrior Peak from near Home Lake (Konrad Schwenke)

Note that several less-prominent easterly gullies, which could be confused with the proper one in bad weather, end in impasses. From the saddle, ascend steep snow on the NW side of the SE peak. The first rock pitch above the snow is fairly difficult. Above this pitch, angle left into a shallow chimney to climb past the last difficulties. From here, a 10-minute scramble leads to the summit. Time: 5 hours up from Boulder Shelter Camp.

Route 2. I, 3. First ascent 1983 by K. Page and J. Sanborn.

Continue past the couloir of Route 1 and follow the most easterly gully up and right to a large bench on the right skyline. Traverse ledges N onto the E face and scramble up on good rock to the summit. An excellent climb. Time: 4 hours up from trail.

Northwest Summit   ca. 7285 (2220 m)

Route 1. I, 3. For approach, see Southeast Summit. From the saddle between Warrior's two peaks, climb NW past a pile of spearlike broken rock to the cliff base. Climb the steep, shallow gully slightly right (N) of this point to its head (about 80 ft.). Contour N on ledges to a scree cone at the base of a second gully. Climb the easy gully to the ridge, which then leads to the summit. Time: 5 hours up from Boulder Shelter Camp.

Route 2. I, 3. First ascent 1968 by A. Bloomer, G. Kelsey, R. Latz, H. Pinsch, and K. Spencer.

The route starts at the Warrior Peak-Alphabet Ridge saddle. Early in the season the best approach to this saddle is via the Dungeness River trail. Leave the trail about 1¼ miles S of Boulder Shelter Camp (at the Park boundary) and climb snow and scree gullies to the 6700-ft. saddle. Later in the year when the snow is gone, the easiest approach is to follow the Charlia Lakes way trail to the Boulder Ridge-Alphabet Ridge saddle. Charlia Lakes may also be reached from the east via the North Tunnel Creek game trail (6 to 8 hours).

The Charlia Lakes trail leaves the Dungeness River trail just S of Boulder Shelter Camp. From the end of the trail at the saddle, climb over Cloudy Peak and descend several hundred ft. over easy snow or scree to the Warrior Peak-Alphabet Ridge saddle. Climb the broad ridge S from the saddle. After a short distance the route leaves the ridge crest, contouring onto the W side via ledges and talus. Follow the line of least difficulty past a number of steep chimneys. The ledges end abruptly behind a small pinnacle on the SW corner of the peak. Climb the only avenue of ascent, a short gully followed by easy rock and scree. The next obstacle, a near vertical pitch, is climbed on its right-hand side; the rock is loose. Above this pitch, proceed through an obvious crack in the ridge. Climb to the summit avoiding the airy ridge crest in favor of an easy scramble on the N side of the ridge. Time: 6 hours up from Boulder Shelter Camp; the easiest descent is via Route 1.

Route 3. I, 3. First ascent 1960 by D. N. Anderson, D. Devin, S. Johnson, and J. Munson.

From the Warrior Peak-Alphabet Ridge saddle (see Route 2 for approach), climb the broad ridge S for several hundred yards to the base of one of several prominent chimneys. Climb one of these chimneys to gain the upper slopes of the peak and then continue S over snow and broken rock to the small summit. Time: 6 hours up from Boulder Shelter Camp; 3 hours down via Route 1. References: 1972 *Mountaineer;* August 1972 *Off Belay.*

WARRIOR ARM   ca. 6900 (2103 m)

A major ridge running east from Warrior Peak. This seldom-visited though interesting area offers numerous climbs of varying difficulty on fairly good rock. There is no easy access to this ridge. The east end (e.g., The Squaw and The Papoose) can best be reached from the North Fork of Tunnel Creek (see approach for Mt. Constance Route 5). The west portion (i.e., The Brave and Tower 6700) is most easily reached from Boulder Shelter Camp on the Dungeness River. Only the major summits are covered; they are listed in order from west to east. There are several lesser summits between Tower 6700 and The Squaw.

Reference: 1969 *Mountaineer.*

The Brave   ca. 6900 (2103 m)
First ascent 1968 by A. Bloomer, G. Kelsey, R. Latz, and K. Spencer.

Route. II, 4. From Boulder Shelter Camp, take the Charlia Lakes way trail to the Boulder Ridge-Alphabet Ridge saddle. Climb S to the summit rocks of Cloudy Peak and then descend S over talus or easy snow to the Warrior Peak-Alphabet Ridge saddle. From here, descend the eastern basin about 750 ft. until a moraine on the S side of the valley is reached. Ascend the moraine to reach the lower terminus of a hidden snow basin which descends from the Warrior Peak-Brave col. An alternate approach to this col can be made from N. Fork Tunnel Creek by following a game trail up the Crystal Glacier drainage, N of Mt. Constance. Climb to the col. From the col, ascend easterly over snow, snow and rock mixed, and a short rock pitch to a sloping ledge. Contour left to the base of a hidden chimney. This chimney, the climb's chief difficulty, requires one long lead to surmount. From here, follow a ledge on the N side beneath the ridge crest to a second chimney. Continue past this chimney a few feet and then climb a short exposed pitch past the final difficulties. A short scramble leads to the tiny summit. Time: 8 hours up from Boulder Shelter Camp, 4 hours down.

East Tower of Brave   ca. 6850 (2088 m)
First ascent 1986 by T. Whitney, J. Williams, and S. Williams.

Route. II, 4. For approach, see route for The Brave. Ascend the moraine to reach the hidden snow basin. Cross this basin to an obvious couloir (crampons are recommended; also, the bergschrund becomes difficult to cross late in the summer). Ascend this steep couloir to The Brave-Tower 6700 notch, then climb W for five leads to the summit. These leads are straightforward and difficult. Time: 3 hours up from notch. Descend by rappelling to notch.

Tower 6700   ca. 6700 (2042 m)
First ascent 1982 by R. Bell, K. Lowry, L. Stretz, and T. Whitney.

Route. II, 5.2. For approach, see route for East Tower of Brave. From The Brave-Tower 6700 notch, climb E up rock (5.2) to platform. Then climb S side to summit. Time: 2 hours up from notch.

The Squaw   ca. 6300 (1920 m)
First ascent 1967 by A. Bloomer, G. Kelsey, R. Oram, H. Pinsch, and K. Spencer.

Route. II, 2. Use the North Tunnel Creek approach as described in Mt. Constance Route 5. From the 3900-ft. level, proceed NW through a meadow to the creek flowing from the Crystal Glacier on the N side of Mt. Constance. Cross the creek and climb N through timber a short distance, then bear NE to an old burn. Ascend the burn and then climb through a prominent break in the lower cliffs. Next, ascend westerly, keeping well under the summit of The

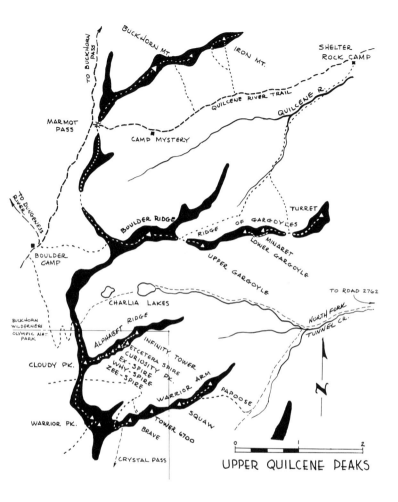

UPPER QUILCENE PEAKS

Papoose to just below The Squaw-Papoose col. An easy scramble leads to the summit. Time: 5 hours up from road.

The Squaw-Papoose col has been reached via a snow chute on the N side after an approach as described for The Brave. Such an approach would be longer.

The Papoose   ca. 6100 (1859 m)
The easternmost summit on Warrior Arm. First ascent 1976 by L. F. Maranville and W. McCleary.

Route. II, 2. See route description for The Squaw. From The Squaw-Papoose col, climb easterly along the broken ridge to the summit. Time: 5 hours up from road.

ALPHABET RIDGE   ca. 7000 (2134 m)

An east-west ridge, consisting of a number of summits and rock spires, bordered by Charlia Lakes on the north and Warrior Peak on the south. The summits are presented from west to east.

The approaches begin at either Boulder Shelter Camp or North Tunnel Creek. From Boulder Shelter Camp, proceed south along the trail for several hundred yards to the unmarked Charlia Lakes way trail. Ascend the trail to the broad saddle overlooking Charlia Lakes. From North Tunnel Creek, Alphabet Ridge can be reached by following the Charlia Lakes drainage to Charlia Lakes.

References: 1969 *Mountaineer;* August 1972 *Off Belay.*

Cloudy Peak   ca. 7000 (2134 m)

The rounded summit immediately above and south of the saddle.

Route. I, 2. Climb S to the summit up steep snow or scree. Time: 3 hours up from Boulder Shelter Camp.

Zee Spire   ca. 6950 (2118 m)

First ascent 1958 by A. Bloomer, R. Oram, and K. Spencer.

Route. I, 3. Traverse the ridge E from Cloudy Peak and climb Zee Spire via the W side.

Why Spire   ca. 6900 (2103 m)

First ascent 1958 by A. Bloomer, R. Oram, and K. Spencer.

Route. I, 3. Continue E from Zee Spire to the summit.

Ex-Spire   ca. 6950 (2118 m)

First ascent 1958 by A. Bloomer, R. Oram, and K. Spencer.

Route. I, 4. Approach from Why Spire. Traverse under the S side and climb the E corner. The shallow Class 5 120-ft. chimney on the S side has also been climbed.

Curiosity Peak   ca. 7000 (2134 m)

First ascent 1958 by A. Bloomer, R. Oram, and K. Spencer.

Route. I, 3. Continue E from Ex-Spire over broken rock to the summit. Time: 4 hours up from Boulder Shelter Camp.

Etcetera Spire   ca. 6900 (2103 m)

First ascent 1968 by A. Bloomer, G. Kelsey, R. Latz, and H. Pinsch.

Route. I, 3. From Curiosity Peak, follow the narrowing ridge NE for about 300 yards. Climb the E side.

Infinity Tower   ca. 6900 (2103 m)

First ascent 1968 by D. Muntz and R. Olson, Jr. This party threw a codline over the top and accomplished a prusik ascent. The first free ascent 1985 by D. Blythe, S. Rowe, L. Stretz, and D. Tennant.

Route. II, 5.6. From Curiosity Peak, follow the narrowing ridge NE to Etcetera Spire. Traverse along the N side of Etcetera Spire and then follow the narrow broken ridge about 300 yards to the tower's base. Traverse on a ledge from SW corner and then ascend the W face (only side not overhanging) one lead up rotten rock with poor protection. Rappel S face.

BOULDER RIDGE   6852 (2088 m)

Located 1 mile south-southeast of Marmot Pass above the headwaters of the Quilcene River.

Mt. Constance, Inner Constance, and Warrior Peak from near Ridge of Gargoyles (Rich Olson)

Route 1. I, 3. Leave the Quilcene River trail at Marmot Pass and climb S over heather and scree for about ¾ mile to an upper basin at the base of Boulder Ridge, which runs E from this point. Climb SE to the notch W of the summit. This notch is just W of a large chimney with a huge chockstone in it. Proceed through the notch and then traverse E along the S side to the summit. Time: 2 hours up from Marmot Pass.

Route 2 (Southeast Shoulder). I, 2. First ascent 1968 by R. Etten, K. Heathershaw, and K. Spencer.

For approach, see the Upper Gargoyle route description. From the Upper Gargoyle-Boulder Ridge saddle, climb WNW over scree and broken rock to the easy summit. Time: 7 hours up from Quilcene River road.
Reference: August 1972 *Off Belay.*

RIDGE OF GARGOYLES   ca. 6400 (1951 m)
A string of sharp rock summits lying immediately southeast of Boulder Ridge forming the south wall of the upper Quilcene River. These summits are described in order from west to east.
References: 1969 *Mountaineer,* 1969 *American Alpine Journal.*

Upper Gargoyle   ca. 6400 (1951 m)
First ascent 1968 by R. Etten, K. Heathershaw, and K. Spencer.

Route. II, 3. Leave the Quilcene River trail at Shelter Rock Camp (ca. 2½ miles from the road). Follow the N riverbank for about ⅔ mile and then cross the stream to a rockslide. Traverse the rockslide W for several hundred yards and then contour into timber for a short distance until reaching the creek (S Fork) flowing from between Boulder Ridge and the Ridge of Gargoyles. Late in the year the creek may be dry. Follow the S Fork through timber to just below a small water cascade formed by a side creek (several meager camp-sites can be found in this general area). Continue climbing along the main stream; the going here is steep and brushy. The easiest passage is high, just below the cliffs on the S side of the canyon. Above the cliff band the gradient lessens. Continue along near the creek, generally following the easiest path. Note that this creek flows from the S side of Boulder Ridge; therefore be alert to traverse SW into the scree and snow basin separating Boulder Ridge and the Ridge of Gargoyles. Climb to near the Upper Gargoyle-Boulder Ridge saddle; then climb a prominent snow-and-rock couloir on the NW corner of Upper Gargoyle. About ⅔ of the way up this couloir bear left over broken rock to a gully system. Climb this system and the steep rock pitch immediately above it. Some scrambling and several short rock pitches lead to the summit. Time: 7 hours up from Shelter Rock Camp.

The ridge from Lower Gargoyle to Upper Gargoyle was traversed in 1976 by R. Chelgren and K. Pearce but is not recommended.

Headwaters of Big Quilcene River; Ridge of Gargoyles in the foreground
(courtesy Olympic National Park)

Lower Gargoyle   ca. 6250 (1906 m)
First ascent 1976 by R. Chelgren and K. Pearce.

Route. II, 5.0. The route starts at the chockstone ⅔ of the way up the chute on the E end of Minaret (see Minaret for approach). Climb past the chockstone to a point near the ridge crest. Angle right and climb the steep gully to the notch at its top. Descend about 200 ft. on the S side to get under the upper cliffs of Minaret. Next, traverse W past scree and scrub trees to the first narrow gully (ca. 300 yards). Climb this gully which leads to the notch between Minaret and Lower Gargoyle. There is less rockfall danger by taking the right branch. Upon reaching the notch, climb W directly up the face to the top (one long exposed lead). Time: 6 hours up from Shelter Rock Camp.

A more direct route might be possible by traversing W under the N face of Minaret, and then climbing directly to the notch between Minaret and Lower Gargoyle. The difficulty is unknown.

Minaret   ca. 6200 (1890 m)
First ascent 1973 by H. Dawson, P. Beaumier, T. Whitney, and D. Mittage.

Route 1. II, 5.3. This route starts at the water cascade mentioned in the Upper Gargoyle route description. Climb the right side of the water cascade to avoid brush, and then bear left to miss a lower cliff band. Above the cliffs, climb generally S over brush, boulders, scree, and snow to the base of the broad N face of the Turret. From this point, bear right over a spur ridge and then descend slightly into the basin between Turret and Minaret. Climb S out of this basin toward a prominent scree or snow chute descending from the E end of Minaret. This chute is identified by a large chockstone completely blocking it about ⅔ of the way up. Climb this chute, past the chockstone, to a point near the ridge crest. Next, angle right and climb the steep gully. From the top of the gully, two moderate rock pitches lead to the lower E summit. Follow the ridge W, descending slightly onto the N side when the ridge becomes impassable. Several leads on the N side bring one to an airy promontory overlooking the summit tower. From here, either rappel or climb down steep exposed slab on the N side to the gully separating the promontory from the summit tower. Next, climb the Class 3 gully to the notch. From here, one long Class 5 lead is required to reach the summit. Time: 6 hours up from Shelter Rock Camp.

Route 2. II, 4. First ascent by D. Colwell, K. Horn, J. King, K. Lowry, F. Stinchcliff, J. White, and T. Whitney.

Climb to the Lower Gargoyle-Minaret col (see Lower Gargoyle). Scramble to the W face of the summit ridge and traverse to the summit. Time: 7 hours up from Shelter Rock Camp.

Turret   ca. 6350 (1935 m)
First ascent 1967 by R. Etten, K. Heathershaw, and K. Spencer.

Route. I, 3. The route starts at the water cascade mentioned in the Upper Gargoyle route description. Climb the right side of the water cascade to avoid brush, and then bear left to miss a lower cliff band. Above the cliffs, climb generally S over brush, boulders, scree, and snow to the base of the broad N face of Turret. From this point, bear right over a spur ridge and then descend slightly into the basin between Turret and Minaret. Climb S out of this basin to the low point in the ridge separating Turret and Minaret. Keep left of the several chutes descending from the E flank of Minaret. From the Turret-Minaret col, climb the ridge E. The false summit can be bypassed on the N side via slabs. A short scramble then leads to the summit. Time: 5 hours up from Shelter Rock Camp.

MT. BUCKHORN   6988 (2130 m)

A double-summited peak located approximately 1 mile northeast of Marmot Pass. So named because the twin peaks resemble deer horns. The Southwest Peak is higher, but the Northeast Peak is a more challenging climb. Reference: August 1972 *Off Belay.*

Southwest Peak   6988 (2130 m)

Route. I, 2. From Marmot Pass, climb NE over heather and scree nearly 1 mile to the summit. Time: 2 hours from Marmot Pass.

Northeast Peak   6956 (2120 m)

Route. I, 3. Leave the Quilcene River trail about ½ mile E of Camp Mystery and climb snow or steep talus to the col between Buckhorn's two peaks. From here, climb the steep exposed ridge NE to the summit. This peak can also be reached by descending from the Southwest Peak. Time: 3 hours up from trail.

IRON MOUNTAIN   ca. 6750 (2057 m)

A multi-summit rock peak located ½ mile northeast of the Northeast Peak of Mt. Buckhorn.

Route. I, 3. Leave the Quilcene River trail about 1 mile above Shelter Rock Camp where the trail completely leaves the trees. Climb up scree or snow and then up a major gully system to the notch between and just below the main peaks. The SW summit is the highest. Time: 6 hours up from Quilcene River Road.

MT. WORTHINGTON (COPPER PEAK)   ca. 6900 (2103 m)

Located ¾ mile northeast of Iron Mountain and ¾ mile east of Buckhorn Lake.

Route. I, 3. Leave the Quilcene River trail at Shelter Rock Camp (ca. 2½ miles from road) and climb due N to the 6100-ft. saddle in the E-W ridge connecting Mt. Worthington and Hawk Peak. Climb NW to the summit over steep rotten rock. Time: 5 hours up from road.

HAWK PEAK   ca. 6550 (1996 m)

Located ¾ mile northeast of Mt. Worthington and ½ mile west-southwest of Silver Lake.

Route 1. I, 2. From the Worthington-Hawk Peak saddle (see Mt. Worthington for approach), follow the ridge E to the easy summit. Time: 4 hours up from road.

Route 2. I, 2. Approach from Silver Lake and ascend to the broad saddle E of the peak. This saddle may also be reached from Big Quilcene River trail.

WELCH PEAKS   ca. 6100 (1859 m)

Located 1¼ miles south of Mt. Townsend.

Route 1. I, 2. Approach via the S side Mt. Townsend trail, #839 (see Quilcene River approach). From Camp Windy, follow the new trail to the Welch Peaks-Mt. Townsend saddle. Leave the trail and climb the ridge S ½ mile to the highest summit. Time: 2 hours up from Camp Windy.

Route 2. I, 4. First ascent 1967 by D. Moss and R. Olson, Jr.

From Camp Windy, climb SE to Upper Windy Lake through brush via stream beds. Next, climb the large talus fan at the base of the chute leading from the main Welch Peak. About ⅔ of the way up this chute, a chimney on the right with a tree at its base signals the start of serious climbing. Climb the chimney to a large comfortable ledge. Next, climb up a wide chimney for three rope leads to just N of the summit. The rock is friable and there is danger of rockfall. Time: 3 hours up from Camp Windy.

MT. TOWNSEND   6280 (1914 m)

This northeastern cornerpost of the Olympics is a north-south ridge bordered by Bon Jon Pass on the north, Silver Creek on the west, and Sink Lake on the southeast. It is becoming increasingly popular as a winter and spring climb due to easy access. A trail runs across the summit.

Route 1. I, 1. Early in the season when the Bon Jon Pass road (#2909) is closed by snow, leave the upper Little Quilcene River road (#2812) 2.6 miles above the 2812-2909 junction. Follow service road #030 to its head and then climb through timber northwesterly to the upper road (#2892). Next, climb WSW generally following trail #835 to Little River Summit. Most early spring groups leave the trail at Little River Summit and climb SSW up the ridge to the N summit. The S summit is slightly higher.

Later in the year, continue on road #2909 past its junction with road #2812. Proceed over Bon Jon Pass. Immediately after reaching the pass, turn left on road #2892 for 3.4 miles to the start of the Mt. Townsend trail (#835). Follow the trail about 3 miles to the N summit. Time: 4 hours up from road.

Route 2. I, 1. Leave the Big Quilcene River-Townsend Creek road (#2812) about 15 miles in from U.S. 101 (0.8 mile S of Skaar Pass). Take spur road #2764 0.8 mile to its end. Follow the S side Mt. Townsend trail (#839) approximately 2½ miles to Camp Windy and another 1½ miles to the S summit. Time: 4 hours up from road.

MT. ZION 4273 (1302 m)

Located approximately 1½ miles north-northwest of Bon Jon Pass. While unimportant as a summit climb, the 500-ft. cliffs of the southwest face offer almost unlimited technical rock climbing. *Lichen Spire,* located ½ mile down the trail from the summit, also provides rock climbing on its northeast and west faces.

Route. I, 1. At Bon Jon Pass, leave road #2909 and follow road #2849 2 miles to the start of the Mt. Zion trail (#836). Climb the 2-mile trail to the summit. Time: 1-2 hours up from road.

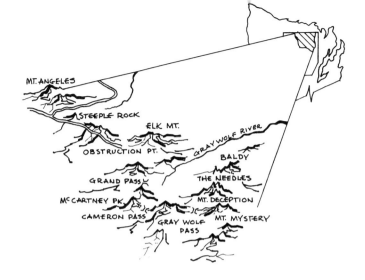

Gray Wolf - Hurricane Ridge Group

The peaks of the Gray Wolf Ridge, extending from Tyler Peak south through Mounts Mystery and Little Mystery, lie between the Dungeness and Gray Wolf rivers. These peaks provide a wide range of climbs on tilted pillow lava.

The rock is generally similar in appearance and quality to that of the Constance-Buckhorn Group to the east. A variety of snow routes exist until mid July in most years. Rock routes are accessible as soon as the Dungeness road is free of snow (early May to early June). The Gray Wolf area enjoys the same northeast corner "rain shadow" weather as does the Constance-Buckhorn area. Hurricane Ridge, Mt. Angeles, and environs on the western edge of the group receive more of the moist Pacific air, and severe storms may occur on these high ridges at any time of year. The most important glaciers are the Cameron Glaciers at the head of Cameron Creek, small glaciers on the north sides of Mt. Deception and Mt. Mystery, and Lillian Glacier (little more than a remnant) on McCartney Peak.

APPROACHES

1. *Dosewallips River.* This approach is used for the S and W side routes of Mt. Deception, Mt. Mystery, and Little Mystery. See Dosewallips Group, page 83 for details.

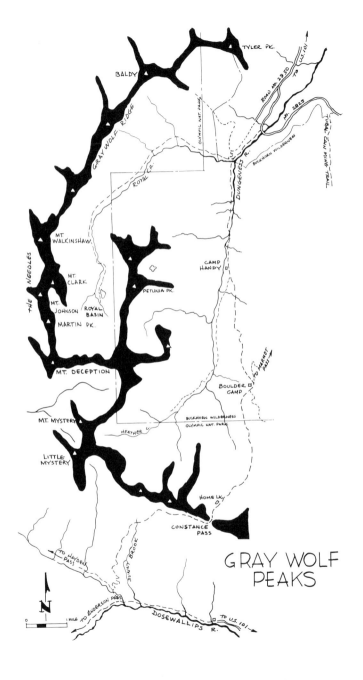

TYLER PK.

BALDY

GRAY WOLF RIDGE

ROAD NO. 2950

NO. 2825

TO U.S. 101

OLYMPIC NAT. PARK

DUNGENESS R.

BUCKHORN WILDERNESS

TUBAL CAIN MINE TRAIL

ROYAL CR.

THE NEEDLES

MT. WALKINSHAW

MT. CLARK

MT. JOHNSON

ROYAL BASIN

MARTIN PK.

PETUNIA PK.

CAMP HANDY

MT. DECEPTION

TO MARMOT PASS

BOULDER CAMP

MT. MYSTERY

BUCKHORN WILDERNESS

OLYMPIC NAT. PARK

HEATHER CR.

LITTLE MYSTERY

HOME LK.

CONSTANCE PASS

TO HAYDEN PASS

SILVUY BROOK

GRAY WOLF PEAKS

N

0   1 MILE   TO ANDERSON PASS

DOSEWALLIPS R.

TO U.S. 101

2. *Dungeness River.* This approach serves for the entire Gray Wolf Group. Leave U.S. 101, turning left at Sequim Bay State Park. In about 1 mile the road ends at a T intersection with the paved county road. Turn left up the county road, which becomes Forest Service Road #2909 at the Olympic National Forest boundary. At 7.5 miles from U.S. 101, road #2950 (Dungeness River road) branches right and descends to the Dungeness River. After crossing the lower Dungeness River bridge, road #2950 climbs 7 miles past several numbered spur roads to a junction with road #2825 which branches left, descends 1.6 miles to the upper Dungeness River bridge and the start of the Dungeness River trail. This road continues into the upper Silver Creek drainage, providing another approach to the Tubal Cain Mine-Dirty Face Ridge area (see Constance-Buckhorn Group, page 97).

The Dungeness River trail follows the river to Royal Creek (1 mile) and a junction with the Royal Basin trail (6 miles to Royal Lake). The Dungeness trail follows the river 2.3 miles to Camp Handy and then climbs 2.8 miles to Boulder Shelter Camp and a junction with the Marmot Pass trail (see Constance-Buckhorn Group). From Boulder Shelter Camp the upper Dungeness River trail continues 3.8 miles past Home Lake to Constance Pass (5800 ft.) and then descends to the Dosewallips River.

The main road (#2950) climbs 1.7 miles past its junction with road #2825. From the end of the road, a trail continues 3.4 miles to the Gray Wolf Ridge. The Royal Basin trail can be reached by a way trail which branches left 1 mile past the end of road #2950.

3. *Gray Wolf River.* While not widely used, this approach is an alternate to the Deer Park trail for reaching the W side of The Needles and the N and W sides of Mt. Deception.

The Gray Wolf River road (#2958) leaves the lower Dungeness River road about 7 miles in from U.S. 101. It descends 0.9 mile to Dungeness Forks campground and then continues another 0.8 mile to a junction with road #2927. Take the right fork (#2927) for nearly 2 miles, then turn left on #050 0.7 mile to the start of the Gray Wolf River trail (#834).

After following the N side of the river about 2 miles, the trail crosses to the S side and eventually climbs to Gray Wolf Camp and a junction with the Deer Park trail (8 miles). The river trail then climbs through the upper Gray Wolf drainage another 9.5 miles to 6150-ft. Gray Wolf Pass. Campsites include Gray Wolf (8 miles, 2000 ft.) and the Falls (13.5 miles, 3900 ft.).

4. *Northern High Approaches.* The Deer Park road leaves U.S. 101 5 miles E of Port Angeles and climbs to the summit of 6007-ft. Blue Mountain. From Deer Park (18.1 miles) the Three Forks trail connects with the Gray Wolf Pass trail, reaching the 6150-ft. pass in 14.5 miles. Campsites are located at Deer Park, Three Forks (4.5 miles, 2100 ft.), Gray Wolf (5 miles, 2000 ft.) and the Falls (10.4 miles, 3900 ft.).

The Hurricane Ridge road leaves U.S. 101 in eastern Port Angeles and climbs 17.8 miles to 5225-ft. Big Meadow. A restaurant, visitor center, and ski facilities are located here. A spur continues 7.8 miles SE to Obstruction Point (6150 ft.). From this point, a trail climbs, then drops to Grand Lake (3.5 miles, 4750 ft.), and continues on to Moose Lake (4.1 miles, 5200 ft.). The trail then climbs to Grand Pass (6.0 miles, 6450 ft.) and descends 1.9 miles to the Cameron Creek-Cameron Pass trail to the Dosewallips River.

RANGER STATIONS

None. Check with Forest Service district ranger station at Quilcene or National Park Service headquarters at Port Angeles regarding limits on size of party and the use of campfires.

CAMPGROUNDS

Dungeness River road: Dungeness Forks, el. 1000 ft. (located on road # 2958 1 mile off road # 2909 ca. 6½ miles in on road # 2909 from U.S. 101); East Crossing, el. 1050 ft. (on road # 2950, ca. 10 miles from U.S. 101).

Deer Park road: Deer Park, el. 5400 ft. (18 miles from U.S. 101).

Hurricane Ridge road: Heart O' the Hills, el. 2000 ft. (5 miles from Port Angeles).

VANTAGE POINTS

Deer Park, Hurricane Ridge, and Obstruction Point can be reached by road. Mt. Townsend, Klahhane Saddle, and Hurricane Hill can be reached by trails (no water).

MAPS

Olympic National Forest/Olympic National Park; USGS 30-minute Olympic National Park and Vicinity; the following 15-minute USGS and Green Trail quadrangles: Tyler Peak and Mt. Angeles; the following Custom Correct Maps: Buckhorn Wilderness and Hurricane Ridge.

MT. MYSTERY   7631 (2326 m)

A bulky peak located between Deception Creek and the head of Heather Creek, a tributary of the Dungeness River.

Route 1A. I, 3. From 1 mile beyond Dose Forks on the Dosewallips River trail, take the Constance Pass trail to a shallow pond about 5500 ft. (good campsites). From the pond traverse benches, then open woods westerly to a basin at the head of upper Twin Creek (2-3 hours).

Climb about 45 minutes to Gunsight Pass between Mystery and Little Mystery. Turn right and climb steep shale 450 ft. to Del Monte Ridge at the base of Mt. Mystery. Climb the ridge, then shale slopes on the W face. Contour N approximately ¼ mile at the top of the shale to the summit block. Next, cross the ridge to the E side (right) and climb back on snow slopes and good rock to the summit. Time: 3 hours up from Gunsight Pass.

Mt. Mystery and Mystery Glacier from the northeast (courtesy Olympic National Park)

Route 1B. From the pond in Sunnybrook Meadows, traverse the meadows westerly and climb the spur ridge NW to the low point of Del Monte Ridge (W of Point 6666). Traverse the ridge about 1½ miles to the intersection with Route 1A 450 ft. above and to the right of Gunsight Pass (6350 ft.).

Route 2. I, 3. Leave the Dosewallips River trail 50 yards above Deception Creek (ca. 8 miles from road) and climb E paralleling the creek following a faint way trail. Climb to just below the confluence of the two branches of Deception Creek where camp can be made. From camp, climb SE about 1½ miles to reach Gunsight Pass and a junction with Route 1A.

Route 3. II, 3. From the Deception Creek camp of Route 2, ascend the left fork into lower Deception Basin (beautiful camp spot). Climb right (SSE) up the stagnant glacier to its head. Turn right (W) and ascend a rock ridge to the summit block. Time: 5 hours up from Deception Creek camp.

North Peak   ca. 7600 (2137 m)
First ascent 1974 by J. Braden, J. Gray, D. Maranville, L. Maranville, and T. Sloan.

Route. I, 4. From Mt. Mystery summit, traverse NW generally following the ridge crest. Climb the short lead on the S corner of the summit block.

LITTLE MYSTERY   6941 (2116 m)
Located immediately south of Mt. Mystery.

North Peak   6941 (2116 m)

Route. I, 3. Ascend benches on the Deception Creek side of Gunsight Pass traversing upward to the gully leading to the plateau N of the tower complex directly above Gunsight Pass. Traverse left (S) behind these towers, continue to a gully in the next tower group. Ascend this gully and climb left to the summit. Seen from Gunsight Pass, the summit is the highest point in the towers just left (S) of the pass. An ascent has been made directly from Gunsight Pass. Time: 2 hours up from pass.

South Peak   6900 (2102 m)

Route. I, 3. Ascend the snow or scree basin facing the upper Twin Creek drainage to a gully leading to a notch about 100 ft. left (S) of the South Peak. Cross the notch and traverse to the peak. Time: 2 hours up from Upper Twin Creek Basin.

MT. FRICABA   7134 (2174 m)
An elongated double-summited peak located northeast of Mt. Mystery at the head of Deception Basin. First recorded ascent 1957 by D. Bechlem (northeast summit) and J. Newman (southwest summit).

(1B)

Mt Mystery

Little Mystery

(2)

(3)

Mt Deception

(5)

(4)

Gilhooley Tower

(3)

(3V)

(6)

Deception

Glacier

(3)

Martin
Peak

Ial
Basin

Surprise
Basin

DM

Mts Deception and Mystery
from north

Route. I, 2. Climb E from upper Deception Basin. The peak can also be approached from either Royal Basin (see Needles for approach) or Del Monte Ridge. Time: 3 hours up from upper Deception Basin.

HAL FOSS PEAK   7100 (2164 m)

Located between Mt. Mystery and Mt. Fricaba. Named after Hal Foss, the first Washington State Search and Rescue co-ordinator.

Route. I, 2. Descend SW from the summit of Mt. Fricaba to the base of Hal Foss Peak. Then climb the NW side of the peak to the summit. Time: 1-2 hours up from Mt. Fricaba.

MT. DECEPTION   7788 (2374 m)

The highest peak in the eastern Olympics even though it cannot be seen from Seattle. It is located 1½ miles northwest of Mt. Mystery between Deception Creek and Royal Creek.

Route 1. I, 2. Leave the Dosewallips River trail about 8 miles from the road (ca. ½ mile below Camp Marion). Ascend the ridge separating Cub Creek and Deception Creek to alpine meadows. At about 5500 ft. bear diagonally right (NE) off the ridge; a long but easy talus and broken rock slope leads to the summit. Time: 6 hours up from trail.

Route 2. I, 2. From a camp just below the confluence of the two branches of Deception Creek (see Mt. Mystery, Route 2), climb N first through meadows, then up wooded hillside and finally over talus slopes to an eventual intersection with Route 1 at about 6000 ft. Time: 4 hours up from camp, 6 hours up from trail.

Route 3. I, 2. From Shelter Rock (see Needles for approach) climb S then SW to the small tarn in upper Royal Basin (camp could be placed here). Make an ascending traverse westerly over talus and easy rock to the low point in the Deception-Martin Peak ridge. Cross to the W side of the ridge and descend S to the glacier. Continue S climbing past a bergschrund and up a steep (40°) but short snow slope to the summit ridge. From here, bear left (E) and climb the easy ridge to the summit. Time: 6 hours up from Shelter Rock.

Route 4 (Honeymoon Route). I, 3. First ascent 1965 by A. Bloomer and D. Bloomer.

The route starts at the low point in the Mt. Deception-Martin Peak ridge (see Route 3). Bear left (E) of the severe ridge crest into a steep (45°) snow gully which climbs S toward the summit. Climb this gully to its exit on the ridge just below the summit. Time: 5 hours up from Shelter Rock.

Route 5 (Northeast Face). I, 3. First ascent 1962 by K. Hilton, J. Merkel, J. Munson, and J. Parolini.

From Shelter Rock (see Needles for approach), climb S then SW to the small tarn in upper Royal Basin (camp could be placed here). Climb SW over glacial moraine for nearly 1 mile to the base of a large snow (or mud) slope on the W edge of the NE face. Climb the steep slope to its head, then directly up to the summit. Rockfall is a problem. Time: 5 hours up from Shelter Rock.

Route 6. I, 2. Climb 3½ miles from the Dosewallips River trail to Gray Wolf Pass (6150 ft.). Traverse E from the pass in alpine meadows on the S side of the ridge for about 3 miles to where Route 1 is joined in alpine meadows. Time: 4 hours up from Gray Wolf Pass.

Route 7 (Southeast Gully). I, 3. First ascent by K. Leibert.
From the flat in Deception Basin, ascend scree and talus NW and then ascend the left (W) of two gullies just right of a large rock buttress. Follow the gully system to the E ridge 150 yards SE of the summit and follow the ridge to the top. Time: 3 hours up from Deception Basin.

Gilhooley Tower   ca. 7400 (2256 m)

A prominent tower located ¼ mile northwest of Mt. Deception. First ascent 1963 by D. N. Anderson, H. Pinsch, and J. Pinsch.

Route 1. I, 4. Climb from the SW corner. The first lead is the most difficult. Time: 1 hour up from the base.

Route 2. I, 4. First ascent 1972 by V. Johnson and G. Lockwood.
Climb the N side via a 2-ft. wide chimney with chockstones on N side.

Snifter Spire   ca. 7000 (2134 m)

This blocklike rotten spire is located on the E flank of Mt. Deception just above the Deception Basin-Royal Basin divide. See Needles for approach. First ascent 1962 via Route 1A by K. Hilton, J. Merkel, J. Munson, and J. Parolini.

Route 1A. I, 5.3, A2. From Shelter Rock climb to the small tarn in upper Royal Basin. Proceed S over glacial moraine nearly 1 mile to the pass just E of Mt. Deception (Royal Basin-Deception Basin divide). From the pass, climb W to the base of Snifter Spire and then traverse the N side via Class 4 slabs to the W side of the Spire. Climb 40 ft. up the W corner of the block (5.3) and then traverse steep slab right to the overhang which requires aid. Above the overhang, 50 ft. of 5.2 climbing leads to the top. Time: 5 hours up from Shelter Rock.

Route 1B. I, 5.3. First ascent by M. Clarke and P. Lathrop.
After climbing 40 ft. up the W corner, continue upward to where the ridge meets the summit block. Step out left onto the N face and ascend 20 ft. to the summit slab (rotten rock will not readily accept pitons or nuts).

THE NEEDLES   ca. 7650 (2332 m)

An extensive north-south ridge of rock peaks and pinnacles located between
Mt. Deception on the south, the Gray Wolf Ridge on the north, and Royal
Basin on the east. This ridge contains the highest collective group of peaks
and spires in the Olympic Range and offers some of the most interesting rock
climbing in the range. The major peaks and many spires are covered in this
description, but innumerable short rock climbs of varying difficulty are
available throughout the area.

Leave the Dungeness River road #2825 or road #2950 and follow the
Dungeness River trail to the Royal Creek trail (see Dungeness River approach). Follow the 6-mile Royal Creek trail to the main meadow in the basin.
A large overhanging boulder called Shelter Rock lies in Royal Basin near the
lake. This boulder is used as a reference point for distances to the surrounding
peaks. A summer ranger station is established in the basin. Royal Basin is
seeing heavy use and one must procure a back-country permit from a
self-service box on the Royal Creek trail (2.3 miles from the Dungeness River
trail).

A climber's way trail crosses the creek just SW of Shelter Rock, climbs to a
swampy meadow which it follows S and beyond up the stream bed and then
right to a tarn in the upper basin close under Mt. Deception and Martin Peak
(ca. 1 mile from Shelter Rock). From camp at the upper tarn, follow the bench
NW (toward the Johnson-Clark gap) to the moraine of Surprise Basin. Times

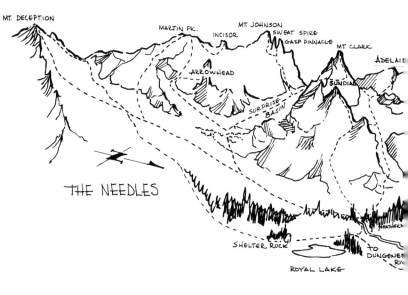

The Needles from Mt. Deception; from left: Mt. Johnson, Sweat Spire, The Incisor, and Martin Peak (Keith Spencer)

to Mt. Deception and Martin Peak will be about 1 hour less than times listed from Shelter Rock (Royal Basin).

Petunia Peak on the east side of Royal Basin offers an excellent vantage point for surveying the entire massif.

Following are route descriptions for the major climbs in the area. These are covered from south to north.

Martin Peak   ca. 7550 (2300 m)

The southernmost peak in The Needles, located 1 mile north of Mt. Deception. First ascent 1940 via Route 3 by E. Johnson and G. Martin.

Route 1. I, 3. From Shelter Rock, cross the meadow W to the waterfall. Climb the left side of the waterfall following a climber's way trail past a boulder fan and left (S) about 20 minutes into a narrow valley. Proceed up the valley to the terminal moraine of Surprise Basin. Continue past the terminal moraine, climbing toward the ridge separating Martin Peak and Mt. Deception. Several hundred yards past the S edge of the moraine turn right and climb directly toward the ridge crest. Several rocky gullies offer relatively easy passage to the upper shoulder of Martin Peak. From the shoulder scramble NW to the summit. Time: 4 hours up from Shelter Rock.

Route 2. I, 3. First ascent 1961 by J. Munson and J. Parolini.
Climb to the top of the terminal moraine of Surprise Basin after an

approach via Route 1. Proceed to the SW boundary of the moraine and ascend a chute to just below The Arrowhead, a prominent 120-ft. spire. Ascend chimneys to the left (S) of The Arrowhead. Above The Arrowhead it is a scramble to the summit. Time: 4 hours up from Shelter Rock.

Route 3. I, 3. Follow the ridge N from the low point in the Mt. Deception-Martin Peak ridge (see Mt. Deception Route 3 for approach). The ascent follows mostly along ledges below the ridge crest. It appears more difficult than it is. Time: 3 hours up from saddle. Descent via Route 1 is recommended.

The Arrowhead   ca. 7000 (2134 m)
A 120-ft. rock spire located on the east flank of Martin Peak. First ascent 1962 by K. Hilton, J. Merkel, J. Munson, and J. Parolini.

Route 1. II, 5.3. Approach via Route 2, Martin Peak. From the notch between Martin Peak and The Arrowhead, a small ledge leads right (S) to the W edge of the vertical S face. Traverse E (across the face) 30 ft. on small holds, then climb to the summit. Time: 4 hours up from Shelter Rock.

Route 2. II, 5.5. From the Martin-Arrowhead notch, ascend an obvious crack and chimney system directly to the summit.

The Incisor   ca. 7350 (2240 m)
A prominent rock tooth located 300 yards north of Martin Peak. First ascent 1958 by K. Heathershaw and R. McKee.

Route. I, 5.4. From the summit of Martin Peak, descend 50 ft. on the E side and then traverse N over snow, ledges, and broken rock below the ridge crest. A short rock climb leads to the SE corner of The Incisor block. From here, make an exposed traverse N, angling up along a slight depression to the low N end of the summit ridge. Straddle the knife ridge to the summit. The E face has been climbed from halfway across the traverse. The N corner has also been climbed. (Variations by M. Clarke and P. Lathrop, 1974.) Descend by rappelling from N end of the ridge. Time: 2 hours up from Martin Peak.

Mt. Johnson   ca. 7650 (2332 m)
The highest peak in The Needles. First ascent 1940 by E. Johnson and G. Martin via Route 2.

Route 1A. II, 4. From Shelter Rock, cross the meadow W to the waterfall. Climb the left side of the waterfall on a climber's way trail past a boulder fan and left (S) about 20 minutes to a narrow valley. Proceed up the valley to the terminal moraine of Surprise Basin. Ascend the moraine and proceed to within 100 yards of the pass at the head of the basin (2½ hours from Royal Basin). Climb W (left) up scree and snow to a sloping ledge that leads S. Follow this ledge to the easy talus gully leading to the snowfields in line with the summit as seen from Surprise Basin moraine. Ascend these, bypassing Sweat Spire on the S. Continue up gullies to the eastern base of the summit block where a 50-ft. chimney leads to the summit (variations have been done on the summit block). Time: 5 hours up from Shelter Rock.

Route 1B. II, 5.1. First ascent 1958 by K. Heathershaw, R. McKee, F. Spencer, and K. Spencer.

This route is recommended if ascent of either Gasp Pinnacle or Sweat Spire is also planned. From the entrance of the snowfield of Route 1A, climb scree and easy rock on the right side of the snowfield toward the notch between Gasp Pinnacle and Sweat Spire. Two Class 5 rock pitches lead to the platform between Mt. Johnson and the spires. From the platform, climb W for 200 ft. to the summit block of Mt. Johnson and the chimney of Route 1A. Time: 6 hours up from Shelter Rock.

Route 2. II, 4. Climb from the S via a traverse of the 1-mile jagged ridge from Martin Peak. Time: 3 hours up from Martin Peak.

Route 3. II, 4. First ascent 1946 by J. Vance and party.

Climb through the gap at the head of Surprise Basin (see Route 1A) and make a descending traverse to the SW. Climb the gully system directly below the summit to just below the top. Time: 7 hours up from Shelter Rock.

Sweat Spire   ca. 7580 (2310 m)

A 200-ft. rock needle located just east of Mt. Johnson. First ascent 1962 by K. Hilton, J. Merkel, J. Munson, and J. Parolini.

Route. II, 5.2. From the platform (see Route 1B, Mt. Johnson) traverse S between the Spire and a large rock flake. Climb to the top on the rib just left of the gully on the SW side. Time: 6 hours up from Shelter Rock.

Gasp Pinnacle   ca. 7540 (2295 m)

Located just north of Sweat Spire. First ascent 1958 by K. Heathershaw, R. McKee, F. Spencer, and K. Spencer.

Route. II, 4. From the platform (see Route 1B, Mt. Johnson) cross boulders to the W side of the pinnacle. Here, a 40-ft. climb leads to a narrow ledge which can be traversed N behind a flake to the summit ridge. Climb the exposed ridge to the summit. Time: 6 hours up from Shelter Rock.

Devil's Fang   ca. 7600 (2315 m)

The prominent pinnacle approximately 100 ft. west of Gasp Pinnacle. First ascent 1972 by B. Caprez, P. Lathrop, and party.

Route. I, 5.2. Approach as for Mt. Johnson Route 1A. Traverse right from near the base of the final chimney to the SE side of the Fang and ascend a 100-ft. lead to the top.

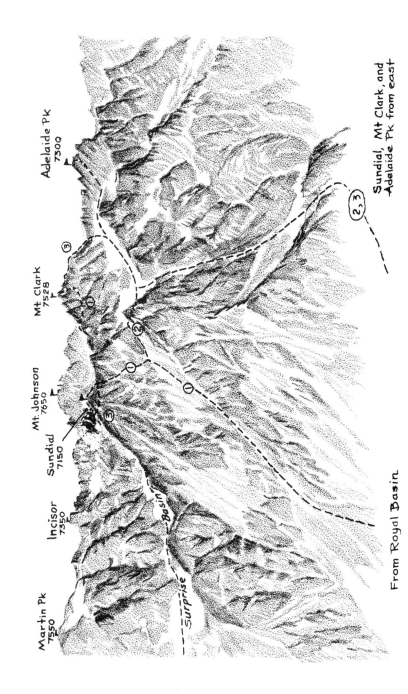

Martin Pk
7550

Incisor
7350

Sundial
7150

Mt Johnson
7650

Mt Clark
7528

Adelaide Pk
7300

Surprise Basin

From Royal Basin.

Sundial, Mt Clark, and
Adelaide Pk from east

Sundial   ca. 7150 (2180 m)

Located at the end of the east-southeast ridge of Mt. Clark directly above and west of the meadow by Shelter Rock. Sundial was named because from Royal Basin the approximate time of morning can be told by watching the sunlight progress down the east face. First ascent 1944 by A. Degenhardt and W. Degenhardt.

Route 1. I, 3. Leave Shelter Rock and cross the meadow W picking up a climber's way trail which ascends the left side of the waterfall to a boulder fan. Climb slightly left (W) through a series of minor cliffs to a buttress forming the right shoulder of a major scree gully. Contour left around the buttress into the gully and climb to the notch at its head. From the notch, traverse S gradually, climbing across the E face over moderately difficult rock to the final short ascent of the two summit blocks. Time: 3 hours up from Shelter Rock.

Route 2. I, 3. From the boulder fan of Route 1, bear right on a broad grassy ledge traversing just below the cliff band for about 20 minutes. Ascend a short gully to a slight notch in a minor E-W ridge. Continue to contour around the cliff band descending slightly into an open meadow. Bear hard left, dropping a short distance into a small snow basin. Ascend the snow finger at its head to the large basin between Mt. Clark and Adelaide (Belvedere Basin). From this basin, traverse SE over permanent snowfields to the N side of Sundial. Climb a chimney-gully system about 300 ft. to the notch mentioned in Route 1. Follow Route 1 to the summit. Time: 4 hours up from Shelter Rock.

Route 3. I, 5.0. First ascent 1975 by J. Gray, T. Sloan, and J. Wilson.

From the base of the summit block on Route 1, contour on the E to the S side and ascend the face.

Route 4. I, 3. From the upper tarn or from Shelter Rock, proceed to Surprise Basin and ascend the basin toward Mt. Clark until approximately under the summit of Sundial. Ascend the SW face. Ascend the summit block by the N (left) or center (Class 3) or S (right) face (Class 5). Time: 4 hours up from Shelter Rock, 2½ hours up from upper tarn.

Mt. Clark (Belvedere)   7528 (2295 m)

This jagged peak, perhaps the best climb in The Needles, is located directly across Surprise Basin from Mt. Johnson. Originally named Belvedere, the peak was officially renamed Mt. Clark in honor of Irving M. Clark, prominent conservationist. First ascent 1940 by E. Johnson and G. Martin via Route 2.

Route 1. II, 3. First ascent 1958 by C. Broberg, K. Heathershaw, R. McKee, and K. Spencer.

From the pass at the head of Surprise Basin (see Route 1, Mt. Johnson) follow a sloping ledge which climbs back SE for 100 yards. At this point, climb a broken rock gully past a large boulder. Above this boulder, climb the right-hand branch gully to a notch in the SE ridge. Cross the ridge and descend to a ledge on the E face. Traverse the E face northerly 200 yards to the NE corner of the peak. Climb a chute of moderately difficult rock and then slab to the summit. Time: 6 hours up from Shelter Rock.

Route 2. II, 4. Follow Route 1 until reaching the S side of the peak. From here, climb steep chimneys in the S face. Time: 6 hours up from Shelter Rock.

Route 3. II, 5.0. First ascent 1961 by J. Munson and J. Parolini.

The route starts in Belvedere Basin immediately E of Mt. Clark (see Sundial, Route 2, for approach to the basin). Ascend the basin to the lowest notch in the Clark-Adelaide ridge. Bear left and climb exposed slab for 300 ft., keeping to the N edge until the ridge is regained. Ascend SE to the summit. Time: 6 hours up from Shelter Rock.

Route 4. II, 5.5. First ascent 1975 by M. Clarke and B. Homes.

Start in Surprise Basin just left (W) of the central S face. Stem the chimney two leads to its conclusion. Climb the broken rock gully of Route 1 for 150 ft. to just past the start of the right-hand branch gully. Ascend the upper S face by what appears to be a slanting crack system to the notch at the top of the crack (two leads). Traverse the sharp ridge left to the base of the summit block. A wide crack on the S side leads to the summit. Time: 5 hours up from upper tarn.

Adelaide Peak   ca. 7300 (2225 m)

Located ⅓ mile north of Mt. Clark at the head of Belvedere Basin. First ascent 1944 by A. Degenhardt and W. Degenhardt.

Route. I, 3. From the S end of Belvedere Basin (see Sundial, Route 2, for approach), proceed to the N end of the basin and Adelaide Peak. Ascent is via the S side of the E ridge over slab and easy rock. Time: 4 hours up from Shelter Rock.

Mt. Walkinshaw (The Citadel)   7378 (2249 m)

The northernmost summit in The Needles, this peak was renamed in honor of Robert B. Walkinshaw, prominent conservationist. First ascent 1961 by J. Munson and J. Parolini.

Route 1. II, 3. Leave the Royal Basin trail 4 miles from the Dungeness River trail at about 4500 ft. Climb W ½ mile through small timber and brush. Continue climbing on easy scree slopes to the saddle between Walkinshaw and the Gray Wolf Ridge. Follow the ridge S and then ascend chimneys and slabs on the N side to the summit. Time: 4 hours up from trail.

Route 2. II, 3. First ascent 1976 by K. Heathershaw and R. Yekel.

Leave the Royal Basin trail 4.5 miles from the Dungeness River trail (1.5

Mt. Walkinshaw (Citadel) from the south (Rich Olson)

miles N from Shelter Rock) at about the 4600-ft. level. Follow a feeder creek W staying 200 ft. left (S) of the creek. Traverse NW into the creek basin and climb a rock slide to open snowfields. Approach the SE base of Mt. Walkinshaw (the small peak to the S can be traversed en route but requires a 100-ft. descent to gain the sharp notch between it and the main peak). Gain the notch and drop 150 ft. on the W side of the main ridge, traverse N and climb a rock gully just S of the summit. Bypass a huge chockstone chute and climb to the ridge until blocked, then traverse left on a tiny ledge that leads around the corner to an easy hidden chute. The top of this chute joins Route 1 about 20 ft. below the summit. Time: 5 hours up from trail.

PETUNIA PEAK   ca. 6900 (2103 m)
Located approximately ½ mile east of Royal Lake. This peak and its slopes are fine vantage points for The Needles.

   Route. I, 2. Climb E from Royal Lake (the lake is ca. 100 yards E and 50 ft. above the meadow by Shelter Rock) over talus and easy rock. Bear slightly N as elevation is gained to avoid rock outcroppings. The final few feet involve rock scrambling. Time: 3 hours up from Royal Lake.

The Royal Shaft   ca. 6000 (1829 m)
A prominent spire located about ½ mile southeast of Royal Lake on the shoulder of Petunia Peak. First ascent 1962 by K. Hilton, J. Merkel, J. Munson, and J. Parolini.

Route. I, 5.3, A1. Ascend SE directly from the lake to a platform on the E side of the spire. The 120-ft. climb to the top includes one aid pitch. Time: 3 hours up from Royal Lake.

GRAY WOLF RIDGE   7218 (2200 m)

A high barren ridge located between the Gray Wolf River and Royal Creek.

Route. I, 2. The highest point is reached by climbing the SE slope after leaving the Royal Basin trail at the 3500-ft. level (ca. 2 miles up trail from Dungeness River). The Gray Wolf Ridge can also be reached by traversing S from Baldy.

BALDY   6797 (2072 m)

Located between the Gray Wolf Ridge and Tyler Peak.

Route. I, 1. Leave Forest Service road # 2950 from its end. Follow the trail 3.4 miles to meadows below the summit. Time: 3 hours up from road.

TYLER PEAK   6364 (1939 m)

Located on the Dungeness-Gray Wolf River divide 3 miles northeast of Gray Wolf Ridge. First ascent by topographical survey party.

Route 1. I, 1. Follow the trail to Baldy and traverse E along ridge between Baldy and Tyler Peak to the summit.

Route 2. I, 2. Leave the Dungeness River road (# 2950) at about 2950 ft. where it crosses Tyler Creek (6.7 miles above the first Dungeness River crossing). Climb W keeping to the N and above the creek bed to avoid heavy undergrowth. At about 3400 ft. contour into and across the creek. Ascend the left bank a short distance until a minor watercourse is reached. Angle left up this watercourse, which drains the E side of the ridge running SE from the summit. Climb to the obvious notch in this SE ridge. Cross through the notch and ascend NW over scree and heather to the easy summit. Time: 5 hours up from road.

McCARTNEY PEAK   6728 (2050 m)

Located at the head of the Lillian River.

Route 1. I, 2. Leave the Moose Lake-Grand Pass trail about 1 mile SW of Moose Lake (5 miles from Obstruction Point) and climb WSW to the 6000-ft. pass immediately S of Point 6753. An alternate approach to this pass is to leave the trail at Moosehead Point (6536, 1½ miles from Obstruction Point) and follow the open ridge S. Cross the pass into the Lillian River drainage and contour southwesterly about 2 miles on the W slope to the Lillian Glacier. Ascend the glacier to its head, then climb easy rock on the S side of the peak to the top. Time: 6 hours up from Moose Lake.

Route 2. I, 2. From Dose Meadows (12.8 miles up the Dosewallips River trail) follow the Lost Pass-Cameron Pass trail to a point 200 yards S of Cameron Pass (2.8 miles from Dose Meadows). Leave the trail and follow the remains of an old trail NW along the ridge for about 2½ miles to a small basin on the S side of McCartney Peak. From here, climb to the ridge and follow it NW to the easy summit. Time: 3 hours up from Cameron Pass.

HURRICANE RIDGE PEAKS   6454 (1968 m)

Lying within 12 miles of tidal saltwater, the peaks and ridges around Hurricane Ridge have long been popular with hikers, climbers, and skiers. The area can be reached on the all-weather Hurricane Ridge road, which is usually plowed on winter weekends so drivers can reach a downhill ski area, day lodge, and cross-country ski trails. The area is aptly named; sudden storms with strong winds can spring up at any time of year.

The peaks around Hurricane Ridge are geologically diverse. Exposed, often eroded outcroppings of volcanic breccia and pillow lava are interspersed with weathered sandstone or other sedimentary formations, offering a variety of challenges to climbers. The rock is often friable, but on several spires and faces difficult technical routes are available for experienced parties.

The area is attracting an increasing number of winter climbers and ski mountaineers. Note that the easy summer scrambles become difficult ice and snow or mixed climbs in winter.

The peaks are described roughly in order, starting with the Mt. Angeles area, then moving east to west.

Mt. Angeles   6454 (1968 m)

The highest peak of this group, Mt. Angeles anchors the west end of Klahhane Ridge and is located 2½ miles northeast of the Hurricane Ridge lodge. It has several summits; the westernmost is the highest. Mt. Angeles is a popular climb in all seasons because it offers routes of varying difficulty and is easy to reach.

Route 1. I, 2. Leave the Hurricane Ridge road 10.1 miles above the National Park boundary (2.9 miles below the visitor center) where the road crosses a major couloir descending from the S side of the peak. Follow the switchback trail up the right side of the creek to its junction with the 3-mile Mt. Angeles-Hurricane Ridge trail. Turn left, following the trail to the Mt. Angeles saddle (¼ mile) and then ascend northerly, keeping on the W side of the peak until just below the summit. Climb gully systems and rock to the top. Time: 3 hours up from road.

Route 2. I, 3. The route starts at the junction of the switchback trail (see Route 1) with the Mt. Angeles-Hurricane Ridge trail. Turn left, following the Mt. Angeles-Hurricane Ridge trail a short distance W until it crosses the main couloir. Climb the couloir until it branches. Proceed up the right

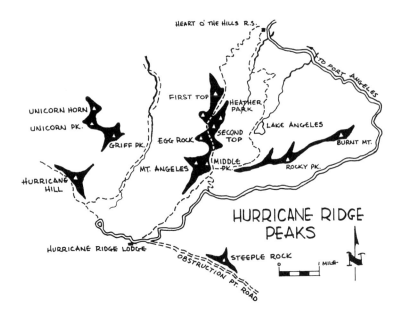

HURRICANE RIDGE
PEAKS

branch, which leads to the E side of the summit block. Time: 3 hours up from road. In winter, under stable snow conditions, the couloir may be climbed in its entirety from the Hurricane Ridge road.

Route 3. I, 2. From the junction of the couloir trail with the Mt. Angeles-Hurricane Ridge trail, turn right and follow the trail eastward and upward to the saddle immediately E of Mt. Angeles (Klahhane Saddle). From this saddle, climb NW, keeping to the S side of the ridge crest, to a point near the summit of the middle peak. From the middle peak, follow the ridge crest W to the main summit. Time: 3 hours up from road.

The E face of the Middle Peak of Mt. Angeles is a ½-mile long N-S face composed of chimneys and gullies of sedimentary rock alternating with tilted ribs of volcanic breccia. These chimneys, gullies, and the adjacent ribs can be ascended to provide routes of varying length and difficulty. From Klahhane Saddle (see Route 3), make a slightly descending traverse N (trail in summer) for about 20 minutes to reach the face. Any of the gullies or the thin adjacent ribs can be ascended. The hardest routes are generally to the N end of ridge. Climbers should expect difficulties ranging from Class 3 through Class 5, depending on the route chosen. From the ridge at the top of the face, follow the crest SW to the summit of Middle Peak.

Mt. Angeles in winter (Frank Chapin)

Rocky Peak   6218 (1895 m)

An elongated massif 4 miles northeast of Hurricane Ridge at the east end of Klahhane Ridge.

Route. II, 3. From Klahhane Saddle (see Mt. Angeles Route 3) follow the Lake Angeles trail uphill, E, for 1 mile to where the trail turns N and begins descending toward Lake Angeles. Continue E along Klahhane Ridge, keeping to the S side to avoid difficulties. At the first of two prominent notches W of Rocky Peak, contour E to avoid the rugged ridge crest and cliff bands. Regain the ridge crest uphill of the second notch using gully and ledge systems. Follow the ridge over easy rock to the summit. Time: 4½ hours up from road.

Numerous minor summits and spires on the summit ridge of Rocky Peak offer short technical climbs. A traverse of the entire Klahhane-Rocky Peak ridge has been done; the route is long and route-finding difficult.

Peak 5550 (Burnt Mountain)   ca. 5550 (1692 m)

A flat-topped peak east of Lake Angeles with an old burn on the east face; prominently visible from U.S. 101 east of Port Angeles. The open eastern slopes contrast with the steep cliffs of the west face. Note that USGS topographic maps identify Burnt Mountain as a minor 4910-ft. peak 1 mile east of Peak 5550, but this is contrary to local usage.

Route. II, 3. From Rocky Peak, descend the steep N face via chimney and ledge systems. The crux is gaining the notch by Point 5310. Careful route finding is necessary to avoid cliffs S of the notch. From Point 5310 climb along the E side of the ridge N to the broad, plateaulike summit ridge. Time: 3 hours from Rocky Peak.

Winter ascents of Burnt Mountain have been made from Lake Angeles. From the lake, cross the logjam at the outlet stream and contour E at about the 4200-ft. level around a subsidiary ridge into a small narrow valley. The massive W face of Burnt Mountain is a series of steep, rocky buttresses bisected by long couloirs. Climb to the foot of the face to gain the base of the southernmost couloir (this S couloir is portrayed by a stream on the Port Angeles USGS 7½-minute quad). Steep, exposed snow and mixed climbing leads to the summit ridge near a bench S of the summit. II, 4. Time: 6 hours up from Lake Angeles. An early start and stable snow conditions are advised.

Other routes on the W face are reported to have been climbed, but no details are available.

Lake Angeles Cirque

The cirque headwall at the southeast end of Lake Angeles is split by a long narrow couloir, which offers a good winter climb under suitable conditions.

Route. II, 4. Ski or snowshoe across the lake to the base of the couloir. Some 1200 ft. of steep snow or ice climbing leads to the top of the cirque headwall. Descend the route or climb diagonally right to gain the ridge followed by the Klahhane Ridge-Lake Angeles trail. Follow the trail N down to the lake. Time: 3 hours up from Lake Angeles.

Heather Park Peaks   6309 (1923 m)

Located approximately 1½ miles north of Mt. Angeles; the peaks surrounding Heather Park can be reached by trail from Klahhane Ridge (see Mt. Angeles Route 3) or a 4½-mile trail from Heart O' the Hills.

First Top   5510 (1679 m)

Located on the north end of the ridge, west of Heather Creek.

Route. I, 1. From Heather Park, follow the trail to Heather Pass and climb easy scree slopes to the top.

Several subsidiary peaks and pinnacles on the ridge between Heather Peak and First Top offer interesting, short rock climbs.

Second Top   6309 (1923 m)

A rock peak just east of Heather Pass. First recorded ascent 1936 by A. Boye, T. Chambers, L. Lander, R. McNabb, O. Nelson, and C. Sarff.

Route 1. I, 3. From Heather Pass, climb E staying on the S side of the summit rock. Easy rock or snow leads to a narrowing rock ramp that allows access to a gap in the summit rocks. A short pitch off the ramp leads to easier climbing and the top. Time: 1 hour up from Heather Park.

Route 2. I, 3. From Heather Park, proceed upvalley SE to the base of the N face. Climb steep snow or rock gullies to the top. Time: 1 hour up from Heather Park.

Egg Rock (The Thumb)   ca. 5485 (1672 m)

A prominent rock spire located about ½ mile south-southwest of Heather Pass. The rock has been reported to have been climbed via a Class 5 route on the east face, but no details are available. The base of the rock can be reached by leaving the Klahhane Ridge-Heather Park trail ½ mile south of Heather pass and following the ridge west.

Steeple Rock   5567 (1697 m)

Located about 2 miles east of the Hurricane Ridge Visitor Center above the Obstruction Point road. This 200-ft. spire is used as a practice area during all seasons. All of the listed routes have been ascended by clean methods: nuts and runners only. Some fixed pins may be found on Routes 2 and 4.

Route 1 (East Ridge). I, 3. From the extreme E end, scramble up over easy rock. The only difficulty is a short exposed traverse on the S side of the lower E summit block. Time: 1 hour up from the Obstruction Point road.

Route 2 (Voile Normale). I, 4. This route ascends the SW spur and is the most popular southside route. From the lowest point of the S face hike to a broken ledge with a tree on the left. From this rope-up spot, climb a debris-covered slab up and left to a wide broken area. Traverse left along terraced ledge systems to the entrance of a gully-chimney on the crest of the SW spur. Follow this gully-chimney to a belay behind a block at its top. A short easy pitch leads to a spacious, broken terrace. Go right to a prominent tree visible from the road. Climb a long crack and chimney system to the notch between two summit blocks.

Route 3 (Pooh Corner). II, 5.2. Follow the initial slab of Route 2 to its top and continue straight up over a steep wall to an area of broken ledges. Climb up and left for two moderate pitches. A short traverse left leads to the tree and final pitch of Route 2.

Route 4 (Direct Finish). II, 5.7. This is a more difficult variation of Route 2. Climb Route 2 to the broken terrace. On the left, a short pitch up an exposed wall leads to a belay in a rock alcove. Climb straight up over steep loose rock to a right slanting ledge. Go around a corner on the right and then finish on easier rock directly to the summit.

Route 5 (Grim Reaper). II, 5.9, A1. This difficult route ascends the overhang at the junction of the S and W faces of the rock. The first pitch leads up a steepening face to the base of a twisting overhanging crack on the right. One long aid pitch, and another moderate free pitch leads to easier climbing and the broken terrace of Route 2.

Route 6 (Pinball Alley). II, 5.7. On the W face, this route ascends the right-hand of two prominent crack systems. Several sustained leads up this crack lead to a junction with Route 2. Warning: the rock on this route is extremely loose.

Route 7 (Wings). II, 5.8. This popular route ascends the left-hand crack system on the W face. This crack system is identified by a small fir growing in the crack about 50 ft. up and a larger tree to the left 120 ft. up. Ascend the crack up and past the first tree, finishing with a difficult layback on white quartzite to a small belay stance atop a pinnacle. The crux is the second pitch: climb straight up on loose, poised flakes and boulders to a bomb-bay chimney. Difficult stemming leads up and over to easier ground. Scramble up and right to the spacious ledge and terrace of Route 2.

Route 8 (Bye Gully). I, 5.0. This is the gully which splits the W face, dividing the main summit rock from a prominent rock horn to the W. It offers a fine snow and ice climb in winter. Start just uphill from Route 7 and climb up a narrowing gully to the larger tree mentioned in Route 7. Proceed up one pitch, then left a short pitch to a stance below a chockstone. A difficult move

Steeple Rock near Hurricane Ridge (Frank Chapin)

around this chockstone leads to the notch. Not recommended during periods of high avalanche danger.

Route 9. I, 2. This N side route is the easiest route up Steeple Rock and offers an easier descent for the preceding routes. From the Obstruction Point road climb heather and scree to the ridge on the W side of the rock. Go through a break in the trees to a small meadow or snowfield. Contour right (E) until directly below the summit and climb heather and grass slopes or steep snow to the top. Time: 1 hour up from road.

This is a consolidation of the most popular routes on Steeple Rock. In all, there are approximately 15 distinct routes or variations that have been identified.

Griff Peak   ca. 5120 (1560 m)

Located approximately 1½ miles northeast of Hurricane Hill, this peak and adjacent Unicorn Peak are very prominent summits viewed from either U.S. 101 entering Port Angeles or from the Mt. Angeles area.

Route. I, 2. Hike the 1½-mile trail to the summit of Hurricane Hill (5757 ft.). Follow a timbered ridge NE to the summit. Time: 2 hours up from Hurricane Hill.

Unicorn Peak   ca. 5100 (1554 m)

Route. I, 3. From Griff Peak, follow the easy rock ridge NW ½ mile to the summit. Time: 3 hours up from Hurricane Hill.

The E side of Unicorn Peak is a steep face with a featureless, smooth rock apron at the base rising from the South Branch of the Little River. Technical climbing opportunities exist for parties willing to make the long trail approach.

Unicorn Horn   ca. 5050 (1539 m)

Located immediately northeast of Unicorn Peak.

Route. I, 3. Climb the broken rock ridge from the main summit of Unicorn Peak.

Olympic owl (George Martin)

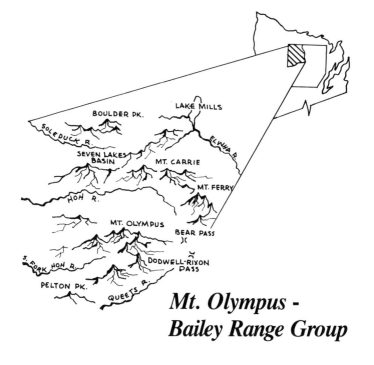

Mt. Olympus - Bailey Range Group

Without question the king of the Olympics, the triple-crowned and glacier-clad 7965-ft. Mt. Olympus thrusts its crest far above the green rain forests on the Pacific slope of the Olympic Peninsula. Included in this group, in addition to Mt. Olympus and environs, are the peaks of the Bailey Range, the isolated peaks surrounding the headwaters of the Soleduck River, and those near the Boulder Creek area. The heavy glaciation of Mt. Olympus results from ocean-born southwesterly winds suddenly striking the Olympics, rising, and losing their moisture. Mt. Olympus has eight named glaciers of the valley type; the longest is 3.8 miles in length. A number of small glaciers are located on the satellite peaks of Mt. Olympus and in the Bailey Range. This group offers the best snow and ice climbing found in the range. Small ridge and plateau lakes are plentiful in the upper Soleduck area.

APPROACHES

1. *Elwha River-Boulder Creek.* This approach provides access to the Boulder Peak-Mt. Appleton area; to the north, central, and south end of the Bailey Range; and to the southeast side of the Olympus Massif.

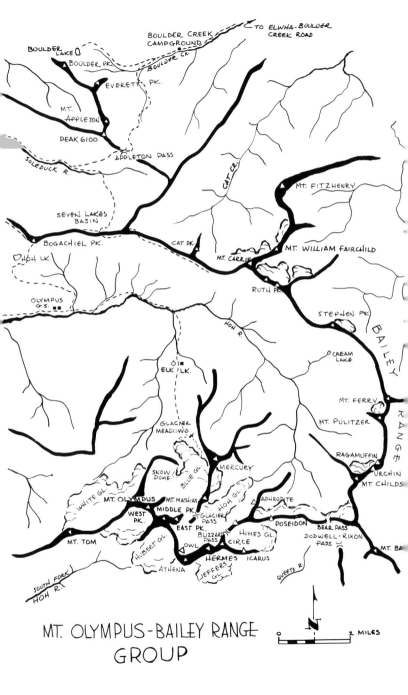

MT. OLYMPUS-BAILEY RANGE
GROUP

The Elwha River-Boulder Creek road leaves U.S. 101 9 miles SW of Port Angeles and ends in 8.4 miles at Deer Creek. There is an additional 2.4 miles to the walk-in campsite at Boulder Creek Campground. This campground is at an elevation of 2061 ft. The Appleton Pass trail continues to 5000-ft. Appleton Pass (5.3 miles from Boulder Creek Campground) and then drops to the Soleduck River trail (7.8 miles from Boulder Creek Campground). A spur road leaves the Elwha River-Boulder Creek road just beyond the Elwha Ranger Station (4.1 miles from U.S. 101) and continues upriver 5 miles to Whiskey Bend and the Elwha River trail (see Quinault Group, page 189 for details).

2. **Soleduck River.** This is the main approach to the High Divide and the north end of the Bailey Range.

The Soleduck River road leaves U.S. 101 30 miles W of Port Angeles just W of Lake Crescent and continues 14.2 miles to the Soleduck River trail (1.7 miles past Sol Duc Hot Springs). Good campsites are located on the trail at Soleduck Falls (0.9 mile, 1900 ft.), Upper Soleduck (5.4 miles, 3200 ft.), and Soleduck Park (7.7 miles, 4500 ft.).

The Deer Lake-Bogachiel Peak trail branches from the Soleduck River trail at Soleduck Falls. Campsites are located at Deer Lake (3.9 miles from road end, 3500 ft.) and at Round and Lunch lakes in Seven Lakes Basin (8.2 miles from road, 4300 ft.). The Deer Lake-Bogachiel Peak trail connects with the High Divide trail and the Hoh Lake trail (8.3 miles from road, 5200 ft.) near Bogachiel Peak. The High Divide trail meets the Soleduck River trail in 2.1 miles near Heart Lake, and then continues 3 additional miles to the S side of Cat Peak, providing the best northern access to the Bailey Range. The Hoh Lake trail provides a 6.5-mile connection between the High Divide trail and the Hoh River trail.

3. **Hoh River.** This is the primary access to Mt. Olympus and environs.

The Hoh River road leaves U.S. 101 12.5 miles S of Forks and extends 19 miles to the Hoh River trail. The 17.4-mile Hoh River trail has campsites at Happy Four (5.7 miles, 820 ft.), Olympus (9.1 miles, 950 ft.), Elk Lake (15.1 miles, 2558 ft.), and Glacier Meadows (17.4 miles, 4200 ft.). The Tom Creek trail branches from the Hoh River trail at 2.7 miles, fords the river, and extends 1.2 miles to a campsite (700 ft.). This trail is not maintained and the river may be difficult to cross.

4. **South Fork Hoh River.** This approach can be used for a difficult access to Mt. Tom, Hoh Peak, the Valhallas, and other seldom-visited peaks west of Mt. Olympus.

The South Fork Hoh River is reached via the Clearwater Corrections Center road which leaves U.S. 101 14.6 miles S of Forks at the Allen Logging Co. Travel E on the Corrections Center road 6.7 miles to road H-1000, then turn left. Stay on H-1000 10.3 miles (mostly gravel and not marked); avoid other marked turnoffs. On H-1000 you will cross the South Fork Hoh River, a campground, and a gravel pit before you reach the trailhead parking area, which is marked. The South Fork Hoh River trail extends about 1 mile to Big Flat Camp (732 ft.) and is maintained for another 2 miles.

5. ***Queets River.*** This approach is of limited value to climbers, but it does provide access to an interesting trail hike.

The Queets River road leaves U.S. 101 7 miles S of the town of Queets and extends 14 miles upriver. The Queets River must be forded at road end to continue on the 15.5-mile Queets River trail. Campsites are at Spruce Bottom (5 miles, 426 ft.), Bob Creek (11.1 miles, 580 ft.), and Pelton Creek (15.5 miles, 800 ft.).

RANGER STATIONS

Elwha (Elwha River road at 4.1 miles); Soleduck District Office (approximately 4 miles N of Forks on U.S. 101); Queets (Queets River road at 12.5 miles); and Hoh (Hoh River road at 19 miles). In summer, manned stations are located at Soleduck (Soleduck River road at 12.3 miles), Seven Lakes Basin (Lunch Lake), Olympus Ranger Station, and Glacier Meadows. Note: Check with ranger regarding limits on size of party and the use of campfires.

CAMPGROUNDS

U.S. 101: Fairholm, el. 550 ft. (W end of Lake Crescent); Kalaloch, el. 100 ft. (5 miles N of Queets on the ocean); Klahowya, el. 800 ft. (spur road 8 miles E of Sappho); Bogachiel State Park, el. 203 ft. (5 miles S of Forks on U.S. 101).

Elwha River-Boulder Creek Road: Elwha, el. 300 ft. (3 miles from U.S. 101); Altaire, el. 400 ft. (4 miles).

Soleduck River Road: Soleduck, el. 1700 ft. (13 miles S of U.S. 101).

Hoh River Road: Hoh, el. 575 ft. (19 miles E of U.S. 101).

Queets River Road: Queets, el. 300 ft. (13.5 miles E of U.S. 101).

VANTAGE POINTS

Hurricane Ridge can be reached by road. Bogachiel Peak, Kloochman Rock, Dodger Point, Kimta Peak, and Mt. Storm King (overlooking Lake Crescent) can be reached by trail.

MAPS

Olympic National Forest/Olympic National Park; USGS 30-minute Olympic National Park and Vicinity; the following 15-minute USGS and Green Trail quadrangles: Mt. Tom and Mt. Olympus; the following 7½-minute USGS quadrangles: Bogachiel Peak and Mt. Carrie; the following Custom Correct Maps: Mount Olympus Climber's Map, Seven Lakes Basin-Hoh, Elwha Valley, and Lake Crescent-Happy Lake Ridge.

MT. OLYMPUS   7965 (2427 m)

The monarch of the Olympics is located between the Hoh and Queets rivers. It was named by John Meares in 1788 for the home of the Greek gods. The West Peak is the highest, with Middle Peak closely rivaling it. The East Peak is slightly lower.

West Peak   7965 (2427 m)

First recognized ascent 1907 by L. A. Nelson and 10 members of The Mountaineers. There is serious doubt of the first-ascent claims of Col. B. F. Shaw and H. D. Clock (1854), Col. M. Simmons (1854), and B. J. Bretherton (1890).

Route 1. II, 3. A 17.4-mile trail climbs 3600 ft. to Glacier Meadows from the Hoh River Ranger Station. Another trail over the High Divide (5200 ft.) from the Soleduck River road (1900 ft.) joins the Hoh River trail (950 ft.) ½ mile E of Olympus Ranger Station, providing a variation in approach.

From Glacier Meadows (4200 ft.), two routes lead to the Blue Glacier; an early summer route and a midsummer route. The climbing routes follow the

Mt. Olympus and Blue Glacier from the northeast (courtesy Olympic National Park)

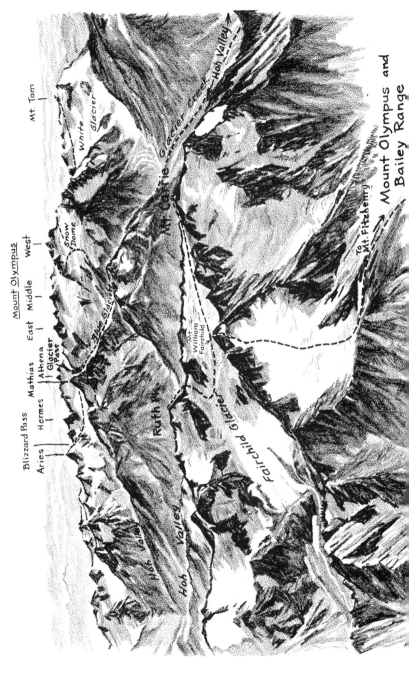

Mount Olympus and Bailey Range

Mount Olympus

Blizzard Pass — Aries — Hermes — Mathias — Athena — East — Middle — West — Mt. Tom

Glacier Pass

Blue Glacier

Snow Dome

White Glacier

Mt. Carrie

Glacier Creek — Hoh Valley

Ruth Pk.

Hoh Pk.

Hoh Valley

William Fairchild

Fairchild Glacier

To Mt. Fitzhenry

trail from Glacier Meadows up to the ranger station (summer only). The early summer route follows a trail just past the station that turns SW (right) and leads to the 4700-ft. level of the Lower Blue Glacier (0.6 mile). Ascending the glacier through the crevasses can provide route-finding problems. The midsummer route continues up the valley past the ranger station to the top (5100 ft.) of the lateral moraine (0.9 mile) on the E side of the glacier. Descend about 150 ft. to the glacier. Ascend the glacier to where both routes join, then cross to the W side of the glacier at 5600 ft. Leave the glacier and climb NW over rock and snow to the crest of the Snow Dome (6600 ft.). Depending on the snow conditions, about 3 hours are required to reach the Snow Dome from Glacier Meadows. From the Snow Dome, proceed on a rising traverse southerly through a 7200-ft. snow pass (see the sketch on page 165). Turn right (approximately 250° TN) and climb to the top of the Upper Blue Glacier. Bear right and this will lead to the saddle between Five Fingers Peak (false summit) and West Peak. Climb a steep snow pitch to the NE side of the rock summit. There may be a problem crossing the moat from the snow onto the rock. Traverse the E side by scrambling over ledges and moderate rock. The final 10 to 15 feet is reached either by climbing up the S side

Mount Olympus - West Peak
from Snow Dome

(Eagle's Nest) or by climbing a crack on the E side to the summit. Time: 7 hours up from Glacier Meadows.

There are early season alternate routes from the Snow Dome: a direct climb to the left of Five Fingers Peak (false summit) or a climb directly to the saddle between Five Fingers and West Peak. Both of these routes can be seen from the Snow Dome (see the sketch).

Route 2. II, 3. From Elwha Basin, climb the Elwha Snow Finger to 4850-ft. Dodwell-Rixon Pass (see Quinault Group, page 187). Descend into Queets Basin and contour W at about the 4500-ft. level to the base of the Humes Glacier (see sketch on page 167). Several streams, including the headwaters of the Queets River, must be crossed. Keep high to avoid crossing problems. Ascend the ridge leading to the center of the terminal snout of the Humes Glacier. Continue up the glacier to Blizzard Pass (6100 ft.).

From here descend right 600 ft. to a fine climber's camp called Camp Pan. This site overlooks the Hoh Glacier from a rock promontory. From Camp Pan descend SW to the Hoh Glacier. Climb W on the Hoh Glacier to 6800 ft. and then NW, climbing over the Middle Peak and traversing to the saddle between Five Fingers (false summit) and West Peak as described in Route 1. Time: 8 hours up from campsite in Queets Basin.

Route 3 (West Ridge). II, 5.3. First ascent 1964 by G. Maykut, L. Miller, and J. Witte.

From the Snow Dome (see Route 1), proceed to the N side of the W ridge at its lowest point. Climb the ridge crest to a large vertical step separating two shallow gullies. Traverse right and climb a 100-ft., Class 5.3 pitch. Continue just below the ridge crest on easy rock to a notch 400 ft. higher. Bypass gendarmes on a ledge on the N side of the ridge to snow at the base of the summit pyramid and continue to the top. Time: 6 hours up from Glacier Meadows.

Middle Peak   7930 (2417 m)

First ascent 1907 by B. H. Browne, W. G. Clarke, G. W. Humes, H. C. Parker, and H. Sisson.

Route 1. II, 3. Go southerly through a 7200-ft. snow pass above the Snow Dome (see Route 1, West Peak) to the Middle Peak over an easy glacier slope. Climb the W side via 100 ft. of rotten rock. Time: 7 hours up from Glacier Meadows.

Route 2. II, 3. Follow Route 2, East Peak, but stay S of East Peak, continuing W to Middle Peak.

Route 3. II, 4. The Blue Glacier icefall offers a challenging route to the Middle Peak. Ascend right of the rock cleaver that divides the icefall. Seasonal conditions will determine the best route. There is some danger from falling debris.

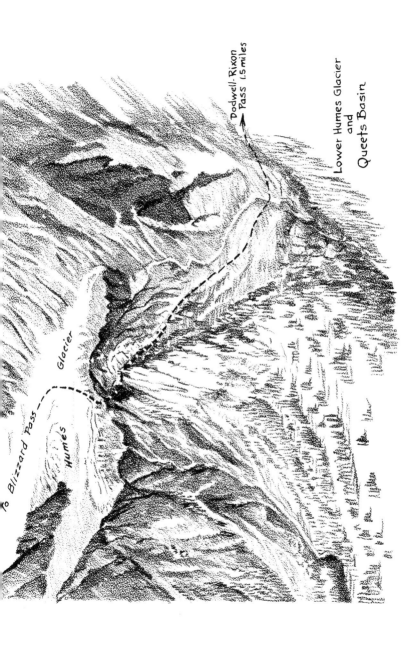

To Blizzard Pass

Humes Glacier

Dodwell-Rixon
Pass 1.5 miles

Lower Humes Glacier
and
Queets Basin

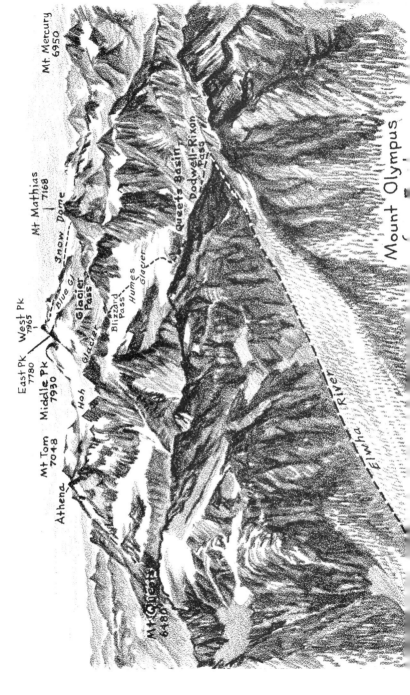

East Peak 7780 (2371 m)

First ascent 1899 by J. McGlone, a member of the Dodwell-Rixon survey party.

Route 1. II, 3. From Route 1, Middle Peak, go over the top of the Middle Peak and ascend the SW side of the East Peak. To descend, drop to the Hoh Glacier to Route 2.

Route 2. II, 3. Climb from Glacier Pass (6200 ft.) by swinging south-westerly around rock buttresses, beneath hanging ice which presents possible avalanche danger, and then up the SE side.

Olympus Traverse

A traverse of the three main peaks of Olympus may be done by climbing West Peak first, then proceeding to Middle Peak, and thence to East Peak, returning to Glacier Meadows through Glacier Pass.

The first recorded traverse was August 1938 by G. Martin, B. Scott, and D. Dooley. They spent three nights on Five Fingers Peak and from this high camp they climbed West, Middle, and East peaks. They also climbed South Peak (later named Athena) and Mt. Tom from this campsite.

MT. TOM 7048 (2148 m)

Located 2 miles west of the summit of Mt. Olympus at the west end of the upper White Glacier. First ascent 1914 by E. Meany and a group of Boy Scouts including T. Martin, for whom the peak was named.

Route 1. II, 3. From the Snow Dome of Mt. Olympus (see Route 1, Mt. Olympus), bear SW keeping close to the West Peak of Mt. Olympus. Cross the crest of a rock ridge running W from the Mt. Olympus summit, just before it drops sharply to the valley. Proceed SW on the crest of the adjoining right-angle ridge for several hundred yards. Turn right into a shallow gully just before this latter ridge breaks sharply, and descend the gully down a steep rock face. Descend the steep snow slope at the bottom of the gully to reach the White Glacier. Traverse the glacier westerly to the summit of Mt. Tom, or bear left to gain the rock ridge leading up to the summit. The highest point is the left-hand peak as seen from the White Glacier. Time: 9 hours up from Glacier Meadows.

Route 2. II, 3. From the end of the Tom Creek trail (900 ft.), proceed up the creek through brush to the headwall (ca. 6 miles). Bear left and climb steep, timbered slopes to timberline, where an excellent campsite exists at lakes on a large bench (5100 ft.). From this bench, the W side of the White Glacier can be easily reached, and the glacier ascended to the summit.

MT. MATHIAS (APOLLO) 7168 (2184 m)

Located between the Blue and Hoh glaciers and northeast of Glacier Pass.

Originally named Apollo, this peak was officially renamed in honor of F. W. Mathias, a prominent Grays Harbor area mountaineer and conservationist, as a result of efforts by the Grays Harbor Olympians of Aberdeen, Washington. First ascent 1957 by Y. Eriksson and J. Hawkins.

Route 1. II, 4. Ascend a steep glacier finger leading from the Blue Glacier to a high col between Mathias and the sharp pinnacle just NE of Glacier Pass. Passage of this finger may be difficult late in the season due to bergschrunds. Attack the steep ridge to Mathias directly, working ledges on the W face as steep pitches near the summit are reached. Eventually gain the opposite ridge just below the summit. The climb is on exposed rotten rock. Time: 8 hours up from Glacier Meadows.

The prominent rock pinnacle between Mathias and Glacier Pass has been climbed via two exposed Class 4 pitches on its north ridge.

Route 2. II, 4. Ascend shallow gullies from the Blue Glacier to the Mercury-Mathias col. Descend the E side of the ridge 200 ft. to a snowfield. Climb S, swinging around a prominent buttress, then regain the ridge crest and proceed to the summit. Time: 8 hours up from Glacier Meadows.

MERCURY   6950 (2118 m)
A triangular peak located 1 mile north of Mt. Mathias. First ascent 1955 by R. Hubley.

Route. I, 3. Proceed to Mathias-Mercury col (Mathias, Route 2) and climb N directly up the ridge to the Mercury summit. Time: 5 hours up from Glacier Meadows.

Both Mathias and Mercury have been climbed from the Hoh Glacier via circuitous routes with danger of rockfall.

A fine climber's high camp, called Camp Pan, is located about 300 ft. above the Hoh Glacier on a rocky promontory at the north edge of the slope which leads from the Hoh Glacier to Blizzard Pass (Hoh-Humes Pass). This camp may be reached in about 4 hours from Glacier Meadows and is a good central location for climbing in this area.

ATHENA (SOUTH PEAK, OLYMPUS)   ca. 7350 (2240 m)
This is the highest point at the south edge of the head of the Hoh Glacier. First ascent 1938 by D. Dooley, G. Martin, R. Peterson, and R. Scott.

Route. II, 3. From Camp Pan, descend to the Hoh Glacier and then climb to its head. Bear SSE along a large snow crest, passing W of Athena's Owl, and continue along the crest to the base of Athena. Circle to the right, and ascend easy rock slightly exposed in places. Reach the summit by climbing the N arête and turning left just below the summit. Time: 5 hours up from Camp Pan.

This peak can also be reached from Glacier Meadows via Glacier Pass, as described in the routes on Mt. Olympus.

ATHENA II ca. 7250 (2210 m)

This companion of Athena, rising adjacent to it on the southeast and about a hundred ft. lower, is of considerable historic interest. Although not conclusive, the evidence strongly suggests this was the peak climbed on September 22, 1890, by B. J. Bretherton, N. E. Linsley, and Private J. Danton, thus making it the first Olympic "seven thousander" to be climbed. The men were members of a party sent to Mt. Olympus by Lieut. Joseph P. O'Neil, commander of an exploring expedition jointly mounted by the U.S. Army and the Oregon Alpine Club (forerunner of the Mazamas). They placed a copper box containing a register book about 400 ft. below the summit, but apparently it has never been found.

Route 1. II, 3. Ascend Athena from the Hoh Glacier (see Athena route description), then descend SE to the saddle between the two peaks. A short scramble up slopes of steep, extremely rotten rock leads to the summit.

Route 2. II, 2. Although much longer, the most feasible route is to approach the peak from lower Queets Basin, generally following the 1890 route. Cross the Queets River headwaters W of the campsite and travel SW through alternate meadowland and forest to an expanse of open country S of the Humes Glacier. Leave the meadow at the S margin and traverse W along a steep, forested slope to a bench above the snow finger below Jeffers Glacier. A short but very steep elk trail descends S directly to the snow. Ascend NW up the snow finger to the glacier, then SW up the glacier to its head (site of the 1890 party's high camp). From this point, climb NW up the S ridge (rotten, broken rock), occasionally traversing moderately steep snowfields, to the summit. Time: At least 2 days up from Upper Queets Basin.

ATHENA'S OWL ca. 7000 (2133 m)

A sharp, double-pronged nunatak located in the Hoh Glacier north of Athena. First ascent 1963 by W. Leggett and G. Maykut.

Route. II, 3. Proceed as for Athena, but leave the snow crest when the W side of the Owl is reached. This short climb is made from the W side after descending a wind-carved moat which describes an arc around the N, W, and S sides of the Owl. Ascend rock to just below the N "ear," where a horizontal traverse leads to the notch between the N and S "ears." The knife-edged summit of the higher S "ear" is reached in two rope leads from the notch by following the E side of the ridge just below the crest. This climb is not difficult, but it is very exposed. Time: 5 hours up from Camp Pan.

HERMES   ca. 6860 (2090 m)

This sharp rock peak is on the south margin of the Hoh Glacier, approximately ½ mile west of Circe. First ascent 1955 by R. Hubley and E. LaChapelle.

Route. II, 3. From Camp Pan, follow the E edge of the Hoh Glacier S to the base of Hermes. Ascend steep, broken ice to the col NE of the Hermes summit. Crossing the schrund may be very difficult late in the season. Ascend a sharp ridge on easy rotten rock W to the summit. Time: 4 hours up from Camp Pan.

CIRCE   ca. 6874 (2095 m)

Located at the junction of three rock ridges which separate the Hoh, Humes, and Jeffers glaciers.

Route. II, 2. From Camp Pan, climb to Blizzard Pass and follow a gentle ridge S to the summit. Time: 2 hours up from Camp Pan.

ARIES   ca. 6400 (1951 m)

Located approximately ½ mile northeast of Circe.

Route. II, 3. From Camp Pan, proceed E to the NW side of Aries; climb to summit via mixed snow and rock. Difficulty with a bergschrund may be encountered. Time: 3 hours up from Camp Pan.

APHRODITE   6254 (1906 m)

Located about 1½ miles northeast of Circe. First ascent 1964 by B. Albro, K. Heathershaw, H. Lee, D. Sicks, F. Smith, B. West, and M. West of the Olympic College climbing class.

Route. II, 3. From Camp Pan, contour NE about 1 mile, keeping above the Hoh Glacier to the W side of Aphrodite where the summit may be gained by easy snow and a rock scramble. A bergschrund may exist late in the season. Time: 4 hours up from Camp Pan.

ICARUS   ca. 6200 (1889 m)

A double-spired peak located approximately ¾ mile east of Circe on the south edge of the Humes Glacier. Both spires appear to be of equal elevation. First ascent 1966 by B. West and M. West.

Route. II, 3. From Camp Pan, climb about 600 ft. through Blizzard Pass and contour S and E around the Humes Glacier (ca. 1 mile). Circle around the N side of Icarus to the E face of the E spire. Climb gully and chimney systems to the summit on loose rock. Time: 3 hours up from Camp Pan. The W spire may be climbed in two Class 4 pitches on the NW side.

Mt. Olympus and the Snow Dome from the northwest (George Martin)

THE VALHALLAS

This interesting but little-known group of peaks is centered 3½ miles southwest of Mt. Olympus, between the Queets River and the South Fork Hoh River. Resembling a miniature Bugaboos, these peaks are an extension of Mt. Olympus' southwest ridge. The central and highest peaks lie in a horseshoe around the Geri-Freki Glacier, whose melt waters provide one of the main sources of the South Fork Hoh River. The central peaks are listed in order clockwise around the Geri-Freki Glacier starting with Bragi in the northeast. The isolated peaks on the ridge, which continues past Woden to *Pelton Peak,*

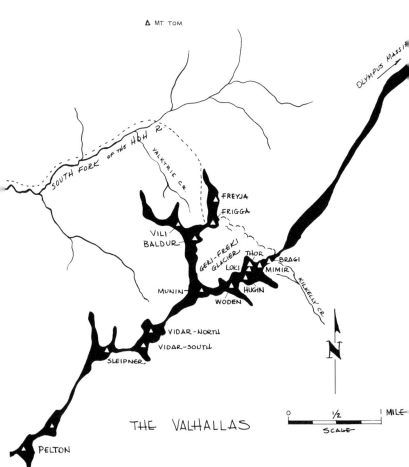

are presented next. The peaks of the Valhallas are named after the gods of Norse Mythology.

The area can be approached from the South Fork Hoh River, from the Queets River, or from Mt. Olympus. The South Fork Hoh River approach is the easiest and is described in detail.

For road access details, see the South Fork Hoh River approach. From the road end, follow a maintained trail for 3.5 miles, passing Big Flat Camp inside the park boundary. From the end of the trail, continue up the north side of the river for another 9 miles to a large boulder field. The main peaks of The Valhallas are approximately one mile southeast of this point. Continue upriver over the moss-covered boulders. Immediately past the boulder field, cross the river and climb the steep wooded slopes on the left side of Valkyrie Creek. Keeping well left of the creek, attain the ridge and then climb it to alpine meadows at 4400 ft. where camp can be made on the crest. From camp, contour into the Valkyrie Creek Basin and then climb up a steep couloir to the col between Frigga on the left and Baldur on the right. Most of the following route descriptions start at this col, which is approximately 45 minutes from camp.

Bragi　ca. 5450 (1661 m)

A 170-ft. pinnacle located near the snout of the Geri-Freki Glacier on its eastern edge, and immediately northeast of its twin, Mimir. First ascent 1978 by J. King, B. Larson, M. Lonac, M. Merchant, R. Stewart, F. Stinchfield, and J. White.

Route. II, 3. From the Baldur-Frigga col, cross the glacier, passing under the N side of Thor (ca. ¾ mile). Leave the glacier and scramble up easy rock to the upper snowfield. From the NE ridge of this pinnacle, run up a rock and heather ramp on the N side to a short belayed pitch to the SW that gains the narrow summit. Time: 1½ hours up from Baldur-Frigga col.

Mimir　ca. 5400 (1646 m)

A 120-ft. pinnacle located immediately northeast of Thor and southwest of Bragi. First ascent 1978 by J. King, B. Larson, M. Lonac, M. Merchant, R. Stewart, F. Stinchfield, and J. White.

Route. II, 4. From the Baldur-Frigga col, cross the glacier to the SE, passing under the N side of Thor. Immediately past Thor, leave the glacier and climb snow to the Thor-Mimir saddle. Climb rotten rock from the saddle, and ascend a 25-ft. narrow chimney to an excellent belay and rappel spot at the top of the chimney. A 15-ft. pitch gains the narrow summit. Time: ½ hour up from Thor-Mimir saddle.

Thor　ca. 5950 (1813 m)

Located above the lower southeast side of the Geri-Freki Glacier approximately ⅔ mile from the Baldur-Frigga col. First ascent 1971 by R. Beckett, D. Haley, G. Kelsey, M. Lennox, D. Michael, D. Stevens, and R. Yekel.

Route 1. II, 3. From the Baldur-Frigga col, contour to the glacier, cross it to the SE, and climb to the Thor-Loki Spire notch. Climb a rotten-rock couloir to the summit. Time: 1½ hours up from Baldur-Frigga col.

Route 2. II, 3. First ascent 1978 by R. Burke, T. Burke, and J. White.

From the Thor-Mimir saddle, scramble up refreshing rock southwesterly to the summit. Time: ½ hour up from Thor-Mimir saddle.

Loki Spire　ca. 5700 (1737 m)

A 300-ft. pinnacle located immediately southwest of Thor. First ascent 1971 by R. Beckett, D. Haley, G. Kelsey, M. Lennox, D. Michael, D. Stevens, and R. Yekel.

Route. II, 3. Climb rotten rock from the Hugin-Loki col after an approach for Thor. The last 10 ft. are climbed flagpole fashion. Time: ½ hour up from Hugin-Loki col.

Hugin　ca. 5990 (1825 m)

Located above the southeast side of the Geri-Freki Glacier approximately ⅔ mile from the Baldur-Frigga col. It is the peak immediately east of Woden. First ascent 1966 by W. Howarth, E. Labistida, I. Lindgren, and J. Wall.

Route. II, 2. From the Baldur-Frigga col, cross the glacier to the SE keeping to the left of Woden. Scramble up rotten rock on the NW side to the summit. Time: 1 hour up from Baldur-Frigga col.

Woden　6038 (1840 m)

This peak, the highest in The Valhallas, is located above the upper southeast side of the Geri-Freki Glacier slightly over ½ mile from the Baldur-Frigga col. First ascent 1966 by E. Labistida and I. Lindgren.

Route. II, 4. From the Baldur-Frigga col, cross the glacier to the SE and then ascend a snowfield to the NE corner of the peak. Climb a jam crack and then traverse to the left under an overhang. Next, ascend a short chimney to the summit ridge. Either climb the ridge to the summit or traverse around to the S face and climb one Class 4 pitch. Time: 1½ hours up from Baldur-Frigga col.

Munin　ca. 6000 (1828 m)

Located near the head of the Geri-Freki Glacier immediately west of Woden. It is approximately ⅔ mile from the Baldur-Frigga col. First ascent 1971 by R. Beckett, D. Haley, G. Kelsey, M. Lennox, D. Michael, H. Pinsch, D. Stevens, and R. Yekel.

Route. II, 4. From the Baldur-Frigga col, ascend the glacier southerly to the Munin-Woden saddle. An interesting rock scramble along the ridge leads to the summit. Time: 1½ hours up from Baldur-Frigga col.

The Valhallas and Geri-Freki Glacier (courtesy Olympic National Park)

Baldur   ca. 5750 (1752 m)

Located above the upper northwest side of the Geri-Freki Glacier immediately southwest of the Baldur-Frigga col. First ascent 1971 by R. Beckett, D. Haley, G. Kelsey, M. Lennox, D. Michael, H. Pinsch, D. Stevens, and R. Yekel.

Route. II, 2. From the Baldur-Frigga col, ascend the NW side of the glacier around the base of Baldur and then climb to the Munin-Baldur saddle. Traverse the easy ridge to the summit. Time: 1 hour up from Baldur-Frigga col.

Vili   ca. 5500 (1676 m)

Located approximately 1/5 mile northwest of Baldur. First ascent 1978 by R. Burke, T. Burke, and J. White.

Route 1. II, 2. From the upper Valkyrie Creek Basin, climb southwesterly to the Baldur-Vili saddle. Ascend easy SE ridge to the summit. Time: 1¼ hours up from upper Valkyrie Creek Basin.

Route 2. II, 2. First ascent of this elevation-saving route 1978 by J. King, B. Larson, M. Lonac, M. Merchant, R. Stewart, F. Stinchfield, and J. White.

From Baldur, descend ridge to the NW and then rappel to the SW for an easy traverse to the Baldur-Vili saddle. Climb the easy SE ridge to the summit. Time: 1 hour from summit of Baldur.

Frigga   ca. 5300 (1615 m)

Located immediately northeast of the Baldur-Frigga col. First ascent 1971 by R. Beckett, D. Haley, G. Kelsey, M. Lennox, D. Michael, H. Pinsch, D. Stevens, and R. Yekel.

Route 1. II, 3. Climb from the Baldur-Frigga col via a short but exposed scramble on rotten rock. In late summer the start onto the rock may be difficult. Time: ½ hour up from Baldur-Frigga col.

Route 2. II, 5.0. First ascent 1984 by G. Bauer, B. Larson, F. Ratliff, R. Teague, and J. White.

From the Geri-Freki Glacier, climb the snow finger, or on exposed rock, to the notch between Frigga and Freyja. Next, make a difficult ascending traverse to SE (left). Gain the ridge and a good belay point behind a tree. Scramble to summit and descend via Route 1. Time: 1 hour up from notch.

Freyja   ca. 5040 (1536 m)

Located approximately 1/5 mile north of Frigga. First ascent 1984 by G. Bauer, B. Larson, F. Ratliff, R. Teague, and J. White.

Route. II, 4. From the Frigga-Freyja notch, scramble up rotten rock to summit. Rappel to notch from tree between true and false summits. Time: 20 minutes up from notch.

Vidar-North   ca. 5650 (1722 m)

Located approximately ⅔ mile southwest of Munin. It is the highest point on the ridge running from Munin to Pelton Peak. First ascent 1978 by B. Larson, M. Lonac, and J. White.

Route. II, 3. From upper Valkyrie Creek Basin, gain the ridge W of Vili and descend on a long southward traverse via good elk trails. Travel high around the head of a basin to avoid major gulleys. Cross over ridge to Queets side for a short distance and cross back over to the Hoh side. Ascend upper snow basin to NE ridge and scramble up rock and heather to the summit. Time: 4 hours up from upper Valkyrie Creek Basin.

Vidar-South   ca. 5600 (1706 m)

Located approximately 1/5 mile southwest of Vidar-North. First ascent 1978 by B. Larson, M. Lonac, and J. White.

Route. II, 3. After an approach from upper Valkyrie Creek Basin as described for Vidar-North, traverse SW on the N side under both Vidars on rock and snow to the Sleipner-Vidar-South saddle. Climb a rotten rock chute northeasterly to the summit. Time: 2 hours up from ridge NE of Vidar-North.

Sleipner   ca. 5550 (1692 m)

Located approximately 2/5 mile west of Vidar-South. First ascent 1978 by B. Larson, M. Lonac, and J. White.

Route. II, 4. From the Sleipner-Vidar-South saddle, scramble up heather and rock on E ridge to a false summit. Belay down to a very rotten narrow notch and then ascend rotten rock chute about 30 ft. to a right-hand ramp with a tree. Follow the ramp a short distance and then climb exposed rock to the summit. The highest point is the easternmost of the two summit horns. Time: 1¼ hours up from Sleipner-Vidar-South saddle.

HOH PEAK   5572 (1699 m)

A prominent, seldom-climbed rock peak located 3 miles west of Mt. Tom. The summit view is striking because of the peak's command of western vistas from Grays Harbor to Vancouver Island.

Route 1. II, 3. Follow the S Fork Hoh River to a point approximately 2 miles WSW of the peak. From camp on the river, climb northeasterly to the 3900-ft. pass NW of Hoh Peak. Ascend the ridge SE a short distance, but when it becomes rocky (ca. 4000 ft.), descend to the N side. Follow game trails and resist the temptation to climb until reaching the meadows W of the N ridge. Cross to the N ridge at just below the upper cliff band. A heavily traveled elk trail on a narrow ledge leads to the N ridge. Continue ¼ mile to a gully. Halfway up the gully, scramble to the E and walk to the summit on the broad ascending ramp between the N cliff band and the E ridge. Time: 8 hours up from camp on the river.

Route 2. II, 3. Ford the Hoh River 2.7 miles above the Hoh Ranger Station (difficult and dangerous during high water), and follow the unmaintained Mt. Tom Creek trail to its end. Continue up the creek for about 2½ miles, staying on the S side. Climb a steep timbered slope along the W side of the outlet creek of Dragon Lake. From Dragon Lake (good campsite), gain the wooded ridge crest and continue SE to the base of the NW ridge. From here, follow Route 1 to the N side. Time: 8-10 hours up from Dragon Lake.

The NW ridge has probably been climbed, but this ridge appears both rotten and difficult.

BAILEY RANGE

This long, curving chain of peaks, paralleling the upper Hoh River canyon, contains summits averaging 6500 ft. elevation. Mt. Carrie, at 6995 ft., is the highest. This isolated range will be presented from north to south through and including Mt. Childs. The southwest slope of the range, bordering the Hoh, presents generally smooth sides, but on the northeast the range is roughly indented and has numerous small glaciers. Named by the Press Party for William E. Bailey, proprietor of the *Seattle Press*.

Mt. Fitzhenry   ca. 6050 (1844 m)

Located between Cat Creek and Long Creek at the north end of the Bailey Range.

Route. II, 2. From the dam at the N end of Lake Mills, take the 2-mile trail which ends at Boulder Creek — may have to climb upstream to cross. From here, follow the lake, keeping high to avoid cliffs. Cross Cat Creek and ascend the dry wooded ridge separating Cat Creek from Fitzhenry Creek, to the 5948-ft. false summit. Drop slightly and continue on to the true summit ½ mile SW. Time: 8 hours up, 6 hours down.

This route may be shortened somewhat by making the approach to Cat Creek via boat on Lake Mills — there is a boat launch at the lake. Fitzhenry has been climbed from Long Creek; however, no details are available.

Mt. William Fairchild   ca. 6950 (2118 m)

Located ¾ mile northeast of Mt. Carrie. Named in honor of pioneer aviator William Fairchild of Port Angeles. First ascent 1963 by D. Baker, J. Christiansen, R. Etten, and D. Pruitt via Route 1.

Route 1. II, 3. From the summit of Mt. Fitzhenry, descend the ridge SW to a saddle, and drop several hundred ft. on the W side of the saddle. Proceed SE to the glacier on the N side of Mt. William Fairchild. Ascend the glacier about 1500 ft. to the highest of several rocky summits and scramble to the top. Time: 3 full days for the round trip from Lake Mills. See Mt. Fitzhenry approach.

Route 2. II, 3. First ascent 1975 by B. Brown, M. Gallager, M. McNerthney, and R. Peffer.

From Mt. Carrie, traverse E down the ridge to the saddle, then S onto the Fairchild Glacier. Descend the glacier easterly about 1200 vertical ft., then contour N past buttresses in the Carrie-Fairchild ridge. Ascend scree and snow to the SW ridge of Fairchild, then directly up that ridge to the summit (one steep spot). Time: 3 hours up from Mt. Carrie.

Jackson Spire   ca. 6650 (2027 m)

A sharp summit on the Carrie-Fairchild ridge, located immediately south of Mt. William Fairchild. This spire is not visible from Mt. Carrie and is best viewed from Ruth Peak or the Ruth-Carrie ridge. First ascent 1975 by P. Janker and G. Wornell.

Route. II, 4. From Mt. Carrie, traverse E down the ridge to the saddle, then S onto the Fairchild Glacier. Descend the glacier easterly about 1200 vertical ft. and contour past buttresses to the bottom of the E ridge of Jackson. Ascend a series of very steep scree gullies to a point about ⅔ the way up the ridge from its base. Next, climb to the ridge crest and follow the crest for four leads to the summit. The descent was via the somewhat easier NE face. Time: 3 hours up from Mt. Carrie.

Mt. Michael   ca. 6750 (2058 m)

Located on the Carrie-Fairchild ridge just south of Jackson Spire and north of the northeast summit of Mt. Carrie. First ascent 1975 by P. Janker, D. Klewin, and M. McNerthney.

Route. II, 3. From Mt. Carrie, traverse E down the ridge to the saddle, then S onto the Fairchild Glacier. Descend the glacier until just below Mt. Michael. Ascend to a notch between Mt. Michael and Mt. Carrie and follow the SW ridge to the summit. The ridge is sharp and rock rotten; the left (NW) side of ridge is used until the last lead, which is done on the SE side. The descent was via the somewhat easier E face and steep scree on the S face. Time: 2 hours up from Mt. Carrie.

Cat Peak   ca. 5940 (1810 m)

A double-summited peak located on the Hoh River-Cat Creek divide.

Route. I, 1. From about ½ mile before the end of the trail (see Mt. Carrie), climb N past the 5600-ft. false summit to the top. Time: 2 hours up from trail.

Mt. Carrie   6995 (2132 m)

The central and highest peak in the Bailey Range located on the Long Creek-Hoh River divide. Named by T. Rixon during the first USGS survey of forest resources, 1898-1900, for Carrie Jones, his wife-to-be.

Route. I, 2. The best approach is from the end of the Soleduck River road, taking the trail through Soleduck Park to the High Divide. Here a branch trail contours E above the Hoh River valley about 3 miles to its end at 5100 ft. between Cat Peak and Mt. Carrie. From the end of this trail, climb to the ridge top (elevation gain ca. 200 ft.) and proceed E along the narrow ridge crest called the "Catwalk." Continue NE along the summit ridge, keeping to the right side on easy shale and heather to the false summit. The main summit is farther E. Time: 5 hours up from Heart Lake.

Ruth Peak   ca. 6850 (2087 m)

A twin-spired peak located ½ mile east-southeast of Mt. Carrie. First ascent 1961 by B. Brown, R. Etten, and V. Nelson.

Route. II, 3. From the summit of Mt. Carrie traverse E down the ridge to the saddle, then S onto the Fairchild Glacier. Cross the glacier and then climb a steep glacial finger about 500 ft. to the ridge crest W of the summit. Follow ledge systems on the S side of the W spire to rotten gully systems leading to the summit. Time: 3 hours up from summit of Mt. Carrie.

Stephen Peak   ca. 6430 (1959 m)

Located on the Hoh River-Long Creek divide 2 miles southeast of Ruth Peak. First recorded ascent 1961 by K. Heathershaw, D. Waali, and R. Wood.

Route. II, 2. From upper Cream Lake Basin, ascend steep heather to the ridge crest at the SE end of the massif. Contour W on snowfields below the ragged crest, and climb a narrow ridge to the summit at the NE end of the peak. Time: 4 hours up.

Stephen Peak has been traversed as part of a Bailey Range traverse, but the route is not recommended.

Mt. Ferry   6157 (1876 m)

Located 2 miles southeast of Cream Lake. Named by the Press Party for Elisha P. Ferry, Washington's first governor.

Route. II, 2. The approach can be made from Cream Lake Basin. Climb from the Mt. Ferry-Pulitzer pass (5800 ft.). The ascent is easy from either the S or E side. Time: 1 hour up from pass.

Ludden Peak   5828 (1776 m)

Located near the south end of the Long Creek-Elwha River divide.

Route. I, 2. From 2 miles up the Elwha River trail, follow the Long Ridge trail to Dodger Point (13.3 miles from Whiskey Bend). Next follow a way trail along the ridge SW, and climb to the summit. Time: 2 hours up from Dodger Point.

Mt. Scott   5913 (1802 m)

Located 1 mile south of Ludden Peak.

Route. I, 2. Follow the trail from Dodger Point approximately 2 miles to its

Mt. Pulitzer (Snagtooth) from southeast (Rich Olson)

end just E of Ludden Peak. Drop about 100 ft. to avoid the cliffs of Ludden's E face, and then climb on elk trails to the saddle between Ludden and Scott where a fine campsite exists. Final ascent is via the N ridge of Scott. Time: 5 hours up from Dodger Point.

Mt. Pulitzer (Snagtooth)   6283 (1915 m)
Located ½ mile southwest of Mt. Ferry. Named by the Press Party for Joseph Pulitzer, publisher of the *New York World*.

   Route. II, 3. From the Mt. Ferry-Pulitzer pass (5800 ft.), ascend the exposed E ridge over extremely splintered rock. Time: 1 hour up from pass.

The Ragamuffin and The Urchin   ca. 6000 (1828 m)
These pinnacles are located ½ mile northeast of Mt. Childs. First ascent 1961 by K. Heathershaw and D. Waali.

   Route. II, 3. Both pinnacles can be climbed on their N ridges. Time for each: ½ hour up from base.

Mt. Childs   6205 (1891 m)
Located 1½ miles northeast of Bear Pass, at the extreme south end of the Bailey Range. Named by the Press Party for George Washington Childs, publisher of the *Philadelphia Ledger*. First recorded ascent 1961 by K. Heathershaw, D. Waali, and R. Wood.

Route. II, 2. Traverse to the E side of the peak from Bear Pass and ascend talus to the summit. Time: 2 hours up from Bear Pass.

Poseidon   6100 (1859 m)
Located ½ mile west of Bear Pass.

Route. II, 3. From Bear Pass follow the ridge W and traverse on the N side to the summit. Time: 3 hours up from Bear Pass.

BOULDER CREEK AREA
The peaks in this area are easy scrambles and offer a fine view of beautiful alpine lakes and meadows.

Boulder Peak   ca. 5600 (1706 m)
A pyramidal peak on the Boulder Creek-North Fork Soleduck River divide, 3 miles west of Boulder Creek Campground.

Route. I, 1. Take the 3.4-mile trail from Boulder Creek Campground to Boulder Lake (4350 ft.) just NE of the peak. Skirt the lake on the E side. Follow game trails, then climb steep heather and rock up the E ridge to the summit. Time: 4 hours up from Boulder Creek Campground.

The summit may also be reached from the Aurora Ridge trail. From Boulder Lake follow the trail to where it intersects the N ridge of Boulder Peak (ca. ½ mile). Climb the steep, easy ridge S to the summit.

Everett Peak   ca. 6200 (1890 m)
Located about 1 mile SE of Boulder Peak.

Route. I, 1. From Boulder Lake, travel SE about 1 mile over a way trail to Three Horse Lake. From the inlet stream of lower Three Horse Lake, follow the creek upvalley (W) 200 yards. Turn uphill (S) and follow a faint way trail through avalanche debris and brush along the E side of the creek which drains the peak's NW slopes. This way trail leads to a small pass on the divide between Three Horse Lake and Blue Lake. Climb a short distance E to the easy, wooded summit. Time: 2 hours up from Boulder Lake.

Mt. Appleton   ca. 6000 (1828 m)
Located on the Boulder Creek-Soleduck River divide.

Route. I, 1. Follow the Boulder Creek Campground-Appleton Pass trail about 4 miles to where it crosses the South Fork of Boulder Creek. Leave the trail and climb W to a 5800-ft. saddle between Mt. Appleton and a slightly higher but unnamed peak to the S. Continue N to the summit. Time: 5 hours up from Boulder Creek Campground.

See description of Boulder Lake-Appleton Pass route under High Alpine Traverses section, page 234, for additional information on this area.

Peak 6100   ca. 6100 (1859 m)
Located about ½ mile S of Mt. Appleton.

Route. I, 1. From the saddle described in the Mt. Appleton approach, the summit can be reached directly. Time: 5½ hours up from Boulder Creek Campground.

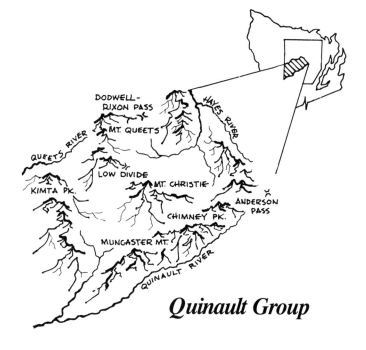

Quinault Group

Clustered around the headwaters of the Elwha River and bordered on the south by the Quinault River is a group of glaciated peaks culminating in the pinnacled summit of Mt. Meany. Two miles north lies the most accessible east-west route of the Olympics, Dodwell-Rixon Pass. While glaciers remain only on Mt. Queets, Mt. Noyes, Mt. Christie, and Mt. Taylor, permanent snowfields abound, some as low as 3500 ft. (Elwha Snow Finger). The lowest of the Olympic passes, the 3602-ft. Low Divide, separates the Elwha from the Quinault River drainage. This pass, crossed by the Press Party in 1890, was an early route for climbers. The ragged ridge of peaks crowded against the east fork of the Quinault River was called the Burke Range by the Press Party. Only one trail along Pyrites Creek, now abandoned, crosses its crest.

APPROACHES

1. *North Fork Quinault River.* This is the shortest approach for Mt. Christie and the Meany-Queets-Noyes Massif. It is also the primary approach for the peaks of Kimta, Lawson, and Zindorf.

The North Fork Quinault River road leaves U.S. 101 about 1 mile N of Amanda Park and extends 18.6 miles to the North Fork Quinault River Ranger Station and campground (500 ft.). The North Fork can also be

Mt. Meany from the north (Kent Heathershaw)

187

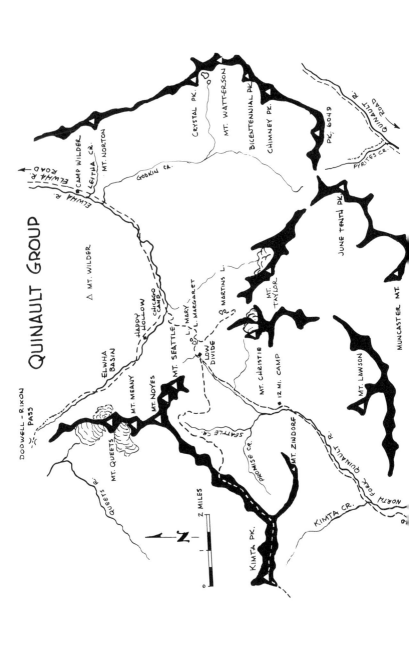

reached on a better road from the S side of Lake Quinault via a bridge 10.5 miles upriver from Quinault. The North Fork Quinault River trail continues 17 miles to Low Divide and drops 2.5 more miles to join the Elwha River trail at Chicago Camp. There are campsites at Trapper (8 miles, 1150 ft.), Twelve Mile (12 miles, 2000 ft.) and Renegade at Low Divide (17 miles, 3600 ft.). The Three Lakes-Skyline trail leaves the North Fork Quinault River road at North Fork Quinault campground and eventually rejoins the North Fork Quinault River trail near Low Divide. A camp is located at Three Lakes (6.6 miles, 3400 ft.).

2. *Quinault River.* This approach is used mainly to reach the Enchanted Valley peaks, including Crystal Peak, Chimney Peak, June 10th Peak, and Muncaster Mountain. Though long, it can also be used as a western approach for Mt. Anderson and environs (see Dosewallips Group, page 91). The Quinault River road leaves U.S. 101 ½ mile SE of Amanda Park near Lake Quinault. It passes along the S side of the lake, follows the S side of the river, and ends 18.6 miles from U.S. 101 at the Graves Creek Guard Station. The Quinault River trail continues 18 miles through the Enchanted Valley to join with the Dosewallips trail at Anderson Pass. The camps are Enchanted Valley Chalet (13.8 miles, 1975 ft.), and, a short distance E of Anderson Pass, a camp affectionately known as "Siberia."

3. *Elwha River.* This approach is gentle and can be used to reach most of the peaks of this group. It is the most practical approach for Mt. Norton, Mt. Dana, Mt. Barnes, and Mt. Wilder.

The Elwha River road leaves U.S. 101, 9 miles SW of Port Angeles, and follows the E side of the river upstream for 9.1 miles to the end of a spur road at Whiskey Bend. The Elwha River trail, starting at Whiskey Bend, extends 32 miles to Dodwell-Rixon Pass, the eastern approach to the Olympus Massif and the southern approach to the Bailey Range. Campsites are located at Mary Falls (8.8 miles, 1200 ft.), Canyon Camp (10.5 miles, 1400 ft.), Elkhorn (11.5 miles, 1500 ft.), Stony Point (11.7 miles, 1500 ft.), Camp Wilder (20.9 miles, 1900 ft.), and Happy Hollow (26.8 miles, 2400 ft.). A trail leaving at the Hayes River-Elwha River junction joins the Dosewallips River trail via Hayden Pass. The trail from Chicago Camp (25.8 miles, 2200 ft.) to Low Divide, joining the Elwha trail with the North Fork Quinault trail, is 2½ miles long and quite steep.

RANGER STATIONS

Quinault, South Shore (USFS); Quinault, North Shore (NPS). Guard Stations: North Fork (North Fork Quinault River), Graves Creek, Enchanted Valley (Quinault River); and Elwha, Elkhorn, Hayes River (Elwha River), and Low Divide. Note: Check with ranger regarding limits on size of party and use of campfires.

CAMPGROUNDS

Quinault River Road: Willaby, el. 200 ft. (2 miles E of U.S. 101); Falls Creek, el. 200 ft. (2½ miles); Graves Creek, el. 540 ft. (18.5 miles).

North Fork Road: July Creek, el. 200 ft. (3.5 miles E of U.S. 101); North Fork, el. 500 ft. (18.6 miles).

Elwha River Road: Elwha, el. 390 ft. (3 miles S of U.S. 101); Altaire, el. 450 ft. (4.1 miles).

MAPS

Olympic National Forest/Olympic National Park; USGS 30-minute Olympic National Park and Vicinity; the following 15-minute USGS and Green Trail quadrangles: Mt. Olympus, Mt. Angeles, Mt. Christie, and Mt. Steel; the following Custom Correct maps: Enchanted Valley-Skokomish, Elwha Valley, Mt. Olympus, and Quinault-Colonel Bob.

MT. NORTON   6319 (1926 m)

Located toward the north end of the ridge separating the Hayes River from the Elwha River, 2½ miles east of Camp Wilder. First recorded ascent 1947 by P. Cummins.

Route 1. I, 2. Leave the Elwha River trail ½ mile S of Camp Wilder after crossing Leitha Creek. Follow the ridge E about 2 miles to open meadows at about 5500 ft. Turn N to gain the ridge crest which is followed to the summit. Time: 4 hours up from Camp Wilder. The north side of Leitha Creek has also been used to gain the ridge.

Route 2. I, 2. Climb the wooded ridge paralleling the trail to Camp Wilder after leaving trail at Hayes River bridge and climbing Norton's ridge to a basin where camp may be made. From camp, climb the sharp ridge on the E side, then cross to the W side past several pinnacles to the summit.

CRYSTAL PEAK   6896 (2102 m)

Located on the Hayes River-Godkin Creek divide 2 miles west of West Peak (Anderson Massif).

Route 1. II, 2. Leave the Elwha River trail ½ mile S of Camp Wilder on the ridge crest immediately after crossing Leitha Creek. Follow the ridge E about 2 miles to open meadows at about 5500 ft. Follow elk trails SE along a series of lakes and a bench system about 3½ miles to Lower Crystal Lake (5700 ft.), where good campsites and wood are available. Climb a talus slope NE to a saddle, bypassing a waterfall that spills from Upper Crystal Lake, and traverse to the main ridge. The summit is reached by continuing N via the ridge or gully systems. Time: 2 hours up from Lower Crystal Lake.

Upper Crystal Lake has also been approached from Hayden Pass by

Enchanted Valley and East Fork Quinault River; Chimney Peak on right, Mt. Muncaster in center background (courtesy Olympic National Park)

traversing the W side of Sentinel Peak, then gaining the long ridge going S to West Peak. After passing Iceberg Lake and Peak 6608, drop 1500 ft. into the headwaters of Hayes River. Traverse SW, then climb through a 6300-ft. pass ½ mile S of Crystal Peak. Time: 12 hours up from Hayden Pass (see High Alpine Traverses, page 241).

Route 2. II, 3. From the saddle between Godkin Creek and West Fork of Anderson Creek (see Route 2, Chimney Peak), follow the ridge N by contouring the first peak of Mt. Watterson on the W side and the second peak on the E. Join Route 1 at Upper Crystal Lake. Time: 8 hours up from Enchanted Valley Chalet.

Route 3. II, 2. First ascent 1976 by G. Bauer, R. Brown, W. Foster, B. Larson, M. Lonac, S. Ritter, R. Teague, and J. White.

Follow Route 1 for Mt. Norton to the Upper Basin (5500 ft.), turn S and climb to a saddle between two small peaks. Follow the ridge crest to the summit. It will be necessary to bypass gendarmes by dropping to the W side.

The ridge crest is heavily corniced on the E side until late summer. Time: 7 hours up from basin on Mt. Norton.
Reference: August 1972 *Off Belay.*

MT. WATTERSON   6600 (2012 m)

Located 1 mile southeast of Crystal Peak. First ascent 1976 by G. Bauer, R. Brown, W. Foster, B. Larson, M. Lonac, S. Ritter, R. Teague, and J. White.

Route 1. II, 2. From Upper Crystal Lake, contour around the S rim of the lake and continue E several hundred yards past the lake. Turn S and climb a steep snowfield to a bench on the NW peak. Turn E and make a short scramble to the summit. Time: 1 hour up from Upper Crystal Lake.

Route 2. II, 2. Follow Route 2, Chimney Peak, to Godkin Creek-Anderson Creek saddle. Climb the ridge N to the summit. Time: 7 hours up from Enchanted Valley Chalet.

BICENTENNIAL PEAK   6722 (2049 m)

Located 1 mile northeast of Chimney Peak. Named in 1976 to honor the United States bicentennial. First ascent 1970 by M. Doherty.

Route 1. II, 3. From the summit of Chimney Peak, descend steep snow NE to a saddle. Climb over broken rock up the S ridge to the summit. Time: 1 hour up from Chimney Peak.

Route 2. II, 4. See Route 2 of Chimney Peak. Time: 9 hours up from Enchanted Valley Chalet.

CHIMNEY PEAK   6911 (2107 m)

Located on the ridge between Godkin Creek and Quinault River, 1½ miles north of Enchanted Valley Chalet. First known ascent 1941 by T. Nelson of USGS.

Route 1. II, 3. Locate the abandoned trail on the N edge of Pyrites Creek (9½ miles from road end on Quinault River trail). Follow this faint trail NW 1½ miles toward the head of a valley. Camp can be made at timberline on the easternmost tributary of Pyrites Creek, 4 hours from the Quinault River trail. Climb above timberline and cross through the 4900-ft. pass just E of Peak 6049. Drop about 1000 ft. to where an easy but long traverse can be made to the central snowfield of Chimney's SW face, staying below several rock ribs. Climb the 40° snowfield to gain the S ridge just below the summit, and continue to the top. Time: 6 hours up from camp.

A longer variation of this route cuts through the 5400-ft. pass W of Peak 6049, then down 2000 ft. to a Godkin Creek bivouac. Godkin Creek is then followed up via snow fingers to join Route 1 on the SW face. Time: 6 hours up from bivouac.

Route 2. II, 4. First known ascent 1962 by D. Pargeter and R. Pargeter.

From the Quinault River trail at the confluence of Anderson Creek and the Quinault River (16 miles from road end), cross the river and follow Anderson Creek 0.4 mile to where it branches out. Continue up the left branch, gaining 3500 ft. in 1.7 miles to the ridge overlooking Godkin Creek. Proceed S 0.2 mile to a small summit about 6300 ft. and continue S, traversing the ridge above steep, exposed snowslopes and rotten rock on the E side of the ridge for another 0.2 mile. After rounding several rock shoulders, the terrain eases to gentle snowslope. Contour SW below Bicentennial Peak for 0.7 mile, passing a small tarn with good water. Proceed SW to the summit via the snow of the N ridge. Time: 9 hours up from Enchanted Valley Chalet.
Reference: August 1972 *Off Belay.*

The Chimney, a prominent tower for which the peak is named, was first ascended in 1970 by M. Banner and V. Johnson. After a camp ½ mile SW of Peak 6049, proceed through a pass S of Peak 6049. Drop 1000 ft. and contour W side of ridge on Chimney Peak. A single 100-ft., Class 5.3 lead up the SE side of the rock tower completes the climb.

PEAK 6049   6049 (1844 m)

Located on the Godkin Creek-Quinault River divide, 1½ miles southwest of Chimney Peak.

Route 1. I, 3. From camp (Route 1, Chimney Peak), scramble up the false summits of the W ridge through sharp upthrusting shale and contorted fir and cedar trees to the top. Time: 2 hours up from camp.

Route 2. I, 4. First ascent 1979 by B. Larson, F. Ratliff, and J. White.

From camp (see Route 1, Chimney Peak), gain the SSE ridge. Stay on exposed crest to the summit block. Time: 4 hours up from camp.

PEAK 5750   5750 (1753 m)

Located approximately ½ mile west-northwest of Peak 6049. First recorded ascent 1981 by G. Bauer, M. Bauer, B. Larson, G. Larson, and F. Ratliff.

Route. I, 3. From 4850-ft. pass (see route on June 10th Peak), scramble ENE up the broad ridge to the false summit. Descend southerly and then climb rotten rock to the lofty NW summit. Time: 1 hour up from pass.

JUNE 10TH PEAK   6019 (1835 m)

Located about 1 mile southwest of the headwaters of Pyrites Creek, on the northwest side of Enchanted Valley. First ascent 1963 by J. Ansell, E. Fukushima, C. Howard, and R. McConnell.

Route. I, 2. From camp (Route 1, Chimney Peak), traverse on elk trails to just below the 4850-ft. pass at the head of Pyrites Creek. Continue around the head of Pyrites Creek to a 5300-ft. col and then ascend the NE ridge to the summit. Time: 3 hours up from camp.

MT. DELABARRE (MT. TAYLOR)   6024 (1836 m)

Located 2½ miles southeast of Martins Lakes. Named for W. R. Delabarre, a Port Angeles banker who financially assisted The Mountaineers' 1907 expedition into the Olympics.

Route 1. Follow the long ridge SE from Martins Lakes to the summit.

Route 2. II, 3. From a camp on the Godkin-Rustler Pass, traverse just above the trees on the SW side of the main ridge until the crest can be gained by slabby rock. Stay on the narrow ridge until a large snowfield on the NE side offers easier going. From the snow, ledges lead directly to the summit. Time: 4 hours up from Godkin-Rustler camp.

MUNCASTER MOUNTAIN   5910 (1801 m)

Located 2½ miles northwest of the O'Neil Creek-Quinault River junction. First known ascent 1941 by T. Nelson of USGS.

Route 1. II, 3. From 2 miles up the Quinault River trail (950 ft.), ascend the ridge on the E side of Fire Creek to Timberline (4700 ft.). Go past a 5624-ft. summit on its W side to a 5150-ft. notch in the ridge. Drop a few hundred ft. to the E side of an open basin and contour NW to regain the ridge at a 5000-ft. saddle SE of Mt. Muncaster. Traverse right to the NE face, and ascend the snowfield to the summit. Time: 8 hours up from trail.

Route 2. II, 4. First ascent 1969 by R. Becker and K. Heathershaw.
From the end of Pyrites Creek trail, contour past June 10th Peak on the N side to a camp ½ mile E of Muncaster on a fork of Rustler Creek. Gain the SE ridge and climb directly to the summit via ledges and a steep couloir. Time: 3 hours up from Rustler Creek camp.

MT. DANA   6209 (1893 m)

Located on the Elwha-Goldie River divide. First ascent 1928 by USGS.

Route 1. I, 2. From Happy Hollow Camp, 1 mile up the Elwha River from Chicago Camp, continue upriver on trail a few hundred yards to gain easier access to slopes leading N. Follow elk trails up a spur ridge 1 mile to the crest of the main ridge joining Mt. Barnes and Mt. Dana at a silver forest burn. The ridge loops around the headwaters of the Goldie River, with Mt. Wilder on a spur separating two forks. From this crest, follow the ridge NE via game trails past Mt. Wilder to the summit. Time: 5 hours up from camp.

Route 2. II, 2. First ascent 1968 by R. Tabor, D. Yeates, and R. Yeates of USGS.

Ford the Elwha River near the first flat N of Hayes River Guard Station, ascending the NE ridge to about 4500 ft. Traverse the N face W, staying below cliffs to a second basin. Climb W to the N ridge and follow it to the summit. Time: 6 hours up from Hayes River Guard Station.

MT. WILDER   5928 (1807 m)
Located 1 mile north of the headwaters of Goldie River.

Route. I, 2. From Happy Hollow Camp (see Mt. Dana, Route 1), gain the crest of the main ridge joining Mt. Barnes and Mt. Dana. Follow the ridge NE about 1 mile on game trails to the small, rounded summit. Time: 4 hours up from camp.

MT. BARNES   5993 (1827 m)
Located on the north side of the head of Elwha Basin.

Route 1. I, 2. Climb E from Dodwell-Rixon Pass 1 mile to the summit over easy rock and snow, or 1 mile SE from Bear Pass along the ridge crest. Time: 5 hours up from Happy Hollow Camp.

Route 2. I, 2. From Happy Hollow Camp (see Mt. Dana, Route 1) climb to the crest of the main ridge joining Mt. Barnes and Mt. Dana, coming out at a silver forest burn. Follow the ridge NW via a game trail 2½ miles to the summit. Time: 4 hours up from camp.

For a different route down, follow a spur ridge SW to the Elwha Snow Finger via elk trails which come out to the river opposite "The Big Snow Hump," bypassing Dodwell-Rixon Pass.

MT. QUEETS   6480 (1975 m)
Located between the Queets and Elwha basins. First ascent 1890 by H. Fisher and N. Linsley of the O'Neil expedition.

Route 1. II, 3. From the end of the maintained Elwha River trail 1½ miles above Happy Hollow Camp, cross the log over the river, then crash through brush to the grassy Elwha Basin. A way trail leads NW up an open basin (3400 ft.), then through bushes and trees down to the Elwha Snow Finger. Follow the snow finger for 1 mile to "The Big Snow Hump," a bulge caused by avalanches off Mt. Queets and Mt. Barnes.

In very dry years, the snow finger may not extend much past "The Hump" and an alternate route can be found on the NE side some 300 ft. up to avoid the deep ravine that the snow usually covers. For more details on the Dodwell-Rixon Pass route, see Queets Basin to Elwha Basin Traverse in the High Alpine Traverses section, page 238.

From the top of the hump, turn SW (left) and follow open chutes and polished rock to an upper bowl. The highest point is a squarish rock

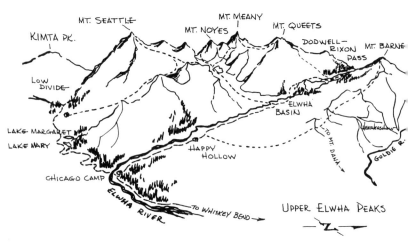

protruding from a rather flat summit snowfield. Time: 5 hours up from Happy Hollow Camp.

Route 2. II, 2. Ascend the Elwha Snow Finger to Dodwell-Rixon Pass and follow the ridge S to the summit. Time: 6 hours up from Happy Hollow Camp.

Route 3. II, 4. From Queets Basin, ascend the Queets Glacier to the summit. Time: 4 hours up from basin.

Route 4. II, 3. Traverse the narrow ridge from Mt. Meany. Time: 1 hour. Reference: August 1972 *Off Belay.*

MT. MEANY   6695 (2041 m)

Located between Mt. Queets and Mt. Noyes. Named for Edmund Meany, longtime president of The Mountaineers and a Professor of History at the University of Washington. First ascent 1907 by A. Curtis, L. Nelson, and P. McGregor.

Route 1. II, 3. From Elwha Basin, cross to Noyes Basin and ascend a gully leading to an upper bench and snowfield at the E base of Mt. Meany. Climb the snowfield to the summit block where a narrow chimney and ledge leads to

Mt. Queets and Queets Glacier from the west; Mt. Meany upper right
(courtesy Olympic National Park)

the broken-up top. The rock climbing is not as difficult as it first appears. Time: 4 hours up from Elwha Basin.

Route 2. II, 3. From Elwha Basin, ascend Noyes Basin to the Noyes-Meany col. Follow the ridge N to the E side of the summit block. Time: 4 hours up from Elwha Basin.

Route 3. II, 3. Traverse the narrow ridge from Mt. Queets. Time: 1 hour from Mt. Queets.
References: 1923 *Trail and Timberline;* 1907-08, 1913, 1920, 1926 *Mountaineer;* 1926 and 1928 *Mazama;* August 1972 *Off Belay.*

MT. NOYES   ca. 6100 (1859 m)
Located between Mt. Meany and Mt. Seattle. First ascent 1907 by A. Curtis and G. Humes.

Route 1. II, 2. Take the Skyline Trail from Low Divide, through Seattle Creek Basin to where the trail switchbacks down to the W (ca. 3 miles). Climb N to the notch in the ridge between Mt. Noyes and Mt. Seattle. Ascend a rotten unsound ridge left to the summit. Time: 4 hours up from Low Divide.

Route 2. II, 2. From Elwha Basin, climb S through Noyes Basin to the notch between Mt. Seattle and Mt. Noyes. Continue up the ridge to the right as in Route 1. Time: 3 hours up from Elwha Basin.

Route 3. II, 2. An easier approach is to turn right from well up the Noyes snowfield to a notch between Mt. Noyes and Mt. Meany. Climb left up the N ridge of Mt. Noyes. A rock scramble leads to the summit. Time: 3 hours up from Elwha Basin.
The rock pinnacle on the ridge between Mt. Seattle and Mt. Noyes is *Cougar Mountain* and involves a Class 3 rock scramble from either side or by either end.

MT. SEATTLE   6246 (1904 m)
Located on the south side of Elwha Basin, 1½ miles west of Low Divide. First ascent 1907 by A. Curtis, G. Humes, and L. Nelson.

Route 1. I, 2. From Elwha Basin, cross left into Noyes Basin. Gain the notch on the N ridge of Mt. Seattle via a brushy gully and snowfields. From the ridge, go around the exposed and rotten E side of the first peak to the S peak which is the higher. Time: 5 hours up from Elwha Basin.

Route 2. I, 2. From Low Divide Ranger Station, climb NNW along the E side of the creek that drains the eastern slopes of Mt. Seattle to a large snow basin. Climb a system of snowfields and rock benches westward to the ridge. The S peak is slightly higher. Time: 4 hours up from Low Divide.
The summit can also be reached via the Seattle Creek Basin, either up the

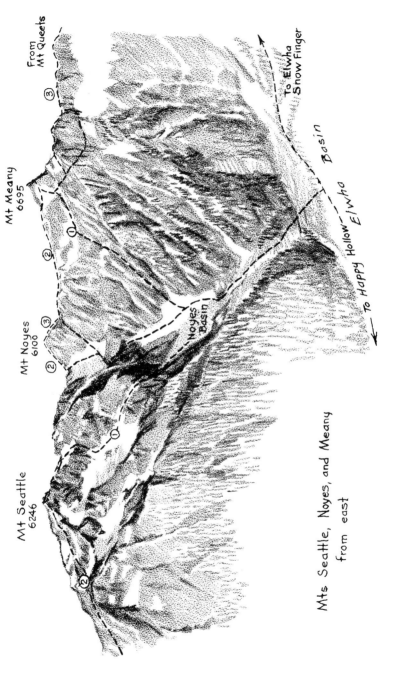

Mts Seattle, Noyes, and Meany
from east

Mt Seattle
6246

Mt Noyes
6100

Mt Meany
6695

From
Mt Queets

To Elwha
Snow Finger

Elwha Basin

To Happy Hollow

Noyes Basin

S ridge or by the Mt. Noyes-Mt. Seattle ridge.
References: 1907-08, 1920, and 1926 *Mountaineer.*

MT. CHRISTIE   6177 (1883 m)

Located 2 miles southeast of Low Divide. First ascent 1907 by A. Curtis and party.

Route 1. II, 3. Take the way trail from Lake Margaret through Martins Park to the head of the cirque where the trail doubles back to the left to Martins Lake. Cross the cirque and ascend the glacier on the NE side of the peak to the ridge crest. Follow the ridge westerly around the head of the Christie Glacier, which flows W to the North Fork Quinault River drainage. The highest point is on the SW side of the massif. Time: 5 hours up from Low Divide.

Route 2. II, 3. From two-thirds of the way up the glacier out of the cirque (see Route 1), turn right up a shallow gully to a saddle on the right of "Bottle Butte." This flat saddle has a USGS monument, with an arrow pointing to the summit across the Christie Glacier. Drop 75 ft. through a snow-finger notch to the large Christie Glacier. Cross the glacier on a near level traverse to a notch in the final ridge (SE) left of the summit. Time: 4 hours up from Low Divide.

Route 3. II, 3. From the lower end of Martins Park (1 mile from Lake Margaret), ascend a wide snow gully with giant boulders in the lower meadow. Continue S to the low point of the ridge that separates Martins Park from the Christie Glacier. Traverse and drop 150 ft. onto the glacier. Ascend S across the glacier to gain the final notch of Route 2. Time: 4 hours from Low Divide.

The rabbit ears at the head of the Christie Glacier are best climbed from their SE sides.

KIMTA PEAK   5399 (1646 m)

Located on the Queets-North Fork Quinault River divide at the head of Kimta Creek. The summit is just off the Skyline Trail 11 miles from Low Divide, or 16 miles from North Fork Quinault campground.

Route. I, 2. Leave the Skyline Trail at the head of Promise Creek, 2 miles E of Kimta Peak. Follow the easy E ridge until it turns jagged. Drop to scree and snowfields on the N side and traverse past the first summit to climb a shoulder to the second and highest summit. Time: 2 hours up from trail.

MT. ZINDORF   5539 (1688 m)

This large massif, prominently seen 4 miles to the southwest from Low

Delabarre Glacier and Mt. Delabarre from the north (courtesy Olympic National Park)

Divide, is located between Promise Creek and the North Fork Quinault River. It was named by the Press Party Expedition.

Route. I, 2. Leave the Skyline Trail at the head of Promise Creek 2 miles E of Kimta Peak. Follow the easy ridge E just less than 2 miles to the summit. The second of two peaks is the higher. Time: 7 hours up from Low Divide.

MT. LAWSON   5401 (1646 m)

Located on a spur between Geoduck Creek and Rustler Creek.

Route. I, 2. From ½ mile S of Geoduck Creek, cross the North Fork Quinault River and climb SE to parallel the N ridge. Gain the easy ridge and follow it S to the summit. Distance is 3 miles from Twelve Mile camp. Time: 3 hours up.

Wynoochee Group

In this southernmost portion of the Olympic Range, all the peaks are below 6000 ft. They are neither massive nor glaciated. Because they lie close to timberline, brushy approaches are common. However, road building in the national forest has shortened some approaches, making it possible to enjoy climbing some peaks heretofore virtually unknown.

With more than 12 feet of precipitation each year, this is one of the wettest regions in the United States. The main drainages are the north and south forks of the Skokomish River, which drains east into Hood Canal, and the Wynoochee and Quinault rivers, which drain south and west into the Pacific Ocean. Each river forms a broad, lush valley en route to the sea. Roads enter the interior along these valleys.

The peaks are generally listed in order of their approaches, beginning with those that can be reached from the North Fork Skokomish River.

APPROACHES

Some of the roads are passable in all weather, but most are slick when it rains and likely to be blocked by snow or downed trees in winter, when they are not patrolled.

Local inquiry should be made before entering during bad weather, and one should be on the lookout for soft spots, washouts, rocks, or downed trees on the road.

Mt. Church — telephoto from Wonder Mtn. (Paul Plevich)

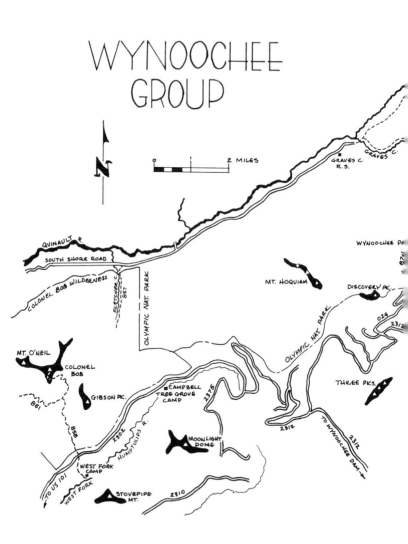

WYNOOCHEE GROUP

N

2 MILES

GRAVES C.

GRAVES C.
R.S.

QUINAULT R.

SOUTH SHORE ROAD

WYNOOCHEE PK

COLONEL BOB WILDERNESS

FLETCHER C. 887

OLYMPIC NAT. PARK

MT. HOQIAM

DISCOVERY PK.

OLYMPIC NAT. PARK

024

23/2

MT. O'NEIL

COLONEL
BOB

GIBSON PK.

CAMPBELL
TREE GROVE
CAMP

THREE PKS.

851

2375

858

2302

HUMPTULIPS R.

MOONLIGHT
DOME

2312

TO WYNOOCHEE DAM

2312

TO US 101

WEST FORK
CAMP

WEST FORK

STOVEPIPE
MT.

2310

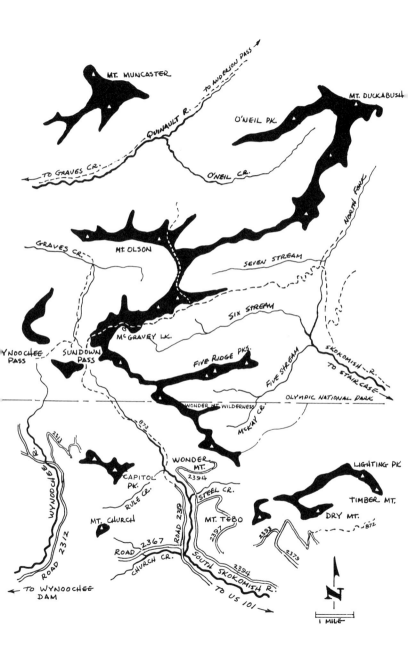

Note: Due to wildlife-area closures, Mt. Church, Capitol Peak, Wonder Mountain, Mt. Tebo, and their respective approaches are closed to auto traffic from October 1 through April 30.

1. **Skokomish River (North Fork).** See Skokomish-Duckabush Group, page 41, for approach details.

2. **Skokomish River (South Fork).** This approach is used principally to reach Mt. Tebo, Mt. Church, Capitol Peak, and other peaks in the eastern half of the group.

The South Fork Skokomish River road (which becomes Forest Service road #23) leaves U.S. 101 near the hook of Hood Canal at George Adams Salmon Hatchery. It follows upstream on the W side of the river, crosses the ridge to Spider Lake, and ends at Grisdale on the Wynoochee River. Branches and spurs lead into high country sites such as Dennie Ahl, Brown Creek, Rule Creek, Pine Lake, and Satsop Lakes. Most of the main and spur road intersections are well marked by Forest Service and Simpson Timber Company numbers, but it is important to have an up-to-date map before entering the area.

3. **Wynoochee River.** This approach can be used as the primary approach for Three Peaks, Discovery Peak, and Mt. Hoquiam. It also provides a second approach to Capitol Peak.

The Wynoochee Valley road (becomes Forest Service road #22) leaves U.S. 12 just W of Montesano where the freeway ends. It generally follows the river valley N about 36 miles, eventually reaching a junction with Forest Service roads #23 (South Fork Skokomish River road) and #2312. At this point road #22 turns left passing Wynoochee Dam in about 1 mile.

The main road (#2312) continues upstream passing along the SE side of Wynoochee Reservoir, past a junction with itself (6.4 miles), past Wynoochee Falls (8.7 miles), and finally to a junction with road #2313 (10.5 miles). From here, road #2312 crosses the river, climbs steeply, completely encircles Three Peaks, and eventually returns to the aforementioned junction.

Since logging operations in the area are now closed, many of the roads will eventually become hazardous to drive and impassable. It appears that road #2312 is being maintained.

4. **Humptulips River.** This approach is used primarily for access to Colonel Bob, Gibson Peak, Moonlight Dome, and environs.

The Donkey Creek road (becomes Forest Service road #22) leaves U.S. 101 3.6 miles N of the town of Humptulips. After 8.9 miles the national forest boundary and a junction with Forest Service road #2302 (West Fork Humptulips River road) is reached. Turn left onto #2302, immediately passing the Humptulips Guard Station, and continue to a junction with road #2310 and the end of the pavement (12.2 miles from U.S. 101).

Road #2310 crosses Humptulips Ridge S of Stovepipe Mountain and eventually ends in the headwaters of the East Fork Humptulips River.

From the end of the pavement, road #2302 drops to the high bridge and then continues up the W side of West Fork to the Pete's Creek trailhead (20.8 miles) and the Campbell Tree Grove campground (24.1 miles). It turns left at an intersection with road #2375 (27.7 miles) and finally ends high on the ridge north of the river.

Road #2375 climbs steeply around the head of the basin and continues about 4 miles to a point east of Moonlight Dome.

5. *Quinault River.* See Quinault Group, page 189, for approach details.

RANGER STATIONS

U.S. Forest Service ranger stations are located at Hoodsport (just off of U.S. 101) and Quinault (SE side of Lake Quinault off U.S. 101). National Park Service ranger stations are located at Hoodsport, Staircase (N end of Lake Cushman), Graves Creek (Quinault River, summer only), and Enchanted Valley (summer only).

CAMPGROUNDS

Lake Cushman-Staircase Road: Lake Cushman State Park, el. 750 ft. (7 miles W of Hoodsport); Staircase, el. 770 ft. (16 miles W of Hoodsport).

South Fork Skokomish River Road: Brown Creek, el. 600 ft. (15 miles NW of George Adams Salmon Hatchery); Church Creek, el. 900 ft. (20½ miles NW of George Adams Salmon Hatchery); Camp Harps, el. 900 ft. (21 miles NW of George Adams Salmon Hatchery).

Wynoochee Lake Area: Tenas (4 miles NE of Grisdale, Forest Service road #2312); Coho (2½ miles N of Grisdale, Forest Service road #2294); and Chetwoot (3 miles N of Grisdale, Forest Service road #2294).

Humptulips River Road: Campbell Tree Grove (15 miles N of Humptulips Guard Station, Forest Service road #2302).

VANTAGE POINTS

Dennie Ahl and Dusk Peak have roads to vantage points, as does a site at the end of Forest Service roads #2312 and 2313 in the upper Wynoochee Valley. There are several other roads in the LeBar, Brown Creek, Mt. Tebo, Spider Lake, Satsop Lake, and upper Wynoochee Valley which offer good view points.

MAPS

Olympic National Forest/Olympic National Park; USGS 30-minute Olympic National Park and Vicinity; the following 15-minute USGS and Green Trail quadrangles: The Brothers, Mt. Steel, Mt. Christie, Mt. Tebo, and Grisdale; the following Custom Correct maps: Enchanted Valley-Skokomish, Mt. Skokomish-Lake Cushman, and Quinault-Colonel Bob.

LIGHTNING PEAK   4654 (1419 m)

Located approximately 2 miles west of the north tip of Lake Cushman. The summit gives an excellent view of the Sawtooth Ridge and the Five Stream Peaks to the north and northwest respectively.

Route 1. I, 3. Turn left across bridge at upper end of Lake Cushman on road #2451. Drive 3 miles and park near switchback where road crosses Elk Creek. Climb S through brush and timber about ½ mile to an open meadow with a large rock. Follow the main stream, which enters the SW corner of the meadow, up a rocky gully to its source at timberline. Climb left (SW) to rocky summit beyond false summit. The USGS brass marker on the false summit is marked "Timber." Time: 4 hours up from road.

Route 2. I, 3. Follow Route 1 as far as the meadow. Turn left (E) and ascend a steep wooded ridge to its crest. Follow the ridge S to its termination at an avalanche bowl and slide alder. Climb a game trail up the basin to the ridge crest between the true summit and the false summit. Ascend the higher true summit. Time: 4 hours up from road.

An occasionally-climbed alternate route ascends a narrow precipitous rocky gully at the head of the meadow due S, continues W of the bowl mentioned in Route 2, and comes out on the N face of the false summit. In early season a cornice would have to be pierced to gain the false summit; this is not recommended.

All routes have potential avalanche hazard in season.

MT. OLSON   5289 (1613 m)

Located 2 miles northwest of the junction of the Six Ridge and McGravey Basin trails on the crest of Six Ridge.

Route. II, 3. From Staircase Ranger Station, follow the Skokomish River trail 5.6 miles upriver to Six Ridge trail. Climb this dry trail 5.6 miles to McGravey Lakes trail junction. Follow a dim trail W then N near Success Creek-Seven Streams divide, finally dropping into upper Lake Success Basin. When reaching the W side of Peak 5065, avoid tendency to drop excessively. The trail is on the N side 400 ft. above the basin floor. The faint trail leads to Lake Success (3 miles from McGravey junction). At saddles, avoid following game trails into Seven Stream drainage. From Lake Success, go 1 mile NW along the ridge to the E base of Olson. Scramble W to the summit. Time: 2 hours up from Lake Success.

Between Mt. Olson and Mt. Duckabush are many other summits, some above and some below timberline, such as Peaks 4960, 5289, and 5786 (Bumbershoot Peak). Above Belview Basin are Peaks 5065 and 5122. Between Sundown Pass and Snowfield Creek are Peaks 4986 and 4758. This latter highly serrated ridge runs roughly W to E, and the numerous pinnacles make the traverse to gain access to the Five Ridge Pinnacles difficult and slow going from this direction. They will therefore be dealt with from the South Fork Skokomish River even though they have been climbed from this side.

MT. TEBO   4604 (1404 m)

Located 7 miles northwest of Brown Creek Campground, South Fork Skokomish River road and at the head of Four Stream and LeBar Creek.

Route. I, 2. From U.S. 101 at the George Adams Salmon Hatchery, take the South Fork Skokomish River road, which becomes U.S. Forest Service road # 23, past Camp Govey to the Brown Creek bridge. Cross the bridge and follow road # 2325 to a junction with road # 2394. Turn left onto # 2394 and follow it to road # 2397. Take # 2397 1.8 miles. Leave the car here and climb NE on the timbered ridge to a small level basin at about 3600 ft. Bear directly E on steeper terrain, bypassing rocky outcroppings. Gain the SW ridge and follow it a short distance NE, passing a major rock gendarme on the right close to its base. From a small notch scramble to the summit. Time: 2 hours up from road.

An alternate route is from road # 2379, which branches from # 2300 and approaches the S and E sides of Mt. Tebo up LeBar Creek. This route is steeper with more brush and rock outcroppings.

WONDER MOUNTAIN   4758 (1451 m)

A broad northwest-southeast trending ridge of wooded slopes and pinnacles located approximately 10 miles northwest of the Brown Creek campground, near the head of McKay Creek. (A summit register was placed in 1976 by the Olympia Mountaineers.)

Route 1. I, 3. Follow road # 2394 to the last switchback (ca. 7.5 miles from junction with road # 2325) and park here. Traverse E through clearcut to a stream and follow it up (over rocky shelves and through brush) NW to open meadows with goat trails, about 300 ft. from the summit block. Climb through meadow to a rocky gully to the summit. Time: 3 hours up from road.

Route 2. I, 3. Follow road # 2394 to its end, about 8 miles beyond its junction with road # 2325. Leave the car here and climb NNW through wooded slopes (sometimes steep) for about 45 minutes to the two western-most pinnacles of the Wonder Mountain Ridge. This route is essentially a ridge traverse, climbing each pinnacle in turn until the summit is reached at the SE end of the ridge. The summit is reached via a scramble from the SW side of the summit block. Time: 5-6 hours up from road. Descent via Route 1. Route finding on this route is an interesting challenge.

FIVE RIDGE PEAKS   5077 (1548 m)

Picturesque pinnacles on a spur ridge between Six Stream and Five Stream to the east and Sundown Pass and Wonder Mountain just within the southern boundary of Olympic National Park. There is a group of alpine lakes at their southern base.

Peak 5077   5077 (1548 m)

The highest peak in the group. First recorded ascent 1973 by K. Johnson and H. Weaver via Route 1.

Route 1. II, 4. Via an approach from Camp Belview. From between Sundown Pass and Six Ridge, traverse easterly as high as possible to avoid brush, but not on the ridge crest, which is very jagged. The faces are high angle on the S and E sides. The route involves dropping through an obvious notch to the S side and following a small gully system to the top. Time: 5 days from roadhead.

Route 2. I, 4. The second ascent, using this route, was made by E. Parolini and G. Sinrud in 1974 from the South Fork Skokomish River side via the lakes at the park boundary.

Take U.S. Forest Service road #23 to its junction with road #2319. Turn right onto road #2319 and follow it to its end (about 5 miles). Take trail #873 upriver about 1½ miles, then climb the steep wooded slope bearing 35° true north to a notch on the skyline ridge to the left of Peak 4666. Drop to the lake (Wonder #1) on the S edge of the park boundary via a steep talus slope or an existing game trail. A comfortable campsite can be found at this lake. Traverse the bench northward and drop to the neck between the two larger lakes at the base of Five Ridge Peaks. Ascend a narrow gully system to the ridge crest just W of the highest peak. Time: 2 days from roadhead.

On the ridge are several pinnacles over 5000 ft. that involve dropping some distance on the N side and reclimbing to the tops.

Peak 4851   4851 (1479 m)

The highest point on the main ridge between Sundown Pass and Wonder Mountain, located immediately south of the headwaters of Snowfield Creek-Five Stream divide. First ascent 1972 by C. Arnold, B. Craswell, and G. Kelsey.

Route. I, 3. From the upper lake known as Wonder #1 just outside the S boundary of the park (see Peak 5077 approach) ascend to the ridge crest just N of an earthslide area. Continue along this ridge NW to the peak, with a rock scramble to the summit. Time: 2 hours up from Wonder #1 Lake.

MT. CHURCH   4770 (1454 m)

Located 2 miles west of South Fork Skokomish River at the head of Rule Creek and the North Fork of Church Creek. Mt. Church is 1½ miles due east of Wynoochee Falls on the Wynoochee River road. First ascent 1955 by Carlson and Coulter, of Aberdeen.

Route. I, 3. Take Forest Service road #23 from U.S. 101 past Camp Govey. Turn right onto #2319 and follow it to ½ mile N of Church Creek Bridge where #2367 turns left (W) up the N side of Church Creek. Proceed on road #2367 to a spur road (#2368) that leads off the main road to the right. Follow road #2368 to the base of Mt. Church and a logged area. Leave car here (ca. 5 miles from road #2319) and climb a steep uncut area northward on the left-hand side of an avalanche gully to timberline, slightly below the ridge crest. Cross the main avalanche gully and ascend to the SE ridge of Mt. Church, which is followed NW to the rocky summit. Time: 3½ hours up from car.

CAPITOL PEAK   5054 (1541 m)
Located 2½ miles northwest from the end of road #2319 at the headwaters of Startup Creek, which drains to the South Fork Skokomish River, and Schofield Creek, which drains into Wynoochee Valley.

Capitol Peak from its north slope (Kent Heathershaw)

Route 1. II, 3. Take road #23 and #2319 to the termination of #2319. Follow trail #873 (Sundown Pass trail) upstream (N) about 2 miles. This trail crosses the river to the right (E) bank at Rule Creek and returns to the W bank at a fisherman's camp close to Startup Creek. At the second crossing leave the trail and follow a small tributary SW up a steep hillside for 2 hours. To surmount a steep rock and brushy wall, follow a rocky waterfall of the tributary. After another 2 hours of more gentle slopes of vine maple and alder, a large snow basin opens up. Ascend the snow basin to directly below the summit. Climb a steep, rocky chute left of the summit to gain the crest of the S ridge. Follow the S ridge N to an exposed summit. Time: 6 hours up from trail.

Route 2. I, 3. From the roads #2312-2313 junction, follow road #2313 to Copper Creek Pass (just NW of Peak 4965, which lies on the W end of Capitol Ridge). Climb SE up the steep timbered slopes of Peak 4965. From the summit, descend 150 ft. SE to the ridge and follow it about ½ mile to the S side of Capitol Peak. Ascend the brushy gully to the summit block. Time: 5 hours up from Copper Creek Pass.

Route 3. I, 4. From the roads #2312-2313 junction, follow road #2313 to spur road #012. Follow #012 to its end at about 3100 ft. and then traverse southeasterly under the SW side of Capitol Ridge to the main gully, which is the source of Schofield Creek. Climb in the bottom edge of this gully to a notch in the ridge S of the summit. Join Route 1 to the summit. The route is circuitous and brushy. Time: 6 hours up from parking area.

THREE PEAKS   4646 (1417 m)

Located between the Wynoochee River and the North Fork West Branch Wynoochee River. It is 2½ miles west-southwest of Capitol Peak.

Route. I, 2. From the roads #2312-2313 junction (NE side of Peak) follow road #2312 across the bridge and 4.6 miles to the NW side of the peak. Leave the road at about 3300 ft. where it turns sharply right (NW). At this point a creek flows down from an upper valley and the road is still climbing slightly. Prior to June 1 this road will be snowbound not too far above the junction.

Climb southeasterly through the timber, aiming at a point between barely visible cliffs of the middle and S (highest) peaks. After 30 minutes, a boulder-strewn meadow is reached and the upper cliffs can be clearly seen. Stay between the two sets of cliffs, but keep to the right of the obvious vine maple-slide alder slopes. Above the slide alder, the slope steepens and the best path bears slightly right. Climb to the low point in the ridge and then turn right (southerly) toward the S summit. After about ¼ mile of scrambling, keeping mostly to the E side of the ridge, the easy summit is reached. Time: 2-3 hours up from car.

The lower and slightly more difficult (Class 3) middle peak is climbed by turning left at the ridge crest and climbing about 200 yards to the rocky summit.

DISCOVERY PEAK   4837 (1474 m)

Located near the headwaters of the Wynoochee River and approximately 3½ miles west-northwest of Capitol Peak.

Route. I, 2. From the roads # 2312-024 junction, take road # 024 as far as it is open. (As of 1987 it is closed by rockfall after 1½ miles; ⅓ mile before trail # 874 starting point.) Proceed to the trail start (trail # 874 to Wynoochee Pass) and then follow the switchback road left for about ¾ mile to the second switchback. From this point, either climb northerly straight up the mountainside or continue on the road another ½ mile to its end near the NE ridge. Climb to the ridge and then follow it SW to meadows below the summit and a junction with the other route. The first route is more direct; the latter is less arduous. From the meadows, climb to the rocky summit. Time: 2-3 hours up from road.

MT. HOQUIAM   4909 (1496 m)

Named after the city of Hoquiam, this sharp summit is located approximately 1½ miles west-northwest of Discovery Peak. It lies on a spur ridge about a mile north of the ridge that forms the national park boundary.

Route. II, 3. Follow the route for Discovery Peak until reaching the meadows on the S side at about the 4300-ft. level. Contour westerly around the peak to the ridge forming the national park boundary. Proceed southwesterly along this ridge in mostly meadow to a spur ridge (ca. 1½ miles) leading northwesterly. Follow the rocky and broken spur past several small peaks for about 1 mile to Hoquiam's base. The final ascent is a semi-serious climb. Time: 8 hours up from road.

Camp could be placed near the ridge just W of Discovery Peak. Also, as an alternate approach, the peak could probably be reached from road # 2312 at the Chickamin Creek-West Fork Branch Wynoochee divide.

MOONLIGHT DOME   4122 (1256 m)

Located toward the north end of Humptulips Ridge between the west and east forks of the Humptulips River.

Route. I, 3. From the roads # 2302-2375 junction, proceed on road # 2375 for about 3 miles until it crosses the ridge crest (3200 ft.) about 1¼ miles ESE of Moonlight Dome. In early season, the road will likely be snow covered soon after the junction. Leave the road at the pass and climb WNW up the wooded ridge which becomes quite steep. Proceed past Point 3685, following the line of least difficulty, to the rocky but partially tree-covered summit. Time: 3 hours up from road.

This peak can also be climbed from the S after an approach via road #2310. This route, a climb up the steep, brushy mountainside, is much longer.

THE COLONEL BOB PEAKS   4492 (1369 m)

This pleasant area lies 4 to 5 miles east of Lake Quinault. Though low in elevation, the peaks start near sea level and offer a good day's work and a fine view.

The best approach is via the West Fork Humptulips River, using the steep but interesting Upper Pete's Creek trail (#858) for access. The area can also be reached from Lake Quinault via the Colonel Bob trail. This trail leaves the South Shore Quinault road about 6 miles from U.S. 101 and is a much longer approach.

Colonel Bob   4492 (1369 m)

Located on the ridge between the Quinault River and the West Fork Humptulips River approximately 4½ miles east of Lake Quinault. The peak was originally named after John McCalla, an early settler in the Quinault area, and later renamed for Colonel Robert Ingersol.

Route. I, 1. Leave road #2302 and follow the steep but enjoyable Pete's Creek trail 2.4 miles to a junction with the Colonel Bob trail. Follow the Colonel Bob trail about ½ mile to the ridge crest which overlooks Fletcher Creek (3600 ft.). The trail now descends left to Moonshine Flats where camp can be located if desired. Continue northwesterly, climbing through upper Fletcher Creek toward the peak. After about ½ mile, the trail climbs to Colonel Bob's ridge, descends a bit westerly, and then climbs to a point near the Mt. O'Neil-Colonel Bob ridge crest. From here the trail switches E toward the summit. The last few feet of the climb are stair steps hacked out of the rock. Time: 4 hours up from road #2302.

Mike's Spike   ca. 4200 (1280 m)

This impressive spire is located midway along the ridge connecting Colonel Bob and Mt. O'Neil. First ascent middle 1970s by M. Lonac.

Route. I, 4. Where the Colonel Bob trail reaches the ridge crest and switches back easterly to Colonel Bob's summit, leave the trail and follow the ridge westerly. The summit can be reached via one long lead. Time: 5 hours up from road #2302.

Mt. O'Neil   4289 (1307 m)

The prominent rock dome overlooking Lake Quinault and located about ½ mile west of Colonel Bob.

Route 1. I, 3. Where the Colonel Bob trail reaches the ridge crest and switches back easterly to Colonel Bob's summit, leave the trail and follow the ridge westerly. Bypass several rock promontories, including Mike's Spike, following the path of least difficulty (usually on the S side) to the summit. Time: 5 hours up from road #2302.

Route 2. I, 3. Where the Colonel Bob trail crosses Zeigler Creek at about 1900 ft., ascend northerly to the 3600-ft. bench W of the summit. Follow the ridge until it becomes broken and then rappel to the SE. Next, traverse to gullies leading to the NE ridge and then scramble to the summit. Time: 6 hours up from the road.

Gibson Peak 4390 (1338 m)

Located between Fletcher Creek and the West Fork Humptulips River and 1½ miles southeast of Colonel Bob. Gibson Peak is identified on the USGS Grisdale quadrangle as the southernmost high point on the Gibson Ridge. Several of the more northerly points are slightly higher.

Route. I, 2. Leave road #2302 and follow the steep but enjoyable Pete's Creek trail 2.4 miles to a junction with the Colonel Bob trail. Follow the Colonel Bob trail about ¼ mile to the edge of a large talus slope. At this point the Colonel Bob trail turns back into the trees and climbs northwesterly toward Colonel Bob. Make an ascending traverse up the talus (or snow) in an ESE direction, keeping below the cliffs. At a convenient point gain the ridge and continue southeasterly to the rocky S summit. Time: 4 hours up from road #2302.

WINTER TRAVEL

The Olympic Mountains, primarily because of their location, provide a unique and challenging winter experience. In winter, the range is influenced greatly by both the warm, wet prevailing winds off the Pacific Ocean and the arctic air masses which periodically drive south out of northern Canada into the area. This can create wide fluctuations in both temperature and precipitation, with weather and snow conditions varying greatly from day to day and from year to year. The situation is further complicated because precipitation on the wet west side is several times greater than on the relatively dry eastern slope (those portions of the range lying in the rain shadow).

The following snow-depth chart shows some of the diversity one can expect in the Olympics during winter, both on a year-to-year basis and in different areas. The Cox Valley data approximates average Olympic snowfall. The Deer Park data more closely represents the dry northeast corner. Records are not available for the wet west side, but the snowfall on the west side of Mt. Olympus is several times greater than that shown for Cox Valley. The chart provides several other interesting bits of information: 1) snow depth varies greatly from year to year, 2) snowfall appears cyclic, with precipitation in the early to middle seventies much greater than later, and 3) snowfall highs and lows do not always correlate between the two areas.

During one of the infrequent dry years, winter travel may be only a little more arduous than normal spring travel. At the other extreme, Olympic winter travel may turn into a struggle of epic proportions. Hope for the best, but prepare for the worst. The physical condition and experience of the party should be major criteria when selecting a winter trip. If in doubt about party strength, select a less vigorous option. It is also advisable to check road approaches and conditions in the high country with a local ranger before selecting your trip. During some years (periods) roads may be open nearly to the trailhead. Under worst-case conditions, road approaches may be closed to nearly sea level. Note that several feet of snow can fall in a very short period of time, and a car may be snowed in at the trailhead just overnight. Take along an ax, shovel, and tow rope to cover any eventuality. Also make certain that those at home know exactly where you are going.

East face of Mt. Angeles in winter (Rich Olson)

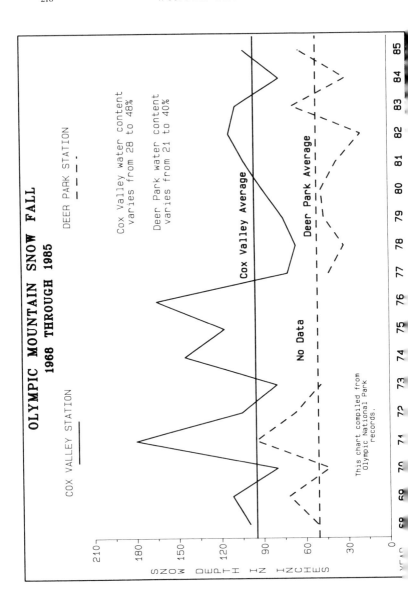

Snowshoes or skis are usually necessary for winter travel into the high country. Route-finding skill and the ability to use a map and compass are extremely important for safe travel during the normal fog- and snow-shrouded winters. Be prepared for both cold and wet conditions; keeping dry is normally a greater problem than keeping warm. Accordingly, double wrap all clothing and sleeping equipment. Since your return could easily be delayed, take extra food, fuel, batteries, and fire starter. If traveling in avalanche country, each party member should have an avalanche transceiver. A suitable radio is another safety device that may become very useful.

History

After the Herculean Olympic crossing by the Press Party during the winter of 1889-1890, the range remained relatively free of winter activity for many years. While a few trappers, miners, and mountain men plied their trade along the edges of the uplift, there was little winter recreational usage or travel until about 1920. This is not surprising, for in those days people were busy just surviving and most were content to sit in their snug houses during the winter. Also, the range was isolated and transportation from the metropolitan areas was a real problem. In addition, the wet and nasty weather, which produces great snowfall, and the long snowbound approaches, leading to generally steep and forested terrain, discouraged all but the most hardy. In truth, the Olympics have never been viewed as a mecca of winter recreation.

Interest in the range for winter use began to pick up in the twenties as groups from The Mountaineers started visiting the area. In 1926, a party consisting of R. Barto, S. Eskanazi, W. Faurot, W. Hoffman, and J. McClellan skied up the south fork of Tunnel Creek, crossed the ridge, and descended into the Dosewallips River valley. A little later, parties which included S. Eskanazi, S. Hall, W. Hoffman, and D. Watson reached both Cat Basin and Seven Lakes Basin. By 1940, groups representing The Mountaineers had penetrated into much of the range, with most of the activity focused on the east and north sides of the range.

By 1930, other groups recognized the area's considerable appeal. The Olympians (an Aberdeen group) could be found touring in the Wynoochee and Quinault areas. While the Enchanted Valley Chalet was built in 1930, there is no evidence that it had significant winter usage.

Meanwhile, the Bremerton Ski Cruisers built a small lodge at Flapjack Lakes and for a number of years spent weekends touring there and in the adjoining Skokomish River area. On the north side of the Olympics, the Klahhane Club (Port Angeles) and later the Olympic Club (a northside ski club) began visiting the Hurricane Ridge and Blue Mountain areas. The high-level tour between Blue Mountain (Deer Park) and Hurricane Ridge was even then considered spectacular. For a period the Olympic Club was quite active and actually engaged in some ski mountaineering. Some of the more active participants included E. Berg, J. Hillyer, W. Hoffman, and D. Watson. Mt. Angeles was probably the first real winter ascent in the Olympics.

The first ski lift, a single rope tow, was built at Deer Park near the summit of Blue Mountain shortly after World War II. It served the Port Angeles area and the Kitsap Peninsula for a number of years until moved to Hurricane Ridge, where it still operates in the only formal ski area on the Olympic Peninsula.

From what is known, interest in serious winter mountaineering first appeared in the thirties. Aside from the Mt. Angeles area, the first winter climbing took place in the southeast corner of the range, where peaks including Washington, Ellinor, Rose, and probably Copper Mountain were climbed. After the war, a group of Bremerton climbers repeated many of these climbs and made attempts on a number of other eastside peaks. It is still fashionable to attempt Mt. Washington on Washington's Birthday; these attempts have usually failed, but several were successful. By 1960, Mt. Washington had been climbed in every month of the year.

While Mt. Olympus was long regarded as a worthy winter objective, there is little evidence that any serious attempts were made prior to World War II. The first recorded attempt took place in 1947 when J. Hieb, P. Schoening, and R. Widrig labored valiantly up the Hoh and reached Elk Lake in a gathering storm. Several later attempts were also unsuccessful, although a 1950 party consisting of C. Allyn and the Schoening brothers got within about 30 feet of the summit. Several feet of rotten rime ice thwarted the party on the final pitch. During the winter of 1957-1958, a party consisting of Y. Erikson, N. Gardner, J. Harkness, E. LaChapelle, and R. Ross wintered on the Snow Dome in conjunction with the International Geophysical Year (IGY). The group did a considerable amount of ski mountaineering and climbed several of the lesser summits in the Olympus area, but not the main peak of Olympus. In all likelihood, Olympus has now been climbed. Unfortunately, there is no record.

In 1964 F. Becky and P. Callis took advantage of a cold, dry winter to make the first winter ascent of Mt. Constance. Several other summits in the Constance massif fell to parties which included R. LaBelle and M. Martin during the 1970-1975 period.

A number of winter ascents of major summits have taken place in recent years. The first known winter ascent of Mt. Deception was accomplished by J. Olson and K. Pearce in 1976. Mt. Mystery (1985), Mt. Anderson (1986), and West Peak (1986) were climbed by parties led by D. Goodman. The other participants, in one or more of these climbs included D. Adams, M. Bebie, M. Bialos, D. Fenstermaker, G. Jones, J. Mason, A. Olson, and N. Reyburn. West Peak, a nasty task under summer conditions, was no small feat.

If readers have factual information on either early-day winter activity or news of significant winter climbs, this data should be relayed to Olympic Mountain Rescue (OMR). However, OMR does not plan on publishing a detailed winter chronology and will be limiting publication of ascent credits to the initial ascent of the major peaks.

Winter Mountaineering

Interest in winter mountaineering has increased significantly in recent years. The normal winter climbing season is December through March. Because of fluctuating winter temperatures, influenced by the offshore flow of warm and moisture-laden air from the nearby Pacific, the freezing level may vary from as low as 2000 to as high as 6000 feet. This moderate weather contributes an abundance of mixed rain and snow. The climber's foremost problem is staying dry. Spare clothing, a necessity, should be double-wrapped in plastic or otherwise protected.

Avalanches are the greatest hazards in this range in the winter. Olympic snowfalls have high water content, even without occasional rainfall, and the combination increases the potential danger. Narrow ridges, heavily corniced, discourage passage, so the winter traveler is forced into the gullies and couloirs, in which he must exercise extreme caution. Some narrow valleys are the scenes of tremendous avalanche activity; the slopes of two opposing mountains can add their shares to the destruction below. However, the peaks tend to unload their burdens in the first day of sunshine following a storm, and the climber can then proceed with the same care that is usually exercised in spring climbing. It is recommended that each party member carry an avalanche transceiver.

Heavy snowfall makes the approaches to most summits inordinately long in most years. The winter climber may find the entire weekend spent snowshoeing or skiing over dreary miles of logging roads. In some areas, the use of snowmobiles may bring Olympic summits within reach, but users should carry emergency gear in case of mechanical breakdown. Snowslide areas, compacted and icy, present tricky traverses for the snowmobile. Road and snow conditions may change quickly, so be prepared for a hasty retreat, particularly if your car is in danger of being snowed in. Remember that both travel time and objective danger increase dramatically under bad or deteriorating conditions.

A listing of winter climbs that are both feasible and enjoyable under proper conditions follows:

Mt. Angeles, Routes 1 and 2. The easiest peak to approach, since the Hurricane Ridge road is kept open during the holiday season and on weekends through April 1. Snowshoes or skis should be taken for the easy one-day ascent.

Mt. Ellinor, Route 1. The Big Creek logging road, with its southern exposure, makes this peak and Mt. Washington approachable most of the time. Conditions permitting, an overnight camp at the head of the Ellinor chute, with a traverse to Mt. Washington, provides an interesting weekend.

Mt. Washington, Route 1. Always a good climb, but the avalanche hazard in Big Creek snow basin is ever-present. Many climbers try its slopes on Washington's Birthday.

Copper Mountain. Though a long one-day trip, under good conditions, the views from this minor summit make the ascent worthwhile. Be careful of the cornice at the saddle.

Mt. Pershing, Route 3. The blanket of snow eliminates the brush found on the approach in the summer. The valley between Pershing and Washington should be avoided during avalanche conditions.

Mt. Thorson, Route 1. The climb provides for a very interesting ridge traverse from the easy summit to the main peak.

Mt. Lincoln, Route 1. Minimum avalanche hazard will be encountered under normal conditions.

Mt. Stone, Route 1. If road and snow conditions allow, this peak can be climbed in one long day.

Mt. Skokomish, Route 1. Beautiful, but notorious for avalanches. The many false summits cause frustration in foggy conditions.

The Brothers, Route 1. Avalanche conditions must be considered up the long, steep gully on this strenuous trip.

Warrior Peak. This is a beautiful climb, but the approaches are usually very long because of snowbound roads.

Tyler Peak. A one-day climb if road and snow conditions allow. The peak presents little avalanche hazard and a splendid view.

Mt. Townsend. A good one-day climb if snowmobiles are available for the logging road approach. The view is magnificent.

Mt. Walkinshaw. This scenic climb in the northern Needles is feasible only if the road is open.

Ski and Snowshoe Tours

This section contains brief route descriptions of the better snow tours available in the Olympic Range. The best season for these is typically December through April or May.

Winter in the high Olympics (Frank Chapin)

Much of the Olympic Range is not ideal for oversnow travel. The snowline is variable and often quite high in elevation. Steep and heavily timbered slopes extend far up most peaks, and upper basins are mostly deep within the range. Many of the high ridges are steep and therefore difficult to travel along for extended distances. Winter weather is a prime consideration with its potential for severe storm and avalanche. Despite possible difficulties and hazards, however, there are some very fine tours, and frequent periods of good weather and snow conditions.

Proper timing is extremely important for maximum success and safety on these tours. Both weather and snow conditions must be good. Be clothed and otherwise prepared for winter conditions, but pack light enough for reasonably fast travel.

Moderate temperatures and steep slopes generally combine to make avalanche hazard in the Olympics more predictable than in colder ranges. Most avalanches occur during or soon after storms, and during sudden or extreme warming periods. High wind with drifting snow can also be dangerous. After a few days of good weather, the snow usually compacts, and skiing is possible again in the former avalanche area.

As in all mountaineering ventures, it is wise to start with easy trips and work up to longer and more difficult ones as knowledge, skill, and strength increase. Most Olympic tours cover steep terrain where snowshoeing and skiing are quite difficult. Few trips offer sustained downhill skiing. For these reasons, equipment is best chosen for traversing steep slopes, not for "schussing." Most of the trips described here have been done on wood Nordic touring skis.

Many of the following tours are approached via secondary or logging roads which are neither patrolled nor plowed in winter. Depending on the elevation of the snowline, upper portions of these roads may be impassable to automobiles for extended periods. In most cases the added distance of a road slog does not put the tour objective entirely out of reach; however, those who wish to avoid the extra oversnow travel should make local inquiry about road conditions before embarking on a particular trip. Remember also that a sudden snowstorm can trap a car until spring.

HURRICANE RIDGE AREA

Several good tours start from this area, which is exceptionally scenic during good weather conditions. Owing to easy access, this is an excellent area to try out equipment and to get the feel of winter travel in these mountains.

A good paved road leaves U.S. 101 at Port Angeles and climbs south 17 miles to 5000-ft. Hurricane Ridge. This is the only place in the Olympics where a road is maintained into the alpine zone in winter. A day lodge and a small ski area are located here. Weather permitting, the road is open during the day each weekend during the winter season. On weekdays it is open when the weather is good and no extra plowing is required. Blizzard conditions occasionally force closure of the road on scheduled open days.

Cars cannot be parked overnight at the visitor center. Overnight parking is allowed in a parking area several miles below the center. The road closes each night, so register in person with rangers for any trip requiring a late return. Use the self-register at the lodge for short trips.

Recommended Maps: Mt. Angeles and Mt. Olympus USGS 15-minute quadrangles; Hurricane Ridge & Vicinity, Elwha Valley, and Gray Wolf-Dosewallips Custom Correct Maps.

Hurricane Hill

This short and enjoyable tour is an excellent way to start Olympic touring. Distance from the parking lot to the summit is about 3 miles, with an elevation gain of about 1000 ft. Under good conditions this is an easy half-day trip.

Start at the W end of the parking lot and follow the snow-covered road for about 1½ miles. The last 1½ miles are via trail along the S side of the ridge. When the snow is stable, an alternate route can be taken through the scenic valley N of the ridge for the last mile. Avoid cornices hanging off the N side of the ridge. There is good downhill skiing from the summit of Hurricane Hill and in basins and on slopes in the area.

Hurricane Ridge to Deer Park via Obstruction Point

This rewarding trip, primarily an above-timberline ridge run, has been done in a single day by strong skiers, but 2 days are recommended. The basic trip to Obstruction Point and return can be done in a full day. It is 8 miles to Obstruction Point, 8 miles farther along the ridge to Deer Park, and an additional 3 to 9 miles down the Deer Park road to the snow line. This route is very exposed to storms. Before starting out, check with ranger regarding conditions.

An unplowed road leaves the E end of the Hurricane Ridge parking area and continues along the ridge easterly for about 8 miles to Obstruction Point. To avoid bad sidehill at the start, leave the plowed main road about ½ mile below the parking lot. Drop down a moderate meadow slope to the Obstruction Point road. Portions of this road are hard to follow in deep drifts. The first 4 miles are moderate to easy in subalpine trees. The ridge then climbs 1000 ft. in elevation to Eagle Point. From Eagle Point to Obstruction Point, the route follows tundralike meadow at about 6000 ft. Except for a little ankle-tiring sidehill, this section is moderately easy. Under most conditions, avalanche hazard is minimal if you stay on the S slopes.

At Obstruction Point, further progress is blocked by the steep, narrow feature that gave the place its name. Passage past this point to Deer Park is recommended only under stable snow conditions. The route of the trail can be followed, but it traverses very steep sidehill under large cornices. The route directly over the top is exposed, steep, and sometimes corniced.

The first 3 miles past Obstruction Point lie along Elk Mountain. This is windswept tundra which is usually free from snow. This unusual alpine area is the location of plants that grow only in this area, some blooming only in winter and early spring.

The road down from Deer Park is not plowed and is usually snow covered for at least the upper 3 miles. Some years the entire 9 miles above the park boundary is snow covered, so local inquiry is advised. The road down can be an enjoyable ski run under good conditions.

Mt. Angeles

This pleasant peak provides an enjoyable ski-mountaineering objective. Under good conditions it is a moderate day trip; either of two good approaches can be used.

For a touring approach, follow the ridge NE from the lodge for about 3 miles to the base of the peak.

If the chief objective is the peak, park the car at a small parking area about 9 miles above the national park boundary (3½ miles down from the Hurricane Ridge parking area). Walk up the road about ½ mile and then climb up to the ridge crest at a low point S of the peak. This, known as "Mt. Angeles Saddle," is where the two approaches join. From the saddle, ascend northerly, keeping on the W side of the peak until just below the summit. Leave the skis here, and climb ledges and gullies to the top.

The total elevation gain using the lower approach is 2000 ft. Of this, about 1600 ft. is good downhill skiing.

QUILCENE AREA

Lying in the rain shadow of the Olympics, this area offers some of the best weather in the range. In recent years both of the following tours have become increasingly popular. Both trips offer considerable downhill skiing on the return, a fairly uncommon situation in Olympic touring. Road conditions are variable and local inquiry should be made. The area is particularly well suited to late winter and early spring trips.

Recommended Maps: Tyler Peak and Quilcene USGS 15-minute quadrangles; Buckhorn Wilderness Custom Correct Map; the most recent Olympic National Forest/Olympic National Park map for road approaches.

Mt. Townsend

This peak offers several scenic trips for the snowshoer as well as a variety of skiing including a number of alpine bowls. The lower slopes of this peak are laced to about 4000 ft. with logging roads which provide access for the various tours. While the following is recommended as a good day trip, other possibilities should not be ruled out. See Climbing Routes, Mt. Townsend, for some of the other routes.

From Quilcene, take U.S. 101 N for about 2 miles. Turn W onto county road # 30 which soon becomes Forest Service road # 2909. Follow this road about 7 miles to a junction with road # 2812. Follow road # 2812 for about 3¼ miles (past a service road, the Little River crossing, and some cliffs) to an unmarked secondary logging road which branches right. Take this road about 1 mile to its end in a logged-off area. From the small creek at the upper end of this logged-off area, climb for 15 minutes along the right side of the creek to a small, flat, open area. Angle right, up a faint gully to the base of some cliffs, and then left through a narrow opening in the timber to an open flat area (approximately 30 minutes more). There is a saddle just above this flat and below a cliff. Climb to this saddle (4700 ft.) which offers a fine view of the skiing bowls above. Drop about 200 ft. into a basin which offers an excellent campsite. The shortest route to the summit leads through a small V-shaped group of trees directly to the top.

Marmot Pass-Mt. Buckhorn
This area of high open peaks and ridges offers very pleasant touring and ski mountaineering. Trail distance is 5 miles to Marmot Pass, and the trip can be done in a long day. However, 2 days, with a camp below Marmot Pass, is recommended.

Leave Forest Service road #2720 at Tenmile shelter approximately 16 miles from U.S. 101 (see Constance-Buckhorn Group, Approaches, page 97, for details on this fairly complex approach). The trail follows the river for about 2½ miles through timber, to Shelter Rock Camp. It then climbs steeply for about 2½ miles to Marmot Pass. A spectacular view of the Ridge of Gargoyles is afforded along this section.

The slopes S of Marmot Pass toward Boulder Ridge and the bowl just E of the pass are the most challenging to skiers and hold snow the longest. Other possibilities from the pass are an easy ascent of Mt. Buckhorn or a traverse N over Buckhorn Pass to Copper City.

BOULDER CREEK AREA
The end of the Elwha River-Boulder Creek road, located about 16 miles southwest of Port Angeles, is the starting point for several interesting tours into the high country. The upper section of the road is not plowed, and the last few miles are often under snow. However, the road is sheltered by big timber and easy to travel.

Recommended Maps: Mt. Olympus and Joyce USGS 15-minute quadrangles; Seven Lakes Basin-Hoh, Hurricane Ridge & Vicinity, and Lake Crescent-Happy Lake Ridge Custom Correct Maps.

Boulder Lake
This trip begins in timber and gradually climbs into scenic, semi-open meadows. If the road is snowed in for several miles, this is a fairly strenuous full-day trip. The trail distance is nearly 6 miles.

From the end of the Boulder Creek road, proceed about 2 miles to the Boulder Creek Campground. Next, follow the trail W for almost a mile to the trail fork. Follow the right fork, which goes to Boulder Lake. This trail climbs gradually in large timber to the upper basin containing the lake. Snow is usually heavy above the 2-mile point even in late spring, but is sometimes sparse below mile 2. The upper basin is semi-open and very scenic in winter. A steep section in heavy timber just below this basin is moderately difficult if icy. The run down is in timber but not difficult unless the snow is icy.

Appleton Pass

This trip begins in heavy timber and climbs into a picturesque alpine setting at Appleton Pass. The trail distance is 7 miles. Two days are recommended when the road is snowed in. This trip is more difficult than Boulder Lake because there are several creek crossings, the route is not well marked, and it is higher and steeper.

From the end of the Boulder Creek road, proceed about 2 miles to the Boulder Creek Campground. Next, follow the trail W for almost a mile to the trail fork. Continue along the main trail past the fork going to Boulder Lake. Two log crossings of Boulder Creek may provide problems. The upper crossing can sometimes be made about 300 yards above the log on avalanche snow that often bridges the creek. As the trail gains elevation, it becomes harder to follow in and out of meadows. The final ascent to the pass is best accomplished using the map, as all signs of the trail will be hidden under the snow. For the last portion to the ridge, follow the valley and then climb up near Oyster Lake. Skiing back down this route is good, and there will be a long alpine run under proper conditions. There are a few steep pitches and much moderate open skiing. This is recommended as a spring trip, when one can drive to the trailhead and walk up through the timbered section. This tour is particularly dangerous during high avalanche hazard conditions.

Happy Lake Ridge

This strenuous 2-day loop is rewarding for the well-conditioned. The route includes some very scenic stretches which provide views of the main Olympic peaks that are seldom seen in winter. While this tour can be accomplished from either direction, it is recommended to go in the Happy Lake trail and out via Boulder Lake, particularly if skiing. Distance is 3 miles to the ridge top, 7 miles along the ridge to Boulder Lake, and 6 miles to the end of the Boulder Creek road. Be prepared for an added 2 to 4 miles down the snow-covered road. This trip is much easier (1 full day) in early spring when the road is open to the trailhead, and the trail is bare much of the way to the ridge crest.

The trail to Happy Lake Ridge leaves the Boulder Creek road about 5 miles above the Elwha Ranger Station. Many winters, this is about as far as the road is open. Since the trail ascends the sunny side of the slope, the snowline is high compared to that of the sheltered road below. The trail is steep with much sidehill near the top.

After 3 miles the broad, timbered ridge crest is reached. Follow the ridge crest westerly to Happy Lake. The ridge is open near Happy Lake but timbered and narrow in many other places. Past Happy Lake divide, take care to stay to the left. There is a tendency to go too far in an open meadow that leads to a dead-end spur ridge. Careful map reading will prevent this. Continue on to a point above Boulder Lake and then descend in semi-open meadows to the lake, where the trail can be picked up. It is advisable to know the route down from Boulder Lake before embarking on this tour. See the Boulder Lake tour for more information.

SEVEN LAKES BASIN LOOP

This very rewarding and scenic tour provides spectacular views of Mt. Olympus in good weather. The trip is not recommended for beginners, and the route should be scouted in the summer first. Wait for good weather and stable snow before starting this loop. The best conditions in both the valley and the basin occur when the snowline is at about 3500 ft. This also allows driving to the trailhead and walking the lower part of the trail.

The time required will vary greatly depending on the party, weather, and snow conditions. Although the trip has been accomplished in 1 day, 2 or 3 days are recommended. The total distance is 20 miles. 10 miles through the high country and 10 miles through forest.

This loop trip starts and finishes at the end of the Soleduck River road (about 2 miles above Sol Duc Hot Springs). A mile up the trail at Soleduck Falls the trail forks. One branch is used as the start of the loop and the other for the return. The Deer Lake start is recommended since there is a chance of getting wet feet in the river crossings between Soleduck Falls and Soleduck Park. Also, by going in via Deer Lake, the high country is reached sooner.

It is 3 miles through timber to Deer Lake. The route from Deer Lake to the divide between the Soleduck and Bogachiel Rivers climbs through pleasant meadow country, with an elevation gain of 1000 ft. From this divide to the Seven Lakes Basin trail junction (ca. 2 miles) stay on the Bogachiel River side, following the trail route through the tree section. About a mile from the junction, the terrain becomes steep, open sidehill which can be avoided by descending several hundred ft. to slight benching. Continue S, climbing back up to the ridge trough (at the trail junction). Next, descend to Round Lake and Lunch Lake in the basin. The slope is steep at the top, but eases off below to provide a good ski run. Do not try to stay high around Bogachiel Peak, because the sidehill there is steep and dangerous.

The basin country is open and the deep snow rounds everything off, making the route E from Lunch Lake easy. Climb NE up a broad draw and hit High Divide at a low point (ca. 5000 ft.) directly above Morgenroth Lake as identified on the 15-minute Mt. Tom USGS quadrangle (misnamed on the 7.5-minute Bogachiel quadrangle). Travel is easy from there along High Divide to Heart Lake Basin. Heart Lake Basin is open, providing good skiing down to Soleduck Park and below. Cross the creek above the headwall leading down from Soleduck Park, just past the large avalanche track from the west. This is where the creek leaves the meadows and starts into a canyon.

The route from the headwall to the main Soleduck River crossing is steep and in timber. There is a footlog at this time (1987) where the trail crosses the main river. If this crossing is difficult, see if an avalanche path in the area has formed a snow bridge. From this point out, there are usually snow patches even in light-snow years.

Recommended Maps: Mt. Olympus, Mt. Tom, and Mt. Carrie USGS 15-minute quadrangles; Seven Lakes Basin-Hoh Custom Correct Map.

OLYMPIC CROSSING VIA HAYDEN PASS

Cross-Olympic trips are seldom done in winter due to difficulty, distance, weather, and avalanche hazard. Of the possible cross-Olympic routes, Hayden Pass from the Elwha River to the Dosewallips River (or reverse) is the best. This trip involves no river crossings, and there is usually a clean snowline on the southern-exposed ascent to the pass, with a good open snow descent on the Dosewallips side.

Total distance for this trip is 40 miles over trails alone, with probable added distance because of snowed-in roads. Snow conditions and snowlines vary greatly with time. The best time to make the trip is with the snowline at about 3000 ft. This provides open roads and allows walking up the low valleys. Under ideal conditions, this trip can be done in 3 days. The Dosewallips River road may be snowed in at times, so local inquiry should be made before the trip.

The trip starts (or finishes) at Whiskey Bend on the Elwha River. Skis or snowshoes may have to be packed up the Elwha River to Hayes River or above (16 or more miles). The climb from Elwha River to Hayden Pass has a good grade, and the trail can usually be followed on snow to the start of the meadows (3 miles below the pass). From there, the pass must be located by landmarks alone, which is not difficult in good weather. Under most conditions, this traverse is safe from avalanche. From Hayden Pass, open slopes lead all the way down to the upper meadows of the Dosewallips River, affording an excellent ski run. A large cornice on Mt. Fromme towers over part of the route. A possible avalanche release zone which must be crossed is near the top of the pass. Once in the vicinity of Dose Meadows there is less avalanche hazard, and there is good skiing for a number of miles. The lower 9 miles of the Dosewallips River trail are in timber, and snow conditions vary greatly.

Recommended Maps: Mt. Olympus, Mt. Angeles, and Tyler Peak USGS 15-minute quadrangles; Gray Wolf-Dosewallips and Elwha Valley Custom Correct Maps.

STAIRCASE-SKOKOMISH AREA

The alpine meadows around and above Flapjack Lakes have long been enjoyed as a winter touring area. Trail distance from the Staircase Ranger Station is 8 miles. A minimum of 2 days is recommended for this trip in winter.

Upper Lena Lake and the false summit of Mt. Bretherton (George Martin)

From Staircase Ranger Station (see Skokomish-Duckabush Group, Approaches, page 41, for approach details), the first 4 miles is easy skiing. The last 4 miles to the lakes is steeper and more difficult.

From the lakes, it is another 1.5 miles to Gladys Divide. The best skiing is found in meadows near the divide, especially in the upper Hamma Hamma drainage, where a 2000-ft. run is available for the hardy. Note that one must climb back out of the Hamma Hamma drainage.

Recommended Maps: Mt. Steel USGS 15-minute quadrangle; Enchanted Valley-Skokomish and Mt. Skokomish-Lake Cushman Custom Correct Maps.

ENCHANTED VALLEY-QUINAULT RIVER

This area is recommended as a spring oversnow trip to view avalanches and spectacular waterfalls off the cliffs of Chimney Peak and vicinity. The trail distance is 12 miles to the Enchanted Valley Chalet, a large public shelter. A minimum of 2 days is recommended for this trip.

The tour starts at the end of the Quinault River road (see Quinault Group, page 189, for approach details) and follows the river in timber most of the way to the chalet. The open meadows above the chalet provide an excellent viewpoint; however, remember that these meadows were formed by avalanche. This trip is best in early spring, when conditions are more stable in the valley, and the road is passable to the trail. Some years, the trail will be bare much of the way to the Chalet.

Recommended Maps: Mt. Christie and Mt. Steel USGS 15-minute quadrangles; Enchanted Valley-Skokomish Custom Correct Map.

HIGH ALPINE TRAVERSES

The traverses described in this section are a form of wilderness travel which is a cross between hiking and climbing. Many of them can be used as approaches to climbs, but they are being recommended for scenery and interest as well as for mountaineering experiences in their own right. Travel is off the trails, mostly in high open meadow, scree, snow, and rock. Some brush is encountered, but this is the exception. Route-finding and map-reading skills are necessary for these traverses. Moderate rock-scrambling ability will suffice. Snow slopes in excess of 30° will be found on some routes, and an ice ax should be carried. Two of the routes, Queets Basin to Glacier Meadows and Hayden Pass to Anderson Pass, cross living glaciers and require full crevasse-rescue skill and equipment.

All route descriptions are based on the 15-minute USGS quadrangle maps. The sheet needed is listed in each traverse. The newly published Custom Correct Maps will also be helpful. Even with a map, guidebook, compass, and altimeter, route-finding ability will still be needed. Anyone in doubt about his skill and experience should start on the shorter and easier routes before trying more extended trips.

Weather is the main hazard for alpine travel in the Olympics. Along these traverses, even hikers knowing the route can become confused in fog, rain, or snow, and be forced to wait out the weather. This possibility should be considered when planning time and equipment for a trip. Some emergency equipment should always be taken for even short trips above timberline. See the section on mountain safety for more information on this subject.

The time required for these trips will vary greatly depending on conditioning, experience, knowledge of the route, and whims of the hiker. Times for very strong and experienced hikers are included in the description to give some idea of what is possible.

Alpine areas are quite fragile and some of the following traverses have been damaged by increased usage. Practice minimum-impact camping, use existing trails, and observe all open-fire bans.

Mt. Childs on the Bailey Range Traverse (Rich Olson)   233

BAILEY RANGE

Through the use of this cross-country route plus the trail from Low Divide to the Quinault River via the ridge between the Queets and Quinault (Skyline Trail), it is possible to cross the Olympics from north to south entirely in high, scenic country. The route is described in sections, but it can be done in one grand traverse, or a few sections at a time. Some segments offer enjoyment as day trips for strong hikers.

This traverse is the classic "Crisler Route" made popular by Herb Crisler, who photographed the Disney film *Olympic Elk* in the Bailey Range in the 1930s and early 1940s. The route was first traveled by Billy Everett, who reached Cream Lake Basin in 1885 at the age of 16. Billy made the traverse many times and may have been the first man to climb Mt. Carrie, Mt. Fitzhenry, and others.

Before the trails were built, travel along the high ridges was easier in many places than crashing up the brushy river valleys. Some of these high routes were followed more often years ago by hunters, trappers, prospectors, and "mountain men" than they are today.

All sections of the Bailey Range traverse are covered on the 15-minute USGS Mt. Olympus quadrangle, and the references to names and elevations are from that map. Seven Lakes Basin-Hoh, Elwha Valley, and Mt. Olympus Custom Correct Maps will also be helpful.

Boulder Lake to Appleton Pass

This entire route is scenic and alpine, with less than 5 miles of off-trail travel. Since both ends of the route join trails from the Boulder Creek trailhead, this makes an excellent loop hike of 2 days, or it can be done in a single day from the road by strong hikers.

From Boulder Lake, 6 miles by trail from road end, the route is southerly to Lower Three Horse Lake, using a contour at or below 4500 ft. Game trails may be followed. Continue up the drainage above Lower Three Horse Lake for several hundred yards to a small creek from the S which drains a basin W of Everett Peak. Hike up into this basin, staying E of the creek on game trails. From the pass in the ridge joining Everett Peak with the main ridge, descend SE through meadows to Blue Lake. From here, the route is S again, on the flat ridge just E of Blue Lake. Follow this ridge S into another basin where scenic Mud Lake lies under the N face of Mt. Appleton. This pool was omitted from the 1956 USGS Mt. Olympus quadrangle. From Mud Lake, climb SW up a permanent 30° snowfield to a notch separating the basin from the Soleduck drainage. If the snow slope is too icy, climb to a saddle via elk trails north of the first notch. Descend scree to the large basins of the tributary of the North Fork Soleduck River. Hold to the upper basin and traverse S to reach the ridge separating this drainage from the main Soleduck River drainage. This ridge should be gained at about 5500 ft. Next, contour the S side of the 6100-ft. summit located NW of Appleton Pass, reaching the Appleton Pass trail one or two switchbacks S of the pass. This unnamed 6100-ft. summit, higher than Mt. Appleton, is located on the main ridge and thus is frequently confused with Mt. Appleton, which is ½ mile to the N.

An alternate route from the upper North Fork Soleduck River is to climb to the saddle between the two peaks and then descend southeasterly to the Appleton Pass trail.

Appleton Pass to Cat Basin

The traverse from Appleton Pass to Cat Basin provides about 5 miles of off-trail travel, and is an easy one-day trip. It can be done from the road by strong hikers in a long day, returning to either the Boulder Creek road via the Appleton Pass trail or to the Soleduck River road via the Soleduck River trail. The total journey involves about 20 miles of trail travel in addition to the traverse.

Appleton Pass is reached via a 7-mile trail from the Boulder Creek trailhead. From the pass, go E and S in scenic alpland along the ridge separating the Soleduck River from Boulder and Schoeffel creeks. In about 2 miles this ridge intersects the ridge bounding Cat Creek on the W at a summit which is avoided by a sidehill traverse on elk trails. The last ½ mile is on the Soleduck side. Traverse to a notch where small ponds can be seen in the Cat Creek drainage. Continue S from this notch in cirques on the Cat Creek side of the ridge, staying above 5000 ft., just under the last upper cliffs on the ridge crest. The last cirque can be located on the map by looking across the ridge SE of Haigs Lake. From the last cirque, ascend to the brushy ridge bounding it on the S to overlook the extensive meadows of upper Cat Basin and the High Divide. Descend through brush to Cat Basin. From the large basin, an old trail leads up to High Divide, or any of several elk trails may be followed to the end of the traverse at the divide.

Cat Basin to Mt. Ferry

Though the distance is less than 10 miles, a full day should be allowed for this section, since route finding between Mt. Carrie and Cream Lake Basin can slow the pace. An early start is advised, for campsites are infrequent and marginal between "Boston Charlie's Camp" and Cream Lake. In addition to the following alpine route, the range can be traversed across the summits of the peaks from the top of Mt. Carrie (see Climbing Routes, page 181).

High Divide, above Cat Basin or Heart Lake, is reached by 8 to 10 miles of trail from Sol Duc Hot Springs. An unfinished trail continues SE to a dead end in rock cliffs between Cat Peak and Mt. Carrie. From the trail end, climb a few hundred ft. to the ridge crest, a narrow, steep, brushy arête known as "The Catwalk," which is less difficult than it appears. Continue SE along "The Catwalk," either on the crest or a few ft. down the N side, allowing an hour to traverse this arête.

Just across "The Catwalk" is "Boston Charlie's Camp," named for an early "mountain man." From "Boston Charlie's" the route gains several hundred ft. in elevation and traverses the grassy S shoulder of Mt. Carrie. Continue SE to the Cream Lake area along the SW side of the Bailey Range at the 5000- to 5500-ft. level, making use of slight game trails. The main difficulties are the many gullies to be crossed and the traverse of steep grass and scree. Avoid going too low, for large gullies draining into the Hoh River can create difficulties.

Once the spur ridge SW of Peak 5978 is reached, the terrain lessens in difficulty. Elk trails lead down to Cream Lake, an old Crisler campsite. From Cream Lake, the route goes upstream to Ferry Basin. This area to the W of Mt. Ferry is open, travel is easy, campsites abound, and tarns dot the landscape.

From Mt. Ferry Basin, there are three possible routes to the crest of the Bailey Range. The summit can be traversed, and though not difficult, this entails the most work. The valley between Mt. Ferry and Peak 6283 (Pulitzer or Snagtooth) is easy to ascend past the remnant glacier. The heather meadows S of Pulitzer are also easy, leading up to the crest of the range at a flat area S of this peak. Once on top, travel is simple to the E of both Pulitzer and Ferry on broad, grassy benches. From the Ferry plateau, routes continue to either Queets Basin or Dodger Point.

Mt. Ferry to Dodger Point

Distance for this easy section is about 4 miles, and it can be traveled in ½ day or less. This is a good route to use either as a retreat from the Bailey Range or to divide the Bailey Range traverse into smaller sections. Dodger Point is 13 miles from the road (Whiskey Bend) via the Long Ridge trail.

From the broad bench E of the summit of Mt. Ferry, descend the ridge E to the saddle at the headwaters of Long Creek. The descent is not difficult, but has one short, steep place. Continue NE in open meadows on the divide between Long Creek and the Goldie River. From this ridge, two routes are possible. One involves climbing over the summit of Ludden Peak and then descending steep cliff bands to the E to gain the trail to Dodger Point. A more moderate route is via open slopes to the flat meadow that lies between Ludden Peak and Mt. Scott, descending just W of Ludden's summit. From the Ludden-Scott saddle, which provides an excellent campsite, descend NE for a few hundred ft., then continue just under the rock cliffs that form the SE side of Ludden Peak. Look up NE for a trail partially blasted out of rock. Ascend at the first opportunity to the unfinished trail, and follow it to the Dodger Point trail. This old trail, seldom shown on maps, stretches along the E side of Ludden Peak to within ½ mile of the Ludden-Scott saddle. There is no water along this trail.

Mt. Ferry to Queets Basin

This section covers about 6 miles and is an easy day in good conditions. However, like most of the Bailey Range, it is very exposed to storms and fog. From the flat ridge top S of Mt. Ferry and Mt. Pulitzer (Snagtooth), ascend a

Tree on the Bailey Traverse (Arnold Bloomer)

snow slope and continue S down the crest of the Bailey Range over easy summits and along ridges. Cut across the top of a snowfield shown on the map just N of Peak 6205 (Mt. Childs). From the snowfield, cross the ridge to the E side of the crest of the range, and pick up broad benches E of Mt. Childs. Follow these benches S to Bear Pass. Bear Pass is a broad shoulder W of Peak 5819, not a true pass. From Bear Pass, open slopes of meadow or snow lead SW down to the vast Queets Basin with its lakelet and numerous campsites.

Queets Basin to Elwha Basin

This cross-country route ends at the terminus of the Elwha River trail in a meadow at the confluence of the Elwha River and the creek draining Mt. Noyes. This location is marked as Elwha Basin on the USGS Mt. Olympus quadrangle. Elwha Basin is 30 miles by trail from the Elwha River road end at Whiskey Bend, and 22 miles by trail from the end of the North Fork Quinault River road and via Low Divide. The route through upper Queets Basin over Dodwell-Rixon Pass and down the Elwha Snow Finger to Elwha Basin is about 4 miles with a 2000-ft. loss in elevation. The descent will take several hours. This is a good route for access to or retreat from the high country, and a good way of ending the traverse. It is also a natural link with the trails or routes out of Low Divide.

Dodwell-Rixon Pass is located in a somewhat hidden notch in the SE corner of upper Queets Basin. This natural approach to the high country was one of the first used by explorers, surveyors, and mountaineers. The position of the pass should be determined and a compass bearing noted before traveling the area, in case of poor visibility en route. From Dodwell-Rixon Pass, the moderate Elwha Snow Finger descends SE to the upper Elwha River. This is not a glacier, but it can be large and may last all year. Avalanches from Mt. Queets, Mt. Meany, Mt. Barnes, and Mt. Noyes pour tons of snow and debris onto the Elwha Snow Finger each year, mostly in winter and spring. Hazards of moats and melt holes exist, especially where streams run under the snow. Descend the snow finger to its terminus. When leaving the snow finger, look for flagging marking the start of a way trail leading to Elwha Basin. Cross to SW side of the river at about 3200 ft. (ca. 1 mile below "The Big Snow Hump"). A faint trail leads up a brushy slope above where the river drops into a gorge, traverses a bench, crosses a ridge, then emerges at open meadows of Elwha Basin near an unnamed stream and waterfalls from the E face of Mt. Queets. Descend open slopes to the river, which must be crossed to reach the end of the Elwha River trail.

In dry years, when the snow finger recedes to "The Big Snow Hump," traverse a meadow on the NE side of the river 100 yards below "The Hump," cross a thin tree band, and follow game trail into the forest 30 ft. above a 15-ft. boulder. The trail rises 100 ft., then traverses, finally dropping to a stream. Cross and continue until trail fades, then descend and traverse toward a meadow visible across the river. Follow game trails to maintained trail.

Queets Basin to Glacier Meadows

This route, across the NE side of Mt. Olympus, crosses three major glaciers and requires mountaineering skill, roped travel, and crevasse-rescue knowledge and equipment. The Custom Correct Mt. Olympus Climbers Map is especially helpful for this traverse. Allow at least a full day for this traverse. For additional details on the area (including campsites), see Quinault Group, page 187. Glacier Meadows is 18 miles by trail from the Hoh River road end.

From Queets Basin, proceed westerly toward the terminus of Humes Glacier. The ascent of its snout can be tricky and the preferred route is to gain the ridge which divides the terminus of the glacier. Climb the ridge to gain the glacier. For more detail, see sketch on page 167. Ascend the glacier to Blizzard Pass, which separates the Humes and Hoh glaciers. From Blizzard Pass, descend steep snow and ice to the Hoh Glacier. Difficulty on the Hoh Glacier will depend on the time of year, and may vary from one year to the next. Cross the Hoh Glacier to the W, and climb to Glacier Pass, which is S of Peak 7168 (Mt. Mathias). From Glacier Pass descend the Blue Glacier on moderate slopes. The route off the Blue Glacier is on the NE side near the snout, where a trail leads to Glacier Meadows. An alternate exit from the glacier is provided by an old trail which follows the top of the lateral moraine E of the Blue Glacier for the last ½ mile. This trail also leads to Glacier Meadows.

DUNGENESS-DOSEWALLIPS AREA

The ranges of the northeast Olympics do not lie in one long chain to form a single traverse as does the Bailey Range to the west. However, some of the routes do link up to form longer trips. Three of the four routes can be done in 2 days or less and offer good trips for the weekender. Most can be worked out to end at the same point as the start, to simplify transportation. All are outstanding mountaineering ventures.

Gray Wolf Ridge to Royal Basin

(USGS· Tyler Peak Quadrangle/Gray Wolf-Dosewallips Custom Correct Map)

This trip has been done in 1 long day from the road, returning by trail from Royal Basin. Distance is about 8 miles off trail, and 7 miles by trail from Royal Basin to the road.

The Dungeness River road, which eventually becomes Forest Service road #2950 is currently open to about Mueller Creek (for approach details see Dungeness River approach in Gray Wolf-Hurricane Ridge Group, page 133). From road end, hike along remains of the old road until it switches back and climbs to the NW. Continue along road for about another ½ mile. At this point, look up for a steep, unmarked cat track leading NW up the ridge. This fire trail follows the general line of the old Maynard Burn way trail. Take the fire trail to about 5000 ft., where it ends at the national park boundary, and continue on the old way trail to timberline. Ascend through easy, open terrain to the summit of Baldy. This summit can also be reached via an abandoned lookout trail which climbs to timberline from Slide Camp on the Gray Wolf River trail.

From Baldy, traverse S at the 6000- to 7000-ft. level in meadow, scree, or snow, all the way to The Needles. Stay on the ridge crest most of the way. Peak 7076 can be climbed by way of a basin between the double summit to avoid a broken ridge. Once past Peak 7076, the next summit is in The Needles, and requires technical climbing. To continue to Royal Basin, descend SE over steep broken slopes and chutes to the Royal Basin trail below the basin.

An alternate, but difficult, route from the ridge top is to work W around Mt. Walkinshaw by way of a basin N of the peak, then climb to the NW ridge of Mt. Walkinshaw at about 6750 ft. From here, drop to the valley W of The Needles. Continue up this valley, which leads into Surprise Pass just SW of Mt. Clark. The climb to the pass is up steep snow or ice, requiring mountaineering skill and equipment. From Surprise Pass, drop into open, snowy Surprise Basin, and continue on easy terrain for 1 mile to Royal Lake.

Royal Basin to Constance Pass

(USGS Tyler Peak Quadrangle/Gray Wolf-Dosewallips Custom Correct Map)

This traverse can be done in a day by a strong hiker coming out the Dosewallips, but 2 or more days are recommended. Distance off trails is about 8 miles.

From Royal Lake (7 miles by trail from the Dungeness River road), hike S up the valley. The brushy section just above the lake is the only difficult terrain in the open, scenic valley. At the head of the valley, ascend a steep slope to the divide E of the remnant glacier on the NE side of Mt. Deception. From this ridge, descend open slopes to the basin at the head of Deception Creek. Continue downstream from upper Deception Basin to the valley leading SE to the notch between Mt. Mystery and Little Mystery. Ascend scree or snow to this notch (Gunsight Pass).

An alternate route leads from Deception Basin to the Dosewallips River trail near Deception Creek. This route stays just out of the canyon of Deception Creek on the NW side.

From Gunsight Pass, traverse E to gain the ridge between the Dosewallips and Dungeness drainages, and follow it to a point where you can drop into Sunny Brook Meadows and the Constance Pass trail. The section between Peak 6666 and Peak 6576 is broken and can be avoided by dropping to the meadows even if you are continuing E to Constance Pass. You can return to the Dungeness River road via Home Lake and the Dungeness River trail, or descend the Constance Pass trail to the Dosewallips River trail and road.

Grand Valley to Lost Basin via Lake Lillian

(USGS Mt. Angeles Quadrangle/Elwha Valley Custom Correct Map)

This trip from Obstruction Point and the return by trail has been completed in one day by strong hikers, but two days are recommended. The distance off trail is about 6 miles.

There is a low, unnamed pass at the head of Grand Valley just above the point where the trail turns SE toward Grand Pass. Leave the trail at the turn (5 miles from the end of the Obstruction Point road) and ascend SW to this broad, unnamed pass. Ignore traces of an abandoned trail, for it leads into the tangled avalanche debris of 1949. Instead, continue into the Lillian drainage to the flat meadows at the base of McCartney Peak, through brush in places. Follow the meadows westerly around the N side of the peak to the creek draining Lake Lillian, where the abandoned trail can be regained and ascended on the E side of the stream to the open basins at the lake. Meadow, scree, or snow lead to the pass above Lake Lillian. Cross the pass into the Lost River drainage and regain the abandoned trail, following it SE below the ridge crest toward Lost Basin. Climb to the ridge crest at Peak 6443, and bypass Peak 6733 a few hundred ft. below the summit on the SW slope. The route joins the Cameron Creek to Dose Meadows trail in Lost Basin a few hundred yards S of Cameron Pass. From Cameron Pass, the Dosewallips River road can be reached in 16 miles via Lost Pass and the Dosewallips River trail, or Obstruction Point can be reached in 12 miles via Grand Pass.

Hayden Pass to Anderson Pass

(USGS Mt. Angeles and Mt. Steel Quadrangles/Elwha Valley and En-chanted Valley-Skokomish Custom Correct Maps)

This rather difficult route involves the ascent and descent of two glaciers and should only be attempted by experienced mountaineers equipped for crevasse rescue. Though the 6-mile distance is frequently done in 1 day, most parties prefer to establish a camp in the alpine meadow near the snout of the Eel Glacier.

From Hayden Pass (15 miles by trail from the Dosewallips River road and 25 miles from Whiskey Bend on the Elwha River road), go S around Sentinel Peak on the W side of the ridge. Contour southerly, bypassing Peak 6301 to the E. Continue S on game trails and meadows, staying high to avoid the brushy cliffs and waterfalls of the Silt Creek canyon. After about 1½ miles, drop gradually to Silt Creek, to where it is a flat outwash from the terminus of the Eel Glacier.

Eel Glacier is moderate, but presents crevasse hazard. Climb to the obvious notch (Flypaper Pass) at the head of the glacier W of the summit of Mt. Anderson. A steep snow chute descends S to the moderate Anderson Glacier from the pass. Descend Anderson Glacier, leaving it at its southeast-ern edge to pass E of a small terminal lake, and climb a moraine SE to a small pond and campsites in meadows. This pond appears on the Mt. Steel quadrangle in the upper drainage of the West Fork Dosewallips River. A good trail leads from the meadow to Anderson Pass. A direct route to the Quinault drainage from the Anderson Glacier should not be attempted, as it involves severe cliffs.

SKOKOMISH-HAMMA HAMMA AREA

Gladys Divide, located above Flapjack Lakes, is 10 miles by trail from
Staircase Ranger Station in Olympic National Park. From Gladys Divide, a
traverse in very interesting alpine country can be made to First Divide and the
Skokomish River trail. It is 13 miles by this trail to the same road end where
the traverse started.

The Putvin trail from county road #25 on the Hamma Hamma River can
be used to enter the traverse in the middle near Lake of the Angels (see
approach to Mt. Stone, Climbing Routes, page 49, for this route). The trail to
Upper Lena Lake (7 miles by trail from the Hamma Hamma River road) can
also be used as a starting or ending point for a traverse in this area. All the
traverses described here are located on the USGS Mt. Steel and The Brothers
quadrangles. The Brothers-Mt. Anderson, Enchanted Valley-Skokomish,
and Mt. Skokomish-Lake Cushman Custom Correct Maps are also helpful.

Total distance for the entire trip to First Divide and return is 23 miles on
trail and at least 8 miles cross-country.

Gladys Divide to Lake of the Angels

This trip can be done in 1 long day from the Skokomish River road. Distance
is 10 miles by trail and about 4 miles off trail.

At Gladys Divide, descend NE into the Hamma Hamma River drainage to
an obvious flat avalanche meadow. It is difficult to contour across without
losing elevation due to gullies and slide alder. A direct traverse over Mt.
Henderson and Mt. Skokomish is long and involves climbing problems.
From the meadow at about 4000 ft., climb NE up a draw to notches in the
ridge extending S from Mt. Skokomish. Cross one of the notches to the
cirque on the E side. Stay high here and cross the ridge N of this cirque to the
next basin, which is the source of Whitehorse Creek. The lake shown on the
map is Lake of the Angels.

Lake of the Angels to First Divide

This pleasant traverse in alpland is about 6 miles, and can be done in a
short day.

From Lake of the Angels, climb a few hundred ft. NW to the pass above.
From this pass, descend the headwall to the basin at the source of the
Skokomish River. Climb N on scree and heather or snow to a saddle just W of
Mt. Stone, which is located exactly on the national park boundary and the
county line. This saddle has been known as "The Great Stone Arrow" due to
rock markings in heather.

It is easy to walk down to Hagen Lake from this pass, then contour WNW
in heather and fir to the basin at the head of Crazy Creek. An easy ascent can
then be made from the basin to the ridge crest S of Mt. Hopper. This point can
also be reached directly from "The Great Stone Arrow" by following the

ridge NW. A way trail leads from this point to the Skokomish River trail at First Divide, which is 13 miles by trail from Staircase Ranger Station.

Upper Lena Lake to Lake of the Angels

This pleasant traverse, largely in alpland, is about 5 miles, and can be completed in a short day.

From Upper Lena Lake, 7 miles by trail from the Hamma Hamma River road, follow way trails southwesterly to the ridge S of Mt. Lena. Continue through the pass approximately 1½ miles SW of Scout Lake to the two lakes on the fork of Boulder Creek E of Mt. Stone. Pass the upper lake and climb SW to a 5900-ft. pass which separates the Boulder and Whitehorse Creek drainages. Moderate snow and scree lead to this pass in the SE ridge of Mt. Stone. Descend and work slightly W to Lake of the Angels at the source of Whitehorse Creek. Lake of the Angels, in open heather, can also be reached via the Putvin trail from the Hamma Hamma River road.

MOUNTAIN SAFETY

*In mountaineering our aim is to make sure of the highest form of
adventure consistent with our sense of proportion.*
— Geoffrey Winthrop Young

This guidebook has been compiled with the assumption that the user is not a
climbing novice — that he has acquired at least a minimum level of skill on
rock and snow, in route finding and wilderness navigation, and in survival,
first aid, and dealing with emergencies. Nevertheless, Olympic Mountain
Rescue feels that some basics need to be stressed repeatedly; also, that in
certain respects the Olympic Mountains differ from other nearby ranges. The
climber needs to adjust his preparation and techniques to cope with these
differences. The following information on accident prevention, survival, first
aid, self-rescue, and rescue, is keyed to the Olympics in an effort to meet
these needs.

Accident Prevention

Climbing mountains is an exciting and satisfying form of recreation for an
ever-increasing number of people. Unfortunately, the probability of accidents
becomes greater as the number of participants increases. However, nearly all
accidents can be prevented. The prudent mountaineer by preparing himself
mentally, physically, and with thorough training, learns to recognize potentially dangerous situations before an accident occurs. If an accident does
happen, he is able to cope with it efficiently.

Unlike most forms of recreation, mountaineering is usually practiced in
remote areas, perhaps days from ready communication, transportation,
outside help, and medical care. Therefore, the importance of developing

Mt. Duckabush from the northwest (Dave Sicks)

mountaineering skills, safe climbing attitudes, and good physical condition cannot be overstressed. Just one person in poor physical condition can endanger an entire party of climbers.

Weather is an extremely important factor in mountaineering. The Olympics generally enjoy a moderate climate, but it is not uncommon to experience a range of temperatures from subfreezing to 90°F, and to see rain, snow, hail, and wind, as well as sunshine, within the space of a few hours. Regardless of the season, clothing for all conditions should be worn or carried. Adequate clothing not only serves to comfort the climber, but adds a large measure of safety. A weatherproof tarp or tent and a good sleeping bag are necessities in the Olympics. A knowledge of emergency shelters is invaluable in case of a forced bivouac.

Skill in the use of map, compass, and altimeter is especially vital in wilderness areas of the Olympics. Finding the way off a fogged-in mountaintop or out of a brush-filled valley bottom may depend entirely on a knowledge of these navigational tools.

Avalanches are most frequent in this range during winter and spring. However, a snow slope can avalanche anytime during the year, given the right set of conditions. The experienced climber learns to recognize conditions that create avalanches and avoids potentially dangerous terrain. Be especially wary of climbing up under snow cornices or beneath rock cliffs topped with heavy winter or spring snow. These masses of snow are certain to fall — don't be a target! Avoid steep, convex slopes, if possible, as they tend to fracture and avalanche when disturbed. Climbing straight up or down these slopes is always preferable to traversing them.

An ice ax should be carried at all times in the Olympics. Snow may be encountered throughout the summer, especially on northern exposures and in gullies, as the range abounds in permanent snowfields and small glaciers. In addition, a party traveling on glaciers must possess a thorough knowledge of crevasse-rescue techniques.

The traveler off the trails in the Olympics will encounter more than his share of loose or friable rock. This condition is further complicated by the presence of wet moss or lichen, especially in the transition zone between forest and peak. The combination makes much of the climbing more than normally hazardous. A hard hat with a secure chin strap is strongly recommended. Take care to stay out of the fall line of climbers above, and keep parties bunched closely when climbing in gullies.

Most of the rock-climbing areas of the range are composed of metamorphic rock commonly called "pillow lava." This rock, while usually solid, has several characteristics that can trap the unwary. Holds are usually large (basketball size), rounded, and sloping. As such, they do not provide the security offered by angularly cleft granite. In addition, the rock structure provides few good belay points. Pillow lava is noted for a lack of cracks, and those present are often shallow or otherwise inadequate.

Early starts are advisable, for the approaches are often exceptionally long and the elevation gain may be great. It is wise to bivouac when off trail, rather than attempt travel by night. Olympic river and stream crossings are usually hazardous, especially in the afternoon when swollen with melt-water. The prevalence of canyons, waterfalls, and insecure snow bridges in the high country adds to the potential danger.

When in the backcountry, it is always advisable to carry the "Ten Essentials": extra food and clothing, fire starter and matches, a compass and map for where you are, a first-aid kit, flashlight, knife, sunglasses and sun cream.

Years of Mountain Rescue experience have shown that several safety recommendations should always be kept in mind:

- Rope up on glaciers
- Keep party together
- Never climb beyond your ability
- Never let your judgment be swayed by desire when choosing a route or turning back
- Leave trip schedule with a responsible person

Survival

The Olympic Peninsula provides some special problems and opportunities for survival. The following paragraphs emphasize some of these for the visitor to the area.

Travel

The Olympic Peninsula, like other wet coastal areas, has heavy undergrowth which makes cross-country travel both slow and difficult. Ridges are generally drier and more open, affording less hazardous and arduous travel than streambeds. Many main drainages in the Olympics have well-maintained trails adjacent to the streams, but there are enough exceptions to make a choice of stream travel questionable. Some major drainages, such as the Goldie, Queets, Tunnel Creek, and Silt Creek are notorious for their box canyons and frequent waterfalls in deep gorges. Many streams have a steep loss of elevation in their upper reaches, with areas of smooth mossy rock and frequent cliffy falls which provide great hazard and result in slow and exhausting travel. When the drainage does bench out, one may have to contend with the notorious "green jungle," a prolific growth of slide alder, vine maple, and devil's club. In selecting a drainage to follow, it may not be possible to determine whether it will lead to the Pacific Ocean, the Strait of Juan de Fuca, or Hood Canal, due to the radial drainage pattern of the range.

Many streams and some major rivers flow into uninhabited areas where there is little chance of obtaining help or of being seen until one reaches the Olympic Highway (U.S. 101).

In most cases, it is advisable to stay high and proceed downstream following broad ridges or alpland near timberline, paralleling a major drainage. This allows you to continue to search for familiar landmarks or fire lookouts, and you may see roads, trails, or logging activity in the adjacent valleys. You may also be in a position to signal searching aircraft with a mirror or bright clothing or tarp. If the ridge that you have chosen terminates at the confluence of two streams, forcing you to the river bottom, check both sides of the river for trails or roads before continuing.

Most large streams are too deep, fast, cold, and slippery to be crossed in any season without the aid of a rope. However, streams which are raging torrents in the afternoon may be fordable in early morning.

The generalization that moss grows on the north side of trees does not apply in this fog-shrouded range. It may grow on all sides, varying only with the prevailing local surface winds.

Self Protection

The hiker should be able to recognize and avoid such plants as poison oak (even its smoke can be toxic), nettles, and devil's club. If inadvertently contaminated, wash with soap and hot water as soon as possible. Rub infected areas with a 10 percent solution of tannic acid or strong tea.

There are no poisonous snakes or reptiles on the Olympic Peninsula, but mosquitoes and biting flies can be a bother. Bees, wasps, and yellowjackets are sometimes a problem in late summer and fall. Ticks are found in the dry rain shadow in the eastern segment of the range, particularly in the spring and early summer. The traveler must protect his food and equipment from the black bear, mountain goats, and a variety of small animals.

Electrical storms are not as common in this range as in other ranges in the nation but are an occasional hazard. If caught in a lightning storm, stay away from lone trees and high points on ridges.

Hypothermia, or the loss of heat from the body core can be serious for the unprepared visitor to these mountains. Extra energy can be a demand in this range due to the rugged terrain and rapidly changing weather conditions. The best prevention of hypothermia is provided by adequate food and clothing and the avoidance of exhaustion. Stay as dry as possible and take shelter on the lee side of rocks, or seek other protection. The inclusion of a storm kit in your pack, with waterproof matches, fire starters, food, and a plastic shelter may save your life. Such a kit can be expanded into a full-scale survival kit by adding a whistle, signal mirror, some simple fishing gear, snare equipment, and a repair kit. This, together with the "Ten Essentials," will be adequate for most emergencies not involving injury.

To summarize, survival in emergencies is dependent on good physical condition, adequate equipment, the conservation and replacement of body heat and energy, and — most important of all — your knowledge combined with common sense, and a calm analysis of the problem.

If You Are Lost

The basic rules apply here, as in other wilderness terrain. First, stop! Whistle or shout to attract the attention of other members of your party. Since panic is your greatest enemy, try to remain calm. Conserve your energy. Carefully review the situation so that you can formulate a plan to solve the problem. After retracing your recent movements in your mind and marking your present location, backtrack to the point where the route is again familiar.

If this fails, give some thought to establishing a camp where you can survive and attract the attention of searchers. Ideally, such a camp should provide an adequate wood and water supply, and natural shelter or the potential for building a makeshift shelter. It should be along the edge of open country where the smudge of a green bough fire will be visible and not be dissipated in the towering trees, and where searching aircraft can be signaled. Make camp at least two hours before sunset and gather plenty of firewood to last through the night.

The scarcity of dry tinder in the damp Olympic Range makes fire-building an exasperating chore in wet weather unless one carries candles or fire starters in his emergency pack. Watch for flakes of pitchy wood on the sides of rotten stumps and dead snags. These will burn even when soaking wet.

If the weather is favorable, a side trip to the most convenient observation point may enable you to locate familiar landmarks. Give the international distress signal (three of anything, audible or visible) frequently throughout the first two days and evenings. Inventory your equipment, food, and other resources. Conserve your strength — important either for finding your own way out or for walking when you have been located by a search party. Ration your food and matches as necessary. If after two days it seems apparent that you will not be found by searchers, it is time to consider walking out. When you break camp, be sure to leave a note or sign indicating the time, date and your direction of travel. When you reach civilization, notify the nearest ranger station so that any search effort in progress can be terminated.

If an Accident Occurs

The enjoyment and challenge of a good climb changes to an unpleasant, dangerous situation if an accident occurs. A small amount of preparation at home can equip a party of four or more to give reasonable treatment to the injured members and enable the party to be evacuated safely. If an accident occurs, take the following steps:

1. Immediately determine if the victim must be or can be moved before treatment. Move if necessary. *Factors to consider:* Danger of further fall,

rockfall danger, weather condition, technical climbing problems, spine or neck injury, bleeding, or difficulty with breathing.

2. Evaluate party capabilities and environmental conditions. *Capabilities:* Party size, first aid and rescue skills, supplies and equipment, fuel, food, shelter. *Environment:* Steepness and type of terrain, weather (precipitation, temperature, wind), distance above timberline and from road end and help.

3. If party size and ability will permit self-rescue, do so. If the party will be delayed beyond the expected return time, send out two people with *written* information to be phoned to family to prevent undue anxiety. If help is needed, send two people with a *written* description of the accident including:

   • Name, address, and age of persons involved.
   • Location and terrain at accident scene and/or present location of party.
   • Extent of known injuries; number of people involved; size, condition, and ability of the remainder of the party; party equipment; weather at the scene.

The message for help should be delivered in person or telephoned to Olympic National Park headquarters or to a park ranger. If outside the park, contact the appropriate county sheriff.

If the phone number of the agency needed is not immediately available, call the operator and secure help in contacting one of the above agencies. The messengers should remain at a rendezvous point agreed on with the agency, for further interrogation or to guide the rescue party to the trailhead or accident site.

The person or persons remaining with the victim (the victim should *not* be left alone) should render first aid and make the entire party as comfortable as possible during the waiting period. Food, fuel, and shelter should be considered as soon as the immediate first aid is rendered. During the waiting period, the most important thing is to keep the victim as comfortable as possible and in good spirits. Extra time can be spent in preparing meals and an especially comfortable shelter, thus improving the spirit of the entire party.

First Aid

The following comments are not designed to teach first aid for mountain travel, but to refresh the reader's memory about important problems to be checked and treated. Anyone indulging in back-country travel should take a standard or advanced first-aid course.

Mountaineering Medicine by Fred T. Darvill, Jr., is a useful pocket first-aid text designed to be carried in the hills. *Mountaineering First Aid,* 3rd edition, by Marty Lentz, Jan Carline, and Steve Macdonald, covers common climbing situations. A third and more comprehensive volume for home study and expeditionary use is *Medicine for Mountaineering,* edited by James A. Wilkerson, M.D.

First aid in mountainous country follows the same rules as elsewhere. Panic is apt to be present and must be controlled. Relax the victim. If unconscious, first establish an open airway; remove anything from the mouth or throat. Treat severe bleeding next; apply pressure dressing over the bleeding site. Next check for neck or spine injuries before attempting to move the victim. When necessary to give mouth-to-mouth respiration give four quick breaths, then free the chest of external pressure from snow, rock, or other debris.

"Splint 'em where they lie" still fits. Traction should not be used. Use fixation splints only, immobilizing the joint above and below the fracture site. Always stabilize the neck in a neutral position by making a neck collar. Stabilize the neck of any person who has been unconscious. Do not bind the chest for damaged ribs, as this restricts breathing and may lead to complications. If the victim is able to walk out, the chest may be bound to relieve pain, if the fracture is not unstable. A puncture through both skin and lung should be sealed immediately with any available windproof material, such as a plastic bag or a wet cloth. This patch should be sterile.

Once the immediate injuries have been cared for, or even during this treatment, preventive measures for traumatic shock should be taken. Remove ALL damp or wet clothing. Reclothe the victim with sufficient dry insulation, such as sleeping bags, parkas, etc., to retain normal body temperature. Provide shelter against rain, snow, and wind. Give liquid sparingly, and only to conscious victims with no abdominal injuries. Avoid causing vomiting.

Accidental hypothermia, the loss of body heat faster than it can be replenished, can occur either in conjunction with traumatic shock or from a combination of fatigue and weather conditions. Hypothermia has been the cause of numerous deaths in the Olympics. The surest treatment is prevention: keep in good physical condition, supply the body's need for food and rest at regular intervals, provide adequate caloric intake, and protect against wet and cold. If the victim is shivering, there will probably be a good response to warm liquids and warm food, dry clothing, and a sleeping bag. If the victim is cold, confused, and not shivering, this indicates a more dangerous state of hypothermia. Apply external heat to sides of the chest with warm bottles or direct nude body contact. Additional warmth can be supplied from a fire, stoves, or lanterns in a shelter or tent.

There is no reason for the prevalence of hypothermia if outdoor groups and climbing parties will observe a few simple recommended principles. They are:

• Dress by the layer system. Cover the head and extremities to keep warm. Avoid wind chill.

- Provide food and rest stops at regular intervals.
- Establish a "buddy system" of observation by party members.

These few simple precautions will eliminate the headline, "Hiker Dies of Exposure."

Note: *The following chart is intended only as a refresher under stress conditions for people with Red Cross or equivalent first-aid training.*

FIRST AID — GENERAL TREATMENT

INJURY	SYMPTOMS	TREATMENT
Severe bleeding	Blood pumping or spurting	Firm direct pressure dressing. Apply tourniquet 1 to 2 inches above wound only as a last resort to stop bleeding.
Suffocation	No sign of breathing	Open airway to mouth and throat. Mouth to mouth respiration. Leave dentures in place.
Broken neck	Pain in neck. Tingling or loss of sensation or inability to move limbs.	Make neck collar and immobilize upper body and head. Do not move victim without aid. Move as a log with direct upward pull on head and neck only when necessary.
Back injury	Pain in back. Tingling or loss of sensation or inability to move limbs.	Immobilize trunk and head in line. Do not move victim without aid.
Bone fracture	Visible deformity. Pain at injury, swelling, discoloration. Pain at injury caused by tapping adjacent joint with hand.	Splint, immobilizing adjacent joints. Check extremities for circulation. Protect extremities from cold. Knee should be splinted slightly bent if possible.
Traumatic shock	Skin pale, cool, then moist. Later, pulse rapid and weak, eyes dull, disoriented.	Victim prone on back and level. Do not give food or liquid until stable. Avoid causing vomiting. Retain body heat by providing dry clothing and complete insulation from cold.

INJURY	SYMPTOMS	TREATMENT
Frostbite (superficial)	No sensation in area, feels doughy. Color white, does not turn red after pressing.	Warm by warming the extremity against companion's armpit or abdomen.
Frostbite (severe)	No feeling in part. Color white. Part feels hard throughout.	Evacuate to location for sterile, rapid rewarming. Walk out on frozen injury if necessary. Stop when foot starts to thaw. Thaw in 104 water (warm to normal hand). Keep injury sterile once thawed. Do NOT use extreme heat (fire). Do NOT rub with snow or treat injury roughly. Do NOT thaw if refreezing might occur.
Head injury	Period of unconsciousness. Check for fluid or bleeding from ears, nose, or mouth. Unequal pupil size. Loss of muscle power in any area. Disoriented.	Question victim to test judgment. When treating for shock, do not elevate feet. If symptoms are present, victim should be carried to aid as soon as possible. If no symptoms, observe patient's balance and walk him out with two or more companions as observers.
Fractured rib	Sharp pain when pressed. Breathing painful. Broken end may be depressed.	Sitting best position. Do NOT bind chest unless necessary to relieve pain for victim to walk out.
Hypothermia (exposure) (excessive loss of body heat)	Exhaustion, same symptoms as shock. Not mentally alert. Cold, but not thinking to warm self. Change in personality, usually disagreeable.	Food and rest in warm, sheltered spot. Warm, dry clothing from skin out. Return body heat to normal by internal and external heat. Hot food and drink (when conscious). Heat near fire, stove, lantern in tent or shelter to raise air temperature. Contact heat from nude companion's body in sleeping bag. Hot water bottle (canteen) against sides of chest.

Self-Rescue

Self-rescue without outside help is a formidable undertaking. However, the organization and implementation of a formal rescue is no simple matter either. Larger parties should consider carefully the possibility of self-rescue, providing the party is in good condition and the terrain is not extreme. If self-rescue is attempted, runners should still be sent for help in case the effort proves beyond the ability of the party.

Many climbing parties will be forced into using some self-rescue if an accident occurs in a site of such hostile nature that the victim must be moved to a safer and more comfortable location. A climber falling into a crevasse or bergschrund, for example, cannot be left there to face inevitable death from hypothermic exposure. Avalanche or rockfall hazard may also necessitate movement of the victim, as may the impending onset of a storm. Beyond this immediate need, a full-scale carryout should be attempted only after a thorough analysis of all pertinent factors, including:

- Can the victim walk or help himself? A carryout is beyond the capability of small parties if the victim is unable to help himself. If the probability of further serious injury is small, an aided walkout is encouraged.
- What is the party size, strength, condition, and technical ability? Two stretcher teams (12 people) will be needed if the distance is more than one mile.
- How long will it take for help to arrive? Distance to the road is a factor.
- Will the victim sustain further injury by transport on makeshift equipment?
- Will delay in getting medical attention seriously threaten his life?
- Is the terrain such that a carryout will place the victim or the rest of the party in undue jeopardy?
- What sort of weather is expected during the carryout? Don't overlook the possibility of a helicopter pickup.

Above all, think! If the decision is to evacuate, movement of the victim must be carefully planned and executed. In exposed areas, secure belays must be used to safeguard those involved in the transport as well as the victim. A handline, firmly anchored, is often a valuable asset. The small or inadequately equipped party can frequently protect its movements by the use of prusiks. The type of injury and the terrain will dictate the method of self-rescue. With a minor injury the victim may be able to descend fairly difficult pitches with only the help of a firm belay and an assisting companion. Keep in mind the danger of belated shock, mental or physical. More serious injuries will necessitate transport of some kind, and it is recommended that an organized rescue be considered.

Accidents tend to occur when the hour is late and the party is tired, or when panic takes a hand. Self-rescue parties should plan each move with care. Decisions must be tempered with good judgment. The need for haste is frequently exaggerated, and serious mistakes are the result. During transport, the victim's welfare is paramount. Move him gently. Maintain his warmth. Check the circulation in his extremities often.

Organized Rescue

If waiting for a rescue party, do not become impatient when help does not arrive immediately. The messengers, though traveling light, will usually take many hours to reach a telephone. After a responsible agency such as the National Park Service is reached, the call for help will usually be relayed to a Mountain Rescue Unit. The organization of the rescue party is time-consuming; and though members can leave on short notice, long hours to the trailhead use up additional time. A small, fast advance party will usually arrive first to provide first aid and organize the details of a carryout or helicopter evacuation.

Those waiting with the victim should use this available time to provide for the comfort and well-being of the victim, and to mark the way to their location from some familiar landmark. Since carryouts are difficult for both victim and rescuers, a path or trail should be cleared if possible. This will speed the evacuation immensely.

Helicopter Rescue

Many rescues today are accomplished with notable efficiency by helicopters. Helicopter rescue efforts can be greatly facilitated by proper ground assistance. The pilot must have a clear area 100 ft. in diameter to land. While waiting for a helicopter liftoff, police the landing or hovering site thoroughly to remove everything that might be sucked into the rotors or otherwise endanger the craft. This includes clothing, tarps, cut brush, and limbs. The pilot must know the surface wind direction. While a smoke bomb is ideal, a smudge fire or a marker can provide this information. Always approach a helicopter from the front, where you can be clearly seen by the pilot; and wait for directions from the crew.

Since the range of a helicopter is limited (dependent on the fuel supply), be ready for the pickup when the craft arrives. Do not allow hope to rise too high. The onset of darkness, poor visibility, or cross winds may delay or prevent the pickup. Success may also be precluded by the terrain or other ground conditions if it has not been possible to transport the victim to a good natural heliport. The party must stay in readiness for liftoff at a moment's notice, for changing weather conditions frequently allow only brief and intermittent air activity.

Because it is extremely difficult for people on the ground to be seen from the air, the presence of smoke, a message stamped in the snow, or bright cloth used as signal panels may determine whether the victim is evacuated one day or the next.

In summary, the chief factor leading to disaster is panic. Don't let this happen to your party. An accident is always serious, yet even the most adverse circumstances can frequently be overcome as long as good judgment and common sense prevail.

PEAK INDEX

OLYMPIC PEAKS 7000 FEET OR HIGHER

Mt. Olympus, West Peak	7965	Mt. Anderson	7321
Mt. Olympus, Middle Peak	7930	Adelaide Peak	7300
Mt. Deception	7788	Warrior Peak, Southeast Summit	7300
Mt. Olympus, East Peak	7780	Warrior Peak, Northwest Summit	7285
Mt. Constance	7743	Athena II	7250
Inner Constance	7670	Gray Wolf Ridge	7218
Mt. Johnson	7650	Cameron Peak	7192
The Pyramid	7650	Mt. Mathias	7168
Mt. Mystery	7631	Desperation Peak	7150
Mt. Constance, South Summit	7600	Sundial	7150
Devil's Fang	7600	Mt. Fricaba	7134
Mt. Mystery, North Peak	7600	Echo Rock	7100
Sweat Spire	7580	Hal Foss Peak	7100
Martin Peak	7550	Point Smith	7100
Gasp Pinnacle	7540	Mt. Tom	7048
Mt. Clark	7528	Peak 7022	7022
Stasis	7500	The Arrowhead	7000
Gilhooley Tower	7400	Athena's Owl	7000
Mt. Walkinshaw	7378	Cloudy Peak	7000
West Peak (Mt. Anderson Massif)	7365	Curiosity Peak	7000
Athena	7350	Point Harrah	7000
The Incisor	7350	Snifter Spire	7000
C-141 Peak	7339		